The
POET
of ARAB WO

The
POETRY
of ARAB WOMEN

A Contemporary Anthology

EDITED BY NATHALIE HANDAL

Interlink Books
An imprint of Interlink Publishing Group, Inc.
New York • Northampton

First published in 2001 by

INTERLINK BOOKS
An imprint of Interlink Publishing Group, Inc.
99 Seventh Avenue • Brooklyn, New York 11215 and
46 Crosby Street • Northampton, Massachusetts 01060
www.interlinkbooks.com

Acknowledgements appear on pages xviii-xxi, which constitute a continuation of the
copyright page.

Library of Congress Cataloging-in-Publication Data

The poetry of Arab women : a contemporary anthology / edited by Nathalie Handal.
  p.cm.
Chiefly translated from Arabic.
ISBN 1-56656-374-7
  1. Arabic poetry--Women authors--Translations into English. 2. Arabic poetry--20th
century--Translations into English. 3. Poetry--Arab authors. I. Handal, Nathalie, 1969–

PJ7694.E3 P64 2000
892.7'160809287--dc21   00-058054

Cover painting "To Everything There is a Season," 1989 by Ghada Jamal, Lebanon.
Artist's Book. Collection of Dr. and Mrs. F. Agrama. Courtesy of International Council for Women
in the Arts/CVAR

Printed and bound in Canada by Webcom.

TO ALL THOSE WHO DREAM AND DARE

Our whole life a translation...
—Adrienne Rich, *Our Whole Life*

How pleasant this hour is! May it extend for me to eternity.
—Anonymous Hieroglyphic Text

CONTENTS

PREFACE

This anthology was prepared to eradicate invisibility: to provide an introduction to Arab women poets, to make visible the works of a great number of Arab women poets who are virtually unknown to the West, to make visible many Arab-American women poets who are marginalized within the American literary and ethnic scenes, and to demonstrate the wide diversity of Arab women's poetry, which extends to other languages besides Arabic and English (as in the case of Arab women poets writing in French and Swedish). This anthology seeks to unite Arab women poets from all over the Arab world and abroad, regardless of what language they write in and whether they were born in an Arab country or not. Its aim is to bridge the religious, linguistic and geographical spaces existing among Arab women worldwide. With the exception of Oman and Sudan, every Arab country has been represented in this volume. Included are Arab women in exile or living in non-Arab countries, and women poets of Arab descent from Europe and North America. The volume incorporates the most accomplished Arab women poets of the twentieth century, including those of the distinctive new generation. It opens a door to a new and fast changing world where women are an extremely vital force in both literary and social terms.

One of the most demanding parts of this project was conducting research on Arab women poets writing today, gathering their poetic oeuvres and locating them personally. I was overwhelmed during my search to have found so many women poets and overjoyed to have discovered such poetic wealth and variety. As for the Arab-American women poets, this was an easier task because of the help of organizations and associations such as RAWI (Radius of Arab-American Writers Inc.), AMEWS (Association for Middle East Women's Studies), AAUG (Association of Arab-American

University Graduates), MESA (Middle East Studies Association of North America, Inc.); and two cardinal anthologies, *Grapeleaves: A Century of Arab American Poetry,* edited by Gregory Orfalea and Sharif Elmusa (Salt Lake City: University of Utah Press, 1988 and Northampton, MA: Interlink, 1999), and *Food For Our Grandmothers,* edited by Joanna Kadi (Boston, MA: South End Press, 1994); and also the important Arab-American newspapers and journals, *Al Jadid, Jusoor* and *Mizna* and the Arabic literature-in-translation journal published in the United Kingdom, *Banipal.* But I must point out that an enormous development took place during these past five years. When I started my research many of these journals were in their beginning stages or were not in existence yet; and RAWI, the most important Arab-American association in terms of literature, was just starting, and thus did not have the membership or the facilities it has today. Furthermore, although when I started researching, many Arab women poets living in the Arab world were still struggling with the fax, within a few years not only were most of them more reachable, but some of them even had e-mail. With newer, easier, and faster means of communication, such as the internet, the Arab world has become more accessible. In addition, there is an openness to the Arab world that did not exist before. Also, the Arab-American lobby is stronger, more dynamic today. This has in turn aided in changing the distorted view the West has of Arab women, and of the Arab world in general. Had I started this project today, my task would have been easier. The francophone poets I knew about because I lived in France and because the ones included are well-known in French literary society. The other poets I discovered through a mixture of circumstances as my research brought me to them or they found their way to me.

The decision of which poets to include was difficult, for apart from the fact that such an undertaking involves perpetual interior and exterior debates, there was the issue that many of the women poets were not established poets yet. Therefore, many of the poets' works cannot, at this point in time, be evaluated in terms of their poetic influence, nor can many of these poets be looked upon as major cultural, social and political figures. It is vital to note, however, that even if the evolution of each poet can not be determined at this point in time, every voice is important in that it contributes to the creation and expansion of Arab women's poetry. Since this volume is an introduction to Arab women poetry, not only poets who have published books but also those publishing in journals, and who have aroused interest among other poets, translators and critics, are included. In this volume, I tried to be as complete as possible. I went to cultural centers, consulates, libraries, bookstores, literary festivals, obtained all the newspapers and journals I could, and contacted critics, translators, friends, and other poets. It is important to point out that in the Arab world, poets' publications are subsidy-based, so anyone can publish a book of poetry. I found extremely lengthy bibliographies of poetry books published by Arab women, but I could not really base my research on bibliographies. Therefore, my main criterion was to include, apart from the well-known poets, most of the poets whom I discovered who were presently in the foreground of poetic activities. Surely, new poets are rising even as I am writing this preface, such as Khuloud al-Mu'alla (United Arab Emirates) and Ashjan al-Hindi (Saudi Arabia), but I had to draw the work to a close. I am painfully aware that there are other poets that could have been added, especially among the francophone North African women poets; lack of space and time led to inevitable absences. Nevertheless, most of the important older and newer contemporary voices are included.

Many of the poets in this anthology are translated and/or published in the West for the first time. I attempted to present unpublished, untranslated poems; however, I have not remained exclusive within those borders as certain published and translated poems have indisputable significant artistic merit, and in some instances I could not find the poet or her books. The responsibility of choosing poems for translation and poems that would work in English was arduous. Some selections were made after discussions—between myself and the translators, myself and the poets. In other cases, when after perpetual persistence, I could not find a substantial amount of work of a particular poet nor could the poet be located, poems were taken from existing translations or we translated what was judged as best (some criteria being: technical, artistic merit, sense of history) from what we had. The space allocated to each writer within the collection does not necessarily indicate a poet's importance. At times difficulty in locating poets and their works influenced how much work by a poet was included. I have tried to remain, throughout the volume, as even as possible in allocating space to each poet.

The distinguished translators and translator/poets come from the Arab world, the United States, Britain and France. There are many discussions, debates and arguments that arise during the translation of any text—has the translator honored the poem, should the translator translate literally or stay faithful to the sense and/or meaning of the poem or perhaps should the translator stray from the exactness of the original text to allow it to stand more poetically in the language it is being translated into? Poetry has its own world in the language it originates from, and poets have their own language; no translation can ever be complete. The translators of these poems did not share set guidelines. Rather, the translating has been a continuous negotiation—between translators, between the poets and the translators, between the translators or poets and myself—and the final consensus differed with every poet and every poem. It could not have been otherwise, for the difference, both culturally and linguistically, between the Arabic and the English is tremendous. The two differ in poetic traditions, ideas, images, religious references, rhyme, rhythm, meter, metaphor, consonance, assonance, and emotion. Thus, the task of bridging the two cultures, translating not only the text but the culture into English, while also allowing the poem to exist as an English text and not only as a translated text, took perpetual negotiating, editing, reading, re-editing, re-reading. All the collaborators in this anthology have tried to maintain the essential elements in each poem.

There were different stages of translating. To begin with, translators were chosen who were rooted in both languages and in a love of poetry; many are poets themselves. The translations were done either by one translator or two translators working together. Then the translations were sent to me, and I made some suggestions and editorial changes. The poems were then sent to second translator/poets who made some minor changes. Then I re-read and re-edited all of the poems again, with the assistance of the British poet and translator Richard McKane and the Syrian critic and translator Subhi Hadidi. Finally all the poems were sent to respected British poets to read as English text. Most of the poems translated by only one translator only carry the name of the first translator even if some changes were made by the second translator or myself. When a substantial amount was changed, "with" was added to the byline. When two translators collaborated on the translation of a poem, their names appear according to the order in which the work was conducted. This is merely a method of presentation; no judgment is intended.

In general, this volume tried to be as objective, inclusive, open, and complete both in the selection and in the translation, although it's impossible to satisfy everyone. The poets are arranged in alphabetical order and their names are translated in as natural a way as possible for the English-speaking reader. The notes to the poems are placed after each poet's poem in the order in which they appear in the poem, and there is also a glossary at the end of the book for the few Arabic words that reappear throughout the volume.

The introduction provides a historical overview for understanding contemporary Arab women's poetry, including the singularity as well as the shared trends and movements in the work of these eighty-three poets.

ACKNOWLEDGEMENTS

First and foremost, I am profoundly grateful to Subhi Hadidi for this support, his valuable advice and insight, and his patience during the production of this anthology. His participation has been of utmost value. He has never failed to believe in this project and in my efforts to realize it, never failed to be there when I needed him. I owe him more than can be expressed.

A warm thank you to Lina Tibi for generously helping me find translators and locate the women poets, which has proved to be a very long and incredibly demanding task because of the geographical scope of this project, and the mobile world we have come to live in. Her presence and assistance has been vital.

I owe a particularly special thank you to Richard McKane, whose poetic vision, expert advice on translation and editing, has been of high importance. He assisted me in the final stages of the anthology, in long and strenuous hours of second translations, editing and re-reading; and he became a major point of reference whom I consulted intermittently.

To my friend, advisor, and emotional supporter, Lisa Suhair Majaj, I offer great thanks. I continuously consulted her for editorial and critical advice while writing the introduction. Her wealth of literary and historical knowledge has been indispensable to me.

My deep gratitude to everyone at Interlink Publishing, and particularly to Pam Thompson and my publisher, Michel Moushabeck, for believing in this project and allowing it to exist; for their understanding and collaboration—it has been wonderful working with them.

To all the distinguished translators, I am deeply thankful—this anthology would not have been possible without their generous contributions and encouragement. They are at the core of this project.

They are admirable not only because of their invaluable work and for their time, but also for their genuine belief in poetry and its dissemination, and their constant attempt to fill the spaces between one language and another, one culture and another. Translators help open the windows between often very different realities, customs, languages, literatures. As we are well aware, translation is an arduous job and a large responsibility to undertake—and because of translators, a project like this one is possible; because of them we are able to glimpse into other worlds and words; for that, I remain indebted. It has been an honor for me to work with all of them, including the readers (those who were involved in reading the final translations and giving me their opinion of the works as English texts) Julia Casterton, Judy Gahagan, Mimi Khalvati, Sarah Maguire, and Carole Satyamurti.

My gratitude goes to all those who have gone out of their way to help me complete this project. Special thanks to Fatma Kandil, Suzanne Haddad, Margaret Obank, Wafa'a Farhat, Ibrahim Abu-Lughod, Elmaz Abi-Nader, Margaret Mullen, and David Gullette; and more particularly, a profound thank you to Michael W. Suleiman, Amjad Nasser, Nouri al-Jarrah, and Samuel Shimon, for their additional attention, continuous support, and generous help.

I would also like to thank the Arab women poets represented in this volume for their vibrant assistance and cooperation, and for continuously reminding me of the importance of this project.

Last but certainly not least, I owe much of everything to my parents. They have always been at the heart of my life—supporting me in every possible way. I extend to them my admiration, infinite gratitude and deep love. To my sister Alexandra, I cannot express my appreciation and adoration—her brilliant artistic and intellectual awareness has been essential in all of my artistic undertakings and her continuous support as a sister and friend has been absolute. To my brother Dimitri, goes my love, for the joyfulness he infinitely projects, which has encouraged me to believe and preserve. To my cousin Paola, whose presence has been a great source of love and support, I thank beyond these words. To all of my dear friends, especially Danielle and Pam, who have been indispensable to me emotionally; and who have shown me throughout all of these years their uniqueness as friends, sisters—endless thank-yous. To Edward, I extend more then these lines can hold… for his endless care, for believing in me and in this project. To my two grandmothers, a warm thank you, for transmitting to me such enthusiasm for life and work—they have been inspirations, always.

INTRODUCTION

Listen to me, sugardaddy: "You can't take a girl for a ride."
—Umm al-Ala bint Yusuf

The literary landscape of Arab women poets, particularly in the latter half of the twentieth century, is one of abundance, diversity and contrasts, manifesting a richness of voices and imagination, and reflecting important changes taking place in the Arab world culturally, socially, politically, and artistically. Arab women writers have contributed to and expressed themselves in almost every writing genre: feminist theory, literary and socio-historical criticism, drama, fiction and non-fiction, poetry and so forth. It is probably in the literary world, however, that Arab women have spoken out the most. Since, as Kanan Makiya notes, "Poetry is the most revered and the most developed art form of the Arab peoples, occupying pride of place in a classical literary heritage which, along with Islam, provides the only persistent tie Arabs have with the past" (45). Thus it is not surprising that this is the genre most chosen by Arab women. As Makiya observes, "No matter how much conflict there may actually be among Arabs, constant invocation of this tradition in modern times—whether literary or religious—has become a powerful basis for asserting Arab identity"(45). Indeed, the enthusiasm for the written word among Arabs manifests itself from ancient times until the twenty-first century, and can be observed by the abundance of their literary production and their impressive literary history, giving to the world numerous great poets. Arab women poets have participated in this illustrious literary tradition since pre-Islamic times (500–622). Some of the most important women poets of these early periods are: Laila bint Lukaiz (d. 483), Al-Khansa (575–646) from Arabia, Laila bint Sa'd al-Aamiriyya (d. 688), Maisun bint Bahdal (d. 700), the mystic poet Rabi'a al-'Adawiyya, better known as Rabi'a the Mystic (712–801) and Laila al-Akhyaliyya (d. 709) from what is now present-day Iraq, and Wallada bint al-Mustakfi (d. 1091). Arab women poets of the earlier periods (from Pre-Islamic through most of the Abbasid period 750–1258) lived and wrote freely about anything they wanted. The participation of women poets in the writing of elegies (from pre-Islamic times up until the beginning of the twentieth century) is well-known, as is the strong oral tradition of composing and reciting poetry among women, which has played an important role in the evolution and literary history of the Arab and Islamic world. In addition, those in Andalucia were far away enough from religious cities such as Mecca, Medina, Jerusalem and Baghdad for them not to be affected by or concerned about social and religious restrictions (Al-Udhari 15). But by the end of the Abbasid period Arab women had practically lost that freedom, and did not regain it until the nineteenth century when Muslim reformers called for women's education and for their social and intellectual inclusion, and women themselves started to revolt.

This anthology focuses on modern Arab women poets, who will be referred to here as *contemporary* Arab women poets. Although poets from the beginning of the twentieth century have been included, the book mainly consists of poets from the latter half of the century, and in particular, from the last two decades or so. In order not to have any confusion in temporal meaning, since we are technically in the twenty-first century while the body of work included in this book was written in the last century, the use of the word *contemporary* seems the most appropriate when discussing these women poets.

This introduction will start with a very brief description of Arab women poets from the Pre-Islamic times until the present. It will then provide a historical briefing of Arab women writers, society and the literary scene, beginning in the nineteenth century and continuing through the contemporary period. This section, "A Historical Briefing: Arab Women Writers, Society and the Literary Scene," will look at the trends in Arab poetry and how modern Arabic poetry has evolved; the place women writers occupied in the literary scene during the nineteenth and twentieth centuries; the rise of feminism and of women's literary salons, activities and associations; the role of women in journalism; the themes women writers were concerned with; and the political and historical tragedies that had an impact on their work. The next section, "The Rise of Arab Women's Poetry," will then look at how and why Arab women poetry gained in prominence in the second half of the twentieth century, in particular over the last twenty years. Although Arab women poets share common themes and are concerned with similar issues and struggles, such as feminism, the struggle against gender inequality and injustice, and the elimination of Arab women's writers' invisibility, they will be discussed by geographical location, for an organizational structure was necessary and given the magnitude of the anthology, this structure seemed the most coherent; in addition, these poets' countries of origin have had the greatest influence on their work. Egyptian women poets will come first; then the Levantine poets will follow, every country having its own section, with Lebanon, Palestine, Syria, Iraq, and Jordan discussed in this order. Women poets from the Arabian Gulf will then be next. Since there are fewer poets represented from each Gulf country, the poets will not be separated into individual countries, but will be discussed in one group, in this order: Saudi Arabia, Bahrain, Kuwait, Qatar, United Arab Emirates, and Yemen. North African women poets will then be discussed; those from Algeria first, then those from Tunisia, and those from Morocco and Libya will be combined together. The final section will be dedicated to Arab-American and Arab-Canadian women poets. The work included in this anthology by each poet will be discussed, as well as these poets' literary social, intellectual, and political influences.

A HISTORICAL BRIEFING: ARAB WOMEN WRITERS, SOCIETY, & THE LITERARY SCENE

It is important to briefly look at the nineteenth century to have a greater understanding of the growth of women writers in the twentieth century, and in particular, the last twenty years. The *Nahdah*, or Arab literary renaissance, started at different periods in different Arab countries, beginning in Lebanon and then moving to Egypt in the latter part of nineteenth century. In Lebanon it focused mainly on prose; it was in Egypt in the second half of the nineteenth century that the poetic renaissance took place. In Egypt, the cultural center of the Arab world, an invigorating force encouraged openness, change, and a break from the more direct and traditional neoclassicists, whose works were linked to classical techniques and rhythms, and who expressed nationalism and longing. Neoclassical poetry was very important to the Arabs, since it was closely linked to a traditional style they were grounded in; thus, a strong struggle was necessary to break away from this literary trend. The avant-garde *Mahjar* (emigrant) poets in the early part of the twentieth century started to change things. The *Mahjaris* came from the *Mashriq* area (Lebanon, Palestine, Syria, and Jordan), and emigrated to the United States and Latin America. The most well-known and influential of them all was Gibran Kahlil Gibran (1883–1931); other important figures included Ilya Abu Madi (1890–1957), Mikhail Nu'aymah (1889–1988), and Amin Rihani (1876–1940). These writers introduced new stylistic, thematic, and linguistic patterns, encouraging the influence of art, Western literature, culture and thought, providing challenging images, reflecting a diverse inner and outer world, and opening doors to a different creativity. Their critical writings also helped solidify their poetic revolution. The *Mahjar* poets, along with the Egyptian poets and the many Arab intellectuals and writers who went to Egypt seeking freedom of expression, all participated in this movement toward change. Women writers and journalists also went to Egypt during that time—in 1870 the Lebanese Zaynab Fawwaz (1850–1914), in 1899 the Lebanese Warda al-Yaziji (1838–1924), whose poetry anthology *The Rose Garden* (1867) was the first book by an Arab woman to be published, and in 1908 the Palestinian-Lebanese poet and journalist born in Nazareth, May Ziyada (1886–1941) (Cooke, "Arab Women" 443). Ziyada played an important role in the feminist cause through her depiction of society and its hypocrisies, and her description of the normal pleasures of life and liberty. She was also the first woman in the early twentieth century to be accepted in mainstream Arabic literature.

The women who wrote in the nineteenth century were mainly educated women from the upper and middle classes, but they were not as advantaged as one might expect. They had to struggle with exclusion on the basis of gender, which led to a feminine literature preoccupied with the fight against and the portrayal of women's discrimination and segregation professionally, educationally, and socially. They emphasized the necessity of social reform in order for Arab society to expand, grow, and evolve. Kept out of the mainstream, women poets occupied a narrow literary scene, publishing in journals and magazines such as Ahmad Lutfi al-Sayyid's newspaper *al-Jarida,* and *al-Mahrusah,* which was edited by May Ziyada's father. Al-Sayyid and the Egyptian judge Qasim Amin were liberal nationalists, and, along with Egyptian Murques Fahmi, and the Islamic reformers, Muhammad 'Abduh and Rashid Rida, fought for women's rights, liberation, and education (Cooke, "Arab Women" 443–444). They insisted on the necessity of women's visibility and freedom, holding these up as the only way for society to advance. Amin's books, *Liberation of Women* (1899) and *The New Women* (1900), and Fahmi's *Women in the East* (1894), were catalysts for the change of Arab women's status. Later on, the Tunisian Tahrir Haddad's *Our Women and Islamic Law and Society* (1929) played the same function in North Africa. These men argued that the subordination of women, gender segregation and wearing the *Hijab* (veil) was not part of Islam, not part of the Islamic *Shari'a*; they argued that the unfavorable social and marital rights of women must change. They fought for women's liberation at every level. Some Arab male poets also took part in this fight, namely the Iraqi poet Jamil al-Zahawi, who was imprisoned in 1911 for requesting that women be freed from social restrictions and supporting the unveiling of women (Badran xix). They emphasized the importance of women's liberty and equality, insisting that the advancement of Arabic society could not come about without the freedom of women, who consisted of the other half of the population. Later on, in the twentieth century, male novelists such as Taha Husain and Najib Mahfuz, under the influence of Western literature and their contact with European societies, used many female characters in their works, thus contributing to the questioning of the female role in society. But few male writers were really able to write about the women's psyche and emotions; few were able to describe women's experiences. Furthermore, most men did not read literary works by women.

Apart from the women poets mentioned above, there were other important women poets during that time and a little later on, including: the Egyptian poets Malak Hifni Nasif, known as Bahithat al-Badiyah (1886–1918); 'Aisha 'Esmat al-Taymuriyya (1840–1902), who was born in Cairo of Turkish/Kurdish ancestry; Malak 'Abdel 'Aziz (b. 1923); and the Iraqi poet Salma al-Mala'ika, better known as Umm Nizar (1908–1953), mother of the prominent contemporary Arab woman poet Nazik al'Mala'ika (b.1923). Although the poetic expression of women of this period did not have strong artistic and personal imprints, it created the foundation necessary for the individualistic, diverse, assertive and highly artistic oeuvres that were to come in the latter half of the twentieth century. And, very significantly, Arab women poets at the time were aware of the importance of collectivity; thus, they started literary salons, women's societies, newspapers, and journals. These activities not only aided the rise of Arab women writers and poets, but helped pose important social and literary questions, such as: what is the role of women? How can it be redefined and what should it be? What are the effects of women's invisibility in Arab society? Why is literary creativity attributed to men only? What can the female creative mind offer, and foremost, does creativity have a gender?

Fortunately, there were many literary activities and associations; unfortunately, too many to list here. Nevertheless, some of the more important ones bear mentioning. Among the first literary societies to be founded was Bakurat Suriya (The Dawn of Syria), established in Beirut in

1880 by the Lebanese writer Maryam Nimr Makariyus (1860–1888); other literary societies then followed in Beirut. In 1898 in Hims, Syria, Nur al-'Afaf (The Light of Virtue) was established. From then on, and especially after World War I, numerous literary and intellectual women's societies emerged, especially in Lebanon and Syria (see Zeidan).

Although much of Arab women's journalism started in Egypt, the main establishers were Lebanese women, and in particular, Lebanese Christian women who emigrated to Egypt with their families in the early 1860s for political, religious and economic reasons (Zeidan 47). Journalism became a vital force not only for literary expression but political and social protest. The first monthly, *al-Fatah*, was established in Alexandria in 1892 by the Lebanese Hind Nawaf. After *al-Fatah*, numerous women's literary journals, magazines, and newspapers were founded, in Egypt, in the rest of the Arab world, and, in the second half of the twentieth century, outside the Arab world. A few of the more recent ones are: in Cairo, *Hawwa* (a monthly from 1955–1957, and then a weekly from 1957–present) founded by Amina al-Said; in Beirut, *al-Hasna* (weekly) founded by George Shami (1970–present), *Mishwar* (weekly) founded by Dar al-Mishwar (1979–present), *Sahar* (weekly) founded by Dar al-Sayyad (1981–present), *Nisa* founded by Dar al-Muthaqqaf al-'Arabi (1981–present), *Fairuz* (weekly) founded by Dar al-Sayyad (1981–present); in Baghdad, *al-Mar'ah* (monthly, 1970–present); in Kuwait, *Usrati* (weekly, 1965–present); in Palestine, *Shu'un al-Mar'ah*; in Qatar, *al-Jawharah* (monthly, 1978–present); in Saudi Arabia, *Sayyidati* (weekly, 1981–present); in the United Arab Emirates, *Hiya* (monthly) founded by Mu'assassat al-Wahdah (1992–present); in France, *al-Sharqiyyah* (monthly) founded by Samira Khashuqji (1981–present) (Zeidan 238–248). The 1990s saw the birth of many innovative and dynamic women's magazines and journals, such as *Tyche* (Jordan), *Noor* (Egypt), *al-Katiba* (London, edited by Nouri al-Jarrah and Lina Tibi), *Hajar* (Egypt), and so forth.

Sukaynah bint al Husayn and Walladah bint al-Mustakfi first established the literary salon hundreds of years before such salons became popular in sixteenth-century Europe. Another 300 years passed before the literary salon was reestablished in the Arab world by Maryana Marrash (1848–1919). A Syrian poet and the daughter of the poet Francis Marrash, she was among the first women to proclaim the freedom of creativity and expression. Many literary salons came into being after her Aleppo salon, the two most important being Princess Nazli Fadil's (d. 1914) in Egypt and May Ziyada's, also in Egypt.

These activities and collaborations, along with the rise of Arab feminism—which began to be conceptualized, especially in Egypt, at the end of the nineteenth century, and then really started at the beginning of the twentieth century—were vehicles for the empowerment women gained by the end of the twentieth century. In Egypt in 1923, The Egyptian Feminist Union was founded and women started voicing their refusal of Arab women's confined position in society. Protesting a society constructed on the invisibility and silencing of women, some women from the upper class unveiled themselves. After the 1920s and up until the 1960s women's public organized movements grew in other Arab countries, including Iraq, Lebanon, Syria, and Sudan. During that time, the Arab Feminist Union was formed in an effort to consolidate pan-Arab feminist thought and consciousness. In the 1950s, Sudanese women took part in the struggle for independence against Anglo-Egyptian rule. But also by the 1950s and 1960s, "states started to co-opt independent feminist movements, repressing but not totally eliminating women's independent, public feminist voices" (Badran xxi).

Beginning in the 1970s, feminist expression revived in Egypt, Iraq, Lebanon, and Syria, and awakened for the first time in other Arab countries. Many Algerian and Palestinian women started to consider themselves to be both feminists and nationalists. In the 1980s pan-Arab feminism, under the leadership of Nawal al-Saadawi in Egypt, resurfaced within the framework of the Arab Women's Solidarity Association (AWSA) (Badran xxviii). Although the rise of Islamic fundamentalists in the last twenty years has been a hindrance in some Arab countries, restraining the advancement of Arab women, feminism has persisted and the 1990s have seen the birth of numerous independent and semi-independent women's organizations and groups in all of North Africa, Egypt, Sudan, Lebanon, the Occupied Territories, and Kuwait.

CHANGE IN ARAB POETRY

Increasing knowledge of European literature and the continuous cultural, intellectual, and social contact with Europe intensified the continued cultural evolution taking place among Arab intellectuals and writers, as they entered a twentieth century filled with complexity and change. Though here it is important to note the catalytic influence Kahlil Gibran had up until the 1930s on most creative minds in the Arab world, and on modern Arab poetry. Gibran's brand of Arab Romanticism was born of the profound need for freedom at every level. His was a poetry anchored in the search for dreams and for interior and exterior liberation; a poetry of individual yearning. Symbolism came in the 1930s, a literary trend that nourished the idea of beauty and the ideal. Throughout this time and into the 1940s and early 1950s, Arab women writers continued to face very solitary times, for they were still not included in the mainstream literary scene. Apparently, their themes, as well as their stylistic constructions and rhetorical styles, made them less appealing to an Arab reader rooted in a more classical literary tradition.

The political upheavals and uncertainties that started with the tragic loss of Palestine in 1948 began to lead Arab intellectuals and writers into a realistic, nationalistic, and humanistic literary sphere. For Arab poets, breaking away from their deeply-rooted history in the traditional form was revolutionary. To understand this, one must be conscious of the importance of form in Arabic poetry. Arab poets' experimentation with form is probably one of the most important changes to note in twentieth century Arabic poetry. The traditional form, literary critic Salma Khadra Jayyusi writes, is "characterized by a two-hemistich monorhymed arrangement and has been the only form used in traditional 'formal' (as opposed to other nonelevated) poetry since time immemorial" (Jayyusi *Modern Arabic* 8). Ahmed al-Tami, Professor at King Saud University points out that,

> within less than half a century more than six poetic forms were the object of widespread experimentation: ash-shi'r al-manthur (prose poetry), an-nathr ash-shi'ri (poetic prose), ash-shi'r al-mursal (blank verse), ash-shi'r al-maqtu'i (strophic verse), ash-shi'r al-hurr (free verse) and qasidat an-nathr (the prose poem) (185).

It was Iraqi poets, Nazik al-Mala'ika and Badr Shakir al-Sayyab (1926–1964), who started a new movement in writing called free verse, a term that was to create conflicting debates among critics and poets. The problems revolving around the usage of the term "free verse" are multiple and the limited space in this introduction does not permit extensive explanation. But it is worth noting, however briefly, the debate surrounding the term "free verse" as it is used in relation to Arabic poetry. The term is a literal translation of the English "free verse," which is defined in the *Princeton Encyclopedia of Poetry and Poetics,* as Ahmed al-Tami mentions, as a poetry

> based not on the recurrence of stress or accent in a regular, strictly measurable pattern but rather on irregular rhythmic cadence or the recurrence, with variations, of significant phrases, images patterns, and the like. The rhyme is treated with a similar freedom and irregularity.

But al-Tami points out, "…the form of poetry al-Mala'ika advocates and about which she theorizes is, in fact, not free: the poet's freedom is limited to varying the number of feet in each line, although he is free to use any scheme of rhyme or none at all" (186).

It was the publication in 1949 of Nazik al-Mala'ika's second collection, *Shazaya wa Ramad* (*Shrapnel and Ashes*), that officially started the free verse movement. The introduction of her book was innovative in that it gave an explanation of the theoretical structure of free verse, explaining why this new form could more efficiently mirror the experiences of contemporary Arab poets, and pointing out the advantages of this new form in contrast with the traditional form. Al-Mala'ika participated in the transformation of Arabic poetry structurally and thematically. She was also an important critic who wrote extensively on modern Arabic literature, on the need for new poetic rules, on the free verse movement and its evolution, and on numerous other literary, artistic, and intellectual issues and developments. Her contributions to the evolution of Arabic poetry and literary thought have definitely made her the most prominent Arab woman poet of the twentieth century. Her poetry demonstrates her evolved expansiveness as it encompasses numerous issues, from a woman's inner turmoil, intellectual suppression, and alienation, to revolution, national struggles and politics, the horrors and catastrophes of humanity, the perplexities of resistance, and profound melancholy. She also wrote poems that portrayed her mystical side, especially her Sufi orientation. Her important poem "Cholera," on the cholera epidemic in Egypt in the late 1940s, demonstrates a significant break with classical verse form. Some critics have claimed that "Cholera" is not a free verse poem, for as the critic Salih J. Altoma points out, poetry "qualifies for free verse only when it does not follow a consistent scheme" (10). But as Altoma also explains, al-Mala'ika had a "broader definition of free verse" (10). Altoma paraphrases al-Mala'ika's definition of free verse "…as any poetry, regardless of its stanzaic structure or rhyme scheme, that departs from the two hemistich line system and that employs the *taf'ilah* (foot) as its basis whether or not it follows uniform scheme" (10). The deep, multiple, yet singular face of sorrow that often surfaces in her lines come through perfectly in this poem. As she writes, "In every heart there is fire,/ in every silent hut, sorrow,/ and everywhere, a soul crying in the dark." Pain and melancholy profusely traverse her work, as the poem "Five Hymns to Pain" reflects. She writes of a pain that exists in nature, in nights and mornings, in the self, in human existence, in the collective consciousness, in a small child, in a country, in questions and answers, in disaster, in joy, in the details and the bigger picture of everything visible and invisible; yet she adds, "We shall forget pain?/ we shall forget it,/ having nurtured it with satisfaction," even if it hides in "our dreams/ in every note of our sad songs." Pain is life and life is pain for al-Mala'ika, yet she declares that we are capable of going beyond its demarcation lines, and those of what we see, think we see, and dare not see, reminding us that we "gathered the bitter teardrops/ and made a rosary."

Another important experiment since the beginning of the twentieth century is that of prose poetry and the prose poem. The prose poem is "based on the rhythms of prose, deriving its rhythmical effects from such techniques as parallelism, repetition, assonance, alliteration, irregular rhyme and return, and resistance to any type of metricality" (Khouri 102). Yet, Salma Jayyusi asserts

> prose poetry differs from the prose poem (poéme en prose) in the following ways: prose poetry, like the prose poem, is without meter and is usually rhymeless, although it might sometimes employ rhyme for decorative reasons. It is written on the page like a poem in free verse with short lines. Often the reader pauses at the end of each line. The prose poem, on the other hand, has the appearance of prose on the page (Modern Arabic 13).

As can be seen, although the terms "free verse" and "prose poem" are used when discussing both Arabic and English poetry, their definitions differ. This is important to note in order to avoid confusion.

Kahlil Gibran and Amin Rihani were the innovators of this new form in their efforts to modernize Arabic poetry. One cannot exaggerate the pioneering importance of their role in shaping modern Arabic poetry. Yet it took until the 1950s and 1960s for the prose poem to be taken seriously. Today many of the newer generation Arab poets, and most of the new generation women poets, write prose poetry. In fact, one of the most heated debates in the past couple decades among some Arab critics and poets is the discussion as to what is "real" poetry: free verse or prose poetry.

Other experiments with poetry, such as surrealism, and other diverse poetic inventiveness with theme, language, imagery, metaphor, mythology, tone, and attitude have taken place from the 1950s until now. Alongside changes in form and technique, political and historical catastrophes have played a major role in transforming Arab poetry. Beginning with *al-Nakba*, or the Palestine disaster of 1948 and post-1948, poets from all of the Arab countries have been touched by the Algerian War of Independence of 1954–1962, the June War of 1967, the Lebanese Civil Wars beginning in 1975, the Iran-Iraq War beginning in 1980, the 1982 Invasion of Lebanon, the mass murder of innocent Palestinian and

Lebanese civilians by Israeli or Israeli-supported operations in Deir Yasin in Palestine in 1948, Tel al-Za'tar in 1976, and Sabra and Shatila in Lebanon in 1982, the Palestinian Intifada starting in 1987, the Gulf War starting in January 1991, the Madrid Conference starting on October 30, 1991, the Oslo Agreement signed in Washington, D.C. on September 13, 1993, and the sanctions on Iraq, which continue at the present time.

The history of colonialism, too, has inevitably affected Arab poetry. The Ottomans ruled the Arab world for more than three centuries. In the early nineteenth century, Egypt was the first Arab country to establish *de facto* independence from them. But by 1882 Egypt was occupied again, this time by the British. The countries of the Levant remained under Ottoman rule until after World War I, when as had been the case in Egypt, the countries of the Levant soon experienced another wave of occupiers. In the 1920s, the Levant was broken up into the states of Lebanon, Syria, Palestine, and Transjordan and fell under British and French mandates. The colonization of these countries altered their educational systems and linguistic expression.

Christian missionaries started establishing French, English, and American schools in the early nineteenth century in Egypt, Palestine, and Lebanon and afterwards in other Arab countries. Arabic remained the language of the majority of the people, and newly established state schools used Arabic as the language of instruction. In most of these countries, Turkish had been the language of the elite, but by the 1920s English and French replaced it. Nonetheless, Arabic still remained the official language, and with these countries' independence in the mid-twentieth century from the British and the French, and with the spread of free, Arabic-taught education through university level, Arabic gained even more precedence (Badran xxv).

Many Lebanese writers write in French due to the influence of French schools throughout Lebanon, even before the French mandate, and while some of them have expressed the positive aspects of this education, others have criticized this influence. It is interesting to note that although a large portion of the Lebanese society speaks French and communicates daily both in French and Arabic, and some have close contact with France, a change took place in the 1990s. The new generation is more and more speaking English as a second language, and American education is becoming more common. Egypt had a somewhat similar situation, for up until the war of the Suez Canal in 1956, most of the women writers from the bourgeoisie were educated in French schools. This explains why Andr(e Chedid, the Egyptian-born poet of Syrian-Lebanese parentage wrote in French, along with other Egyptian women writers, such as the novelist Qut al-Qulub al-

11

Dimirdash (1898–1968). Many North Africans were educated in French schools until the 1950s and 1960s, and were not taught classical Arabic.

THE RISE OF ARAB WOMEN'S POETRY

The first concerns and preoccupations of Arab women poets were, unsurprisingly, their unjust degradation, marginalization, and oppression by the social system, and their boundedness by tradition. The battle for women's rights, equality and inclusion in the literary and intellectual spheres continues today, although women stand far from where they originated. This fight includes Arab women writers in Europe and North America, as we will see later on in this introduction. Their inner and outer struggle for a personal identity, for self-realization, and their preoccu-pation with bipolarity, biculturalism, bilingualism—especially among the women poets writing in French from the Maghreb (North Africa) and Lebanon, and the Arab-American/Arab-Canadian women poets—have not ceased.

The publication of the novel *Ana Ahya* (*I live*) in 1958 by the 22-year-old Lebanese novelist Laila Ba'albaki launched the feminist literary trend. By the 1960s Arab women from all of the Arab countries were writing, and by then Egypt was not the only literary center in the Arab world; Iraq, Syria, Lebanon and Tunisia were also important literary centers. There are important women feminists, activists, and writers who, although not poets, participated in the liberation of women's voices, minds and creative selves. These women played a significant role in increasing Arab women writers' visibility, and in the struggle to recognize and acknowledge the existence of an Arab women's literature. The following are a few of these important women activists and writers: the Egyptians Doria Shafik (1908–1975), Aisha 'Abd al-Rahman (1912–1974) whose pen-name was Bint al-Shati, Zaynab al-Ghazali, Nawal al-Sadawi (b. 1930), Huda Shaarawi (founder of the Egyptian Women's Movement), and Amina al-Said, and the Moroccan Fatima Mernissi. Nizar Qabbani, the famous Syrian poet who died just recently, must be mentioned here, for he played an important role in feminine liberation. His erotic verses participated in freeing the female body and spirit, and in breaking male chauvinist attitudes. In his work he portrayed the positive energy and the wholeness of women. By the 1980s, the vibrancy of Arab women writings from all over the Arab world was growing considerably and was not only gaining visibility, but more recognition in the Arab world and abroad.

Egypt

Egypt has been a pioneering Arab country at many levels, politically, socially, culturally, intellectually, artistically, and certainly, in the struggle for women's advancement. Egyptian women writers have always played an active role in the growth and evolution of the literary scene, and they continue to do so; and poetry written by Egyptian women poets continues to flourish. Egypt started offering secondary school education equally to both girls and boys in 1925, and university education became available to women in 1929. But the event that enabled women writing to find a creative space occurred after the revolution of 1952, when primary education became obligatory for both sexes (Tadie 55).

Some of the Egyptian women poets in this collection live outside of their country: Safaa Fathy and Andrée Chedid live in France and Iman Mersal lives in Canada. Chedid writes in French and the two other poets in Arabic.

Safaa Fathy sails through life in search of enlightening gazes. She finds a certain depth in abstraction, finds passion in observing all that passes by. She wonders where she is as the question is posed to her. She enjoys not knowing even when she knows. A sailor, a stranger, a traveler, she likes to discover and be discovered. She writes, "Strangers lay down across the threshold of homes/ so the sailor would stumble over them..." Iman Mersal in her poem "Solitude Exercises" encounters death and loss, loneliness and tragedy. She questions mortality, justice, love, God. She writes, "...it's not important that God loves me./ No one in this world— even those who do righteous deeds—can provide a single proof that God loves him." She demonstrates courage and hope in the face of darkness, observing that, "this is not a dramatic situation at all." Mersal's poignant last few lines leave us standing still at the edge of the steepest hill inside of us. She leaves us with truth. She writes, "Middle aged mothers are addicted to sadness,/ maybe to get accustomed to mourning before its time./ These touch-ups in the telling/ have a magic/ that can't be understood by those/ who never had to steal sympathy from others."

Andrée Chedid has resided in France for close to thirty years. Lyricism flows throughout her poems, as they question daily life, life itself, destiny, the civil war in Lebanon, the human condition, and ultimately, express greater love. She tells us to "...return to those cities/ where events await..." us, but warns us that *we* might need another clock, even if time does not. Should we not need or want another destiny, should we not want to stop time? Chedid gives us questions that are answers, and answers that are questions, leaving us the breath of our heritage and helping us to "...resurrect/ from hope." She has always considered herself equally of France and of the Arab world, and has always conveyed the fact that writing in French did not transform her identity. Chedid continues to search for all that she writes about.

Fatma Kandil is one of the better-known new generation poets. She struggles to finally unlock the rooms inside of her, rooms that Arab women are often confined in, and attain the freedom that is rightly hers. She writes, "...the key that dies in my pocket/ reminds me it is time/ that I became a reasonable woman/ who lives in a house/ without keys, without doors." She is on a journey to free the darkness that "devours [the] full moon" inside of her, to free herself from all the times she has been defeated, to free herself from her heart. And she will stop at nothing: "I bathed in a language I did not understand..." Kandil does not fear her past, her memories, does not fear being alone: "dragging threads of the horizon from/ memory and weaving a wide net where/ human pictures [fall], and little by little the water's gaze..." widens and widens, and the poet widens and widens.

Hoda Hussein is among the younger generation poets in Egypt. She expresses profound needs; wanting to steal another child's childhood, she writes, "I myself will crawl to steal her childhood away./ I will try to logically persuade her /that losing early things is simple/ as a vaccination." Hussein interrogates incessantly, trying to answer and find new answers to all of her "question and exclamation marks." She recognizes the hypocrisies of society, its unequal structures, its injustices, its demands, and she criticizes them: "I know/ that I do not understand what/ male grownups mean by/ homeland, love, liberty—/ making a toast to the great centers of civilization—royal hats off to honor the epitome of knowledge." What she knows is that these "royal hats" knock her "small head." But one day the poet "will have a room of [her own]" to "remember the grief" when they "were homeless" and to free herself from her questions that concern the many dark, unjust realities she encounters and observes.

THE LEVANT

Lebanon

Beirut has inspired many poets, has risen in many verses. Through most of the second half of twentieth century, Beirut, as we have seen, has been an important cultural, artistic, intellectual, and publishing center in the Arab world. On the April 13, 1975, the Lebanese civil war started, and once again, Beirut found center stage in many literary oeuvres. The war clearly became a forceful and vital factor in the emergence of women writers and the growth of feminist consciousness. The mid-1970s also mark one of the most important periods in the history of international feminist criticism and literature (Cooke "Arab Women" 454). It was also a time that saw an Islamic reawakening as well as the rise of a strong women's activist movement, which helped women become more literate and knowledgeable in Islamic principles. Women not only empowered themselves in socio-cultural terms, but also went on to hold high political positions and other important posts, becoming an important presence in the nationalist and democratic movements in many Arab countries.

During the Lebanese civil war many transformations were to occur, not only in the Lebanese national consciousness, but in the Arab consciousness and in Arab women's and Arab women writers' consciousness. During this time, prose became a vibrant genre in Lebanon. Miriam Cooke refers to the women writers who remained in Lebanon during the war and wrote about the war as the Beirut Decentrists. Their works did not focus on the enemies or revolution, but rather on the harsh, brutal realities of daily life and on the violence that infiltrated their minds and existence, eventually creating a decline in the society and in the people. Throughout the war, the Beirut Decentrists were sharp observers of the new society in creation and of the generation growing up in this war, and this transfigured their works. Their call for essential changes and freedom—to write, to speak out—became a model for other women writers in the Arab world. Women writers from Yemen to the Arabian Gulf found the strength during that time to fight literary invisibility and to revolt against all forms of oppression. In the 1970s, the Saudi poet Fawziyya Abu Khalid was, for example, a strong voice against alienation and for social change. The Iraqi poet Lamea Abbas Amara also participated in the women's struggle at the time and was in Lebanon during the Lebanese civil war. Her poetry during this period portrayed how the war affected women. Many other Arab and Arab-American women poets were affected by the Lebanese war.

Etel Adnan, one of the most renowned Lebanese writers and a pioneer in the Arab-American literary scene, was born in Lebanon of Syro-Greek parents, educated in France, emigrated to the United States, and currently lives in California, Paris, and Lebanon. Adnan writes in Arabic, French and English. She has powerfully portrayed the madness of sexual politics and transmitted the horrors and absurdity of the Beirut war in her work. She writes, "War is our dialogue. It brings explosions at home, debris of/ human limbs, booby-trapped love letters.../ Always the writing, that recorded silent voice which jumps/ generations to claim eternity for blood." She has, with great mastery, described exile and wandering, accommodating herself to nomadism and otherness, and her inner and outer voyages have penetrated the many layers of self and consciousness. As she juggles life in death and death in life, she tells us, "There is a word that never/ makes it./ …that word is *death*." In her latest collection, *There*, written in English, from which passages are included in this anthology, she raises questions of self, of the other, of identity, of womanhood. These questions travel well alongside the themes of war's aftermath and its wounds on the conscious and subconscious, on identity. She tries to convey that identity continuously changes and can be multiple, and that you can be somewhere and long for somewhere else; that once you are culturally multiple you are bound to always be missing something. After all, she has a Muslim father and a Christian mother, speaks and writes in different languages, has lived in different places, and admits to this perpetual sense of longing. She seems to want to transmit that the metaphysical impact between the other and the self is so intense, that at times the other almost becomes the self. From there to here, self to other, one senses that she is trying to unite distance/ exile, rootedness/ home, time and space, "the self and itself." She asks and answers, "What is *here*?: a place or an idea, a circle focused in God's eye…" And *there* "lies the/ confrontation between the self and itself." Adnan knows who she is, though; she does not struggle with her identity like other Arab-American poets. Her identity is clear to her: she is a woman, she is Lebanese, she is an Arab, but her linguistic expression, mainly in English and French rather than in Arabic, leads *others* sometimes to question her settled identity.

Nadia Tuéni is another francophone Lebanese poet. When writing about Lebanon and the war, she was often concerned with the relationship between the individual and the homeland at all levels, and also reflected the ludicrousness of society. Her work explores the themes of childhood, nature, life and death, and her beloved Lebanon. The beauty of her relationship with her country transcends the lines of her poems, carrying the reader to the arms of Lebanon, to Beirut of "a hundred palaces," to Baalbeck "a gift from the world of measures," to Tripoli "Wide as a smile," to the Lebanese mountains and a "child's recollection," to the cedars that she loves "as a man loves breath."

Vénus Khoury-Ghata resides in Paris, and also writes in French. She is strongly influenced by the Lebanese war; her work plays with death. Her poems are rooms filled with graves, images of guns and cannons. In her poems, "Because" and " It was a season tattooed on the forehead of the earth," the death of the individual, of the civilian, of the husband and of the father, of the child, bleed in hearts and on her pages. She writes, "...they loaded their rifles.../ they died from indifference" and "Only the naïve die..." Her poem, "Humbly," is like the faintness of terror at the edge of darkness, from the "Bone driller of every abscess/ clay in lieu of womb/ roots required to hang laundry from the flesh" to "no key to open these stones/ and no cry on his house's shoulder." Although between life and death she tends to walk toward death, for that is the reality she sees, and the pain she endures, she still demonstrates immense courage and survival, honor and dignity; she still holds on to hope.

The French created the category called "francophone" literature, creating a marginal situation for the Arab writers who write in French and who live in France and mostly have French citizenship. As Etel Adnan points out, this category creates a separation between literature that is "native" and literature that is "foreign." Thus, writers such as "...Apollinaire, who was Polish and Italian, born in Rome,...[is] considered [a] French author. But people such as Georges Schehadah, Amin Maalouf... or Aimé Cesaire, Alloula,...etc.,... from the Arab or African worlds, are considered francophone" (quoted in Shimon 61). Though Khoury-Ghata, Andrée Chedid, and the Tunisian poet Amina Said are included in numerous anthologies of French women poets, many Arab-French writers in France are still marginalized or absent in contemporary French discourse, criticism, and literature.

Then there is the case of Claire Gebeyli, who was born in Egypt, has lived most of her life in Lebanon, writes in French and is originally Greek. The interesting thing about Gebeyli is that, although she is not Arab, the Lebanese war intensified her Lebanese identity: Gebeyli wrote for Beirut. Instead of leaving during the war, she stayed and took part in all its realities. A collective Lebanese consciousness is felt when reading Gebeyli's work. She writes fiction, poetry, and *billets* (war correspondence poetry). Her work mirrors the war, evoking its horrors, its every emotion, its every vertebra. She wanted to liberate her adopted country of this dark cloud. She expresses the angry echo of death—death of a country, of a soul, of a body, of the tiniest breath. She writes, "Nothing ahead/ But a cry/ At the heart of... darkness." By portraying a collective consciousness she also transmitted the hopeful collective reconstruction of Lebanon after the war.

Other Lebanese women poets emigrated to the United States, but continued to write in Arabic, like Amira el-Zein. El-Zein is rooted in Lebanon, and exiled melancholy and profound wounds are the mirrors of her land. But she knows that there is no return after war, after exile, after distance has distanced itself. While never being able to divorce herself from her land of mirrors, she declares, "How can I return to you,/ now that you are without memory?" And then, " I shiver with cold and dig up/ the floor of my room/ to see you lying/ in the grave of my memory,/ O land of mirrors!"

Houda al-Na'mani left Lebanon in 1986 for London and Washington, and returned when the division between East and West Beirut, known as the Green Line, was dismantled. She admits to have spent the years of the war in her house, bearing many attacks, but also says that these years brought her closer to her spiritual and mystical self. Her work could not escape the portrayal of war and terror, of violence and human suffering. Her poems are equally, though, a conversation with time, eternity, and fear, a fusion of beauty and love, an immersion into peace. Her images and messages are often grounded yet full of mystery, of the unknown, thus, she writes, "Oh, Fear, drunken and tipsy as a mystical tree.../ By yourself, paralyzed, you stay by the window/ watching the tempest pass,/ the lightning didn't even surprise you—/ the winter curved in your eyes.../ What might perhaps impress you—/ a walking mountain?"

The inner voyage, the lack of understanding men have of women, the absence of real freedom, the frustration and loneliness that often surrounds an Arab woman is not far away from what Therese 'Awwad tries to express. She writes, "My loneliness/ ages like wine./ ...I make love/ to the hunger/ deep inside." And 'Awwad's pessimism concerning the situation of women, of war and injustice seems lasting, "Over my skin/ the echoes of famine/ persist." Traces of 'Awwad's loneliness walk into the poems of 'Enayat Jaber, yet Jaber's words express less vulnerability but perhaps as much sadness as those of 'Awwad. Jaber writes, "I now resemble/ alley cats;/ too miserable to miaow..." She does not escape the ruins of the war as she writes, "He breathed deeply,/ when the street awoke,/ with the very features of yesterday." Nada al-Hage, who is of the same generation as Jaber, is on a journey through the skies of herself, of her life, of poetry and the worlds stretching from these places. She continues to journey without limits. She says, "I continue/ I do not know where/ I do not mind but/ I continue." She seems to be escaping to a spiritual sphere to unite the trees, the sea, to unite all that she loves on earth with what lives in shadows, in the unknown and she "will reach the light/...cross the Secret." This element of transcendence in al-Hage's poetry fades to a somewhat more mathematical horizon in Sabah al-Kharrat Zwein's poetry. Zwein experiments with the "maze of language" and the center of the universe and what exists and might exist in it. She explores the obscure spaces and Space itself, along with the sky, its shapes, and the flaws that can't be located even when they are right there. Her work has an abstractness with a certain direction—Zwein's direction. A mind "always [bending] in that direction" that holds within it the opposite of itself. Zwein writes, "below the arch of the old window, the opposite window/ ...the face is in the sky."

Palestine

Palestinian women's poetry is filled with the dark shadows of blood and death, struggle and resistance, while still being concerned with a multitude of themes from personal quests to love. It is a poetry that rarely escapes the heavy weight of the occupation, of exile both outside and inside their country, echoing the pains and conflicts associated with loss of homeland, and the fact, as the Iraqi-Jewish writer Yizhak Bar-Moshe says, that "A Man without his house is only an illusion" (Berg 112). Fadwa Tuqan is the most prominent Palestinian woman poet, and one of the most renowned Arab women poets. The echoes of Palestinian reality and struggle travel in her work: "...the fishing nets were full/ one thousand slaughtered, two thousand, thousands..." And a perpetual unknown haunts as she continues, "Any more to come?" And the longing never ceases; Palestinian collectivity never fades. She says, "In our hands is a fresh yearning for you." Tuqan's work is also concerned with the repression of women in her society, with the absoluteness of freedom and with breaking away from tradition. One of her most remarkable literary traits remains her insight into the conflicting, often paradoxical, world of emotions.

Salma Khadra Jayyusi is one of the most important women writers and critics in the second half of the twentieth century. Her contributions in the field of Arab literary criticism and Arab literary awareness have been tremendous, and both admirable and commendable. In Jayyusi's poetry, the love of a mother and the love of the motherland meet, and Palestinian resistance is constantly present. In her poem "In the Casbah," the trauma and illusions that war can plant in the fields of one's subconscious are mirrored, while simultaneously revealing the facts and atrocities of war. She writes, "I thought the war was.../ here we died, Mai and I...[Mai is her daughter]/ flattened by armored wheels..." And her vivid consciousness continuously confesses, as she does in "The Sunken Ship," that she is "a mother,/ a woman without love..." who constantly dies "in shame,/ without a heart, without a country,/ without a home."

The Palestinian tragedy is expressed in the works of most Arab and Arab-American writers and poets, but of course it affects Palestinian literature most profoundly. The strains of the Palestinian's daily life, their oppression and dispossession, their fundamental need of a homeland and their fight to resolve their unsettled identity, are struggles that naturally find a place in the works of Palestinian women poets. Palestinian women have always participated in cultural and political movements, and Palestinian women poets have always contributed to literature and their presence has grown tremendously. We are reminded of these poets' Palestinian-ness as we travel through Nidaa Khoury's corridors of youth, as her "...soul craves/ the sour taste of childhood," to the crevice of past memory, the confinement of present reality, and the different corners of the Palestinian diaspora in Siham Da'oud's "I Love in White Ink," where she writes, "from my brow bursts a memory/ smuggled from jail to jail/ scattered like my land's windwisps," to Laila Allush's portrayal of exile and rootedness in "The Path of Affection." This is a path that is conquered but that can never take away the profound affection of the speaker, of any Palestinian. She describes the "mortgaged trees," the "...fresh fertilizers,/ And efficient sprinklers..." to demonstrate Zionist agriculture and conquest, which is imprinted in Palestinian consciousness. The poem carries us from Jerusalem to a *New* Haifa, the old to technology, the past to the present, the free to the occupied, while telling us that even if there are changes, the land still expresses the most essential: "All the poplars and... ancestor's solemn orchards" smile at her "with Arab affection" and the land sings out "...with affection" to her.

The newer generation Palestinian poets did not escape their sober history as we can see in Donia el-Amal Ismail's haunting description of Gaza, as it "...creeps/ with cold hands and feet..." like her "...life in this hot-city/ of sins." Palestinians cannot flee the additional tortures of their changing realities, the irony and absurdness of their reality, as Ismail continues to tell us in a powerfully sarcastic voice: Gaza now "professionally [practices] whoredom/ over traditions of Revolution, fashioning red neckties/ over newspapers in a cloudy morning....[and enjoys] her luxurious pains/ like an old woman complaining about her teeth falling..." The new generation cannot escape the perpetual questions perpetually returning and asking— Why this tragic existence? Why this uprootedness? Why this insanity? Ghada el-Shafa'i asks, "Has it ever happened/... searching the wardrobe of time for a shirt that might fit,/ for lost hours of/ happiness." Sumaiya el-Sousy asks what she already knows, "can we escape?" Mai Sayigh asks, "How many massacres did you survive?" and then concludes with a *new* departure, "...you collect all the wounds, taking refuge with/ death,/ wearing dreams as wings?" But dreams are often difficult to get to, especially if you are a woman. Laila al-Sa'ih writes in "Imitations of Anxiety" about the difficulties of being a woman, of having dreams, a voice, a pen: she says, "You do not know how hard it is,/ transfiguring blood into ink—/ emerging from one's secret dreams/ to voicing the dream." And maybe one day she will be able to add "a single syllable to this existence." Maybe one day Munia Samara will find what she is looking for while going through all the doors of the cities. Maybe one day she will find what she is looking for instead of finding in Jericho "the scandal of this universe," in Jerusalem that "the great gods/ and fairies of the epochs have left," in Gaza "a burning wound in the side of the earth."

The Palestinian disaster of 1948, *al-Nakba*, and then the Six Day War in 1967, led to the fleeing, expelling, exiling, and emigration of millions of Palestinians. Their dispossession led them to many different countries throughout the world, which eventually led them to the inevitable: writing in different idioms. Although, apart from Arabic, Palestinian poets write mostly in English; but Anton Shammas started writing in Hebrew, Rawia Morra writes in Swedish, and surely Palestinian writers will start writing in other languages. Morra's beautifully woven words flow gently on the page; every line is like a breath that liberates and captivates. There is a wholeness in her work as it comes full circle with life and death, with love and oneness. She travels in the different layers of herself, in the different days and nights inside of her. Her work is focused on the world that exists inside and that, in fact, mirrors the preoccupations and realities of the world outside. Every step she takes with her lines is an intriguing and powerful pause: "Powerless" "Inside here/ are those/ who were born too late./ Outside there lie/ those who died prematurely." But her sense of exile and Arabness is not far away as she describes her family: "My grandfather has an ashtray/ a cup of coffee/ tens of grandchildren/ and his turban." As she continues, the absence of homeland surfaces: "The leaves have no tree/ to hang on to." Ultimately, she says, "I have not found my home/ but I have learnt/ to live/ in my voice."

Syria

Many of the better-known contemporary Syrian women poets are living outside of Syria but continue to write in Arabic and partake in the Arabic literary scene. 'Aisha Arnaout, Maram Masri, and Salwa al-Neimi live in Paris, Ghada al-Samman lives between Beirut and Paris, and Lina Tibi lives in London. Hala Mohammad, after numerous years in Paris, has gone back to Syria. Her words are heavy with pain, and love walks with her as she writes, "Every time/ I stepped towards him/ a fleeting moment/ replaced my footsteps…" She leaves us with an endless chase at the door of anticipation, with a man who offers his chest and love, who will always, according to Mohammad, burn out the light or the darkness.

Maram Masri's lines are also filled with the many dark and light journeys of the heart, the many faces of love—love of a man, of poetry. She says, "All the words my love/ are ropes/ and all the smiles/ are masks..." Although "she left her shoes on the shore, and her vision got obstructed and she lost her balance," she "...did/ not fall." There is a simple mysteriousness in Masri's poems that appeals to the reader, a simple language that is beauty. Salwa al-Neimi, on the other hand, uses a more straightforward and raw language. The reality she portrays is like the poem that "falls from the faucet/ like a fish, down onto [her] hands/ while [she washes] the dinner dishes." In her poetry the surreal and the real are side by side, and the fantasia of the mind is in fusion with the elements of daily chores. And al-Neimi has a way of leaving us with Dracula and a ripe fig while she pretends to "watch the passerby."

'Aisha Arnaout stands in a space similar to Sabah al-Kharrat Zwein, as she explores orbits, boundlessness, and the infinite spaces of time. She dives into an unconscious state and explores its beyondness. She unites elements of the earth and the heavens, of life and death, love and mystery. There is a scientific trail in the poems by Arnaout. In the womb of space everything seems to exist: the "cracked soul" and the "gleaming body," the "Absolute nonlogic" and the "Proof of the indefinite." Most of all, there is love and chaos and all that is shapeless. Arnaout's poems are in a sphere of their own, where "spaces zoom by/ and time repositions itself," where we continue to question the "spinal cord" of the world, of our lives, ourselves, our consciousness.

Lina Tibi's work echoes that of Emily Dickinson as well as that of the well-known Syrian woman poet Dade Haddad, in its constant confrontation with death and darkness. Her work also resonates a certain roaming despair that is often found in the work of Syrian poet Saniyya Saleh, who died in 1985. Yet, her work walks in a very unique way. Only Tibi can write the way she does about the lights of darkness, the darknesses of light, about the world inside of herself, inside moments, inside emotions, inside details. She often wants us to "Leave [her] to the night/ to the darkness drifting out of the sun's window..." Her definition of darkness is as mysterious as her God. Her loneliness is both comforting and distant, as she writes, "I will stretch my loneliness/ a bed,/ for you to sleep..." Her meeting with death is both a way to the light and a suicide. And although she often leaves us with light, we mistake it for darkness.

Saniyya Saleh's despair is associated with women's isolation and their suppression. There is also great loss conveyed in her work, mainly for her mother whom she lost at a very young age. She is often in the corridors of grief, and all her life she has "willed to go forward [but has] not/ advanced beyond/ the borders of [her] grave." Her pessimism seems to be never-ending, and although she continues to cry out for her mother, she also tells her to "Go back to [her] death…," which is ultimately where Saleh herself seems to believe she will find freedom.

Ghada al-Samman broadens our views of Arab women. She is better known for her novels and short stories but also writes essays and poetry, and has played an important role in Arab feminism and sexual politics. Her work and activism are geared toward fighting sexual oppression, inequality, and discrimination of Arab women. She calls for a revolution at all levels, for a new definition and reconstruction of the man/woman dynamic in relation to tradition, society, intimacy, and sexuality, and for a change in the economic, ideological, and political system. Her poetry is written in a simple, straightforward, personal style and reflects—apart from the necessity for social reform—the fragmentation of Arab society, religious tension, nationalism, war and defeat, revolution and politics, and of course, the joys and pains of life in Beirut, which became her home away from Syria. However, love and its often complex and multiple faces—love of a man, of a country, of nature, of poetry— is what seems to surface foremost in al-Samman's poetry. Her poems, "The Lover of Blue Writing above the Sea!" and "The Lover of Rain in an Inkwell" are fine examples of this focus. Her feminine voice, her speaking out about pain and love of a man and of Beirut, unite present in the first poem as she insists that even if she is "running alone in the rain, without a man or a nation…" she will leave "traces of [her] step, traces of [her] pens." In the second poem, the echoes of her first poem continue and she unifies herself with ultimate love: "…the sun will rise above my tomb in Beirut!"

Iraq

Many of the well-known Iraqi women poets writing today are also living outside of their country. Amal al-Juburi is in Germany, Dunya Mikhail and Lamea Abbas Amara are in the United States, and May Muzaffar in Bahrain. All three poets follow history and convey it with their own perception, personal experiences and reflections, with mystical and mythical elements. Mikhail interrogates her inner world, and the world of her heart. When reading Mikhail one often encounters pain, anguish and dead ends, as she writes, "Within me is a heart/ in the heart—walls—/ in the walls—cracks/ in the cracks—dead wind." Her lyricism is striking as she witnesses herself: "I had a dream/ in which I was the witness." And she always returns to history, memory, and the states of the heart. She writes,

"The evening is white/ and the heart is an icy carnation./ The evening is white/ history is snow." She also reminds us that her roots are where she left them, in Iraq. Al-Juburi's poem, "Enheduanna and Goethe," mirrors the style and theme found in Enheduanna's poetry (see pages 134–135). It expresses rage against oppression and a sense of crippledness due to this oppressive state. Al-Juburi writes about exile and longing, about her agony vis-à-vis the Gulf War and the horrifying reality that Iraq is facing today. Her poetry is filled with myths and mythic images, history, and the passing of time, and leaves us "in the fleeting moments of lightning…" and in protest. Muzaffar leaves us spinning in "remote lands," leaves us with men that "go past seats that remain empty," leaves us with "Nothing but a resonance/ of [a] distant voice," leaves us with yesterday and the Absent. Her voyage is as infinite as that of a bird, as powerful as her words and images. Her work seems to penetrate the invisible and is held by a reality that is both spiritual and full of "chests of darkness."

Lamea Abbas Amara emigrated to the United States in 1986. Amara's lyrical work has often reflected Arab politics, culture, and civilization as well as the position of women in Arab society. Her poem, "San Diego (On a rainy day)," is filled with inner conflicts. She admires the beauty of San Diego, California where she resides, and a melancholy covers her, for the city and its beauty remind her of Lebanon and Iraq, and of the horrors of the war. She writes, "The beauty of San Diego/ reminds me of Lebanon/ if only the bleeding would stop." Amara's profound longing roams in her recent poems and as she remembers the Arab world she writes, "I wish we could love there/ but time and exile/ separate us." The struggle she faces of living away from her home amplifies with the unfavorable US policies in the Arab world: "How can I live comfortably in a country/ where swords are sharpened for our people?" Many of Amara's latest poems reflect the cruelties of the Gulf War, a war, as we shall see, that affected not only the Arab world and its writers, but became a catalytic factor in forming the identity of Arab-American writers.

Jordan

Jordanian women poets are not numerous; however, with the numerous changes currently taking place in Jordan culturally and socially, surely more voices will surface. Zulaykha Abu-Risha is one of the better-known contemporary Jordanian women poets. Abu-Risha is in agony, looking for "what buries/ our aches/ alive." She journeys to dream, longs for freedom, and speaks of unrest, exile, and her womanhood. She writes, "Come let's dream together of journeying far/ Come, let's not go back/ when the homeland expels us/ and there remains nothing but our tree/ alone/ in the swamp." Mona Saudi writes about the strong love between a mother and a daughter, and how this love conquers her desire to die. In the poems included in this anthology, she carries us to the world inside the different elements of nature, whether it is the night, the air, the trees. She carries us to her darkness, her "Blind City," and to the "weeping pavements," where "life glows in an instant/ born in a puddle of light."

Thurayya Malhas suggests, "everything is false/ under the sun/ above the sun/ and around." Malhas expresses the hypocrisy of her society, the agony of women and the torment of life and isolation. She prays, finds refuge in writing, and questions incessantly: "Where is my way?/ Where is my poem?/ Where is my guitar?"

The Arabian Gulf

> *The female writer should be committed in three ways: as a writer, as a woman and as a third world person; and her womanhood is implicated in all three.*
> —Omolara Ogundipe-Leslie, *The Female Writer*

It was from the Arabian Peninsula that Arab tribes came. They traveled, especially after the coming of Islam, to what became the Arab world, and mixed with the people in these countries. People in the Arab world come from many different origins: Arab, Persian, Turkish, Greek, Roman, Crusader, and so forth. Today, "Arab" refers to a shared culture and language. Also, the Arab world has become predominantly a Muslim world; the number of people from other religious groups is very small.

Although the poetry that stems from the Gulf has its own individual elements, its evolution in terms of form and content has been the same as that of Arabic poetry generally. The Gulf poets have, like other Arab poets, been affected by, participated in, and written about, the joys and achievements, the horrible political happenings, the wars, the psychological turbulence, and the struggles and failures of the Arab people and world. Women poets from the Gulf have shared these concerns, which have transfigured their writing, as well as the specific concerns of Arab women, such as the need to expunge the oppression of women.

Political and social changes in the Arabian Gulf affected the literature of these writers; these changes are reflected as distinctive elements in their poetry. Poets from the Gulf states have looked "nostalgically at the pre-oil past, the past of seafaring and pearl diving, full of toil and hardship, it is true, of endeavors hardly ever requited and hopes hardly ever achieved, yet settled and well-rooted in place and time, and full of contentment and innocence, governed by a spirit of harmony and human brotherhood" (Jayyusi, *Literature* 22). The Gulf War became an important theme to Gulf poets and to most Arab poets. For women poets from the Gulf, most particularly for Saudi Arabian women—since Saudi Arabia is the center of Islam—an important concern has been the difficult task of finding an equilibrium between modernity and the preservation of traditions and culture.

The number of women writers from the Arabian Gulf (Saudi Arabia, Bahrain, Kuwait, Qatar, United Arab Emirates, and Yemen, listed in order by which they will be discussed) has grown tremendously in the last three decades, and the contributions of these writers have accelerated in the last decade. It seems important to mention that equal primary and secondary education for girls in Saudi Arabia was not available until the mid-1950s, and university education only became possible for women in the Gulf in the 1960s.

Women writers from the Gulf are mainly from middle and upper class families, although the door is gradually opening for women writers from other social classes. It is common for these upper class women to sponsor women's literary events, organizations, and projects. It is said that some women from Arabian royal families wrote, particularly in the folk form of Nabti poetry (Arebi 23). However, these women published very little, and if they did, used a pen-name. For Arab women in the Gulf, family support is a determining factor in the development of their writing and the continuation of their creative craft. Most of the women from the Gulf who write are encouraged by their families, and usually these families are interested in and/or have experimented with oral poetry and are knowledgeable about poetry and religion. Most of these women writers are still, however, victims of the social restrictions of their society. They are forced to follow the social and cultural norms, and are often cornered between their point of view and the respect they have for their family. Thus, the choice of themes and views in their writing is inevitably affected, since most of the time they abide by what is acceptable. Nevertheless, as time goes by, women in the Arabian Gulf are challenging themselves, their societies, and institutions even as they have had to endure often very difficult circumstances.

Literature from the Gulf is not considered an independent literature as of yet. As for the status of women's literature from the Gulf, to begin with, it is important to emphasize the extent to which any form of literature in that part of the world is intricately linked with politics, religion, society, and culture. These associations have created a certain pattern in literary history and in the reception of literature. Women writers from the Gulf not only have to fight the same battles that most of the other Arab women face, but in addition, have their specific historical, religious, political, and cultural confrontations. While the general Arab literati have welcomed them and many Arab critics have encouraged their voices and recognized their poetry, women poets from the Gulf are still struggling for their voices to be acknowledged and respected in the Arabian Gulf's literary scene.

Fawziyya Abu-Khalid is one of the most known Saudi poets. She has been active in trying to change the suppressed position of women in Arab society, and her poetry, avant-garde both in content and form, has steered many debates. Her poetry interrogates Arab culture and history, the relationships between the sexes, between poetry and religion, between Islamic society and Western society, while demonstrating a profound insight into a woman's mind and consciousness. Her thematic choices and language usage break boundaries. She describes women's bodies and speaks freely about sex in her work. Her determination to "solve [any] riddle" never ends. She remains hopeful about women's freedom, women's political and social openness, and she continues to dream the possible and impossible. As she writes in her poem, "A Country": " She bathes in rain gushing forth from her lap/ And she dreams."

Another Saudi poet, Thurayya al-Urayyid, journeys inside herself and dares to visit many worlds. Her voyage is at times a search for what she wishes to see, a search for something she is uncertain of or unwilling to acknowledge she is looking for: "Do we see in what we see/ anything but what we wish to be?" At times it is a search for a spiritual or transcendental awakening. As she writes, "My body standing between me and myself,/ how can I transcend it?" At times it is a search for ways to unveil mysteriousness: "Will the mystery remain hostage to my intuition?" And it is a search for ways to eradicate women's silence: "...is my soul killing me with my own voice/ or centuries of forced silence choking my voice?"

Another well-known poet writing from the Gulf is the Bahraini Hamda Khamees. Her work reflects profound vision and inner depth. She has also been very active in the fight for the progress of women and for justice. In her poem, "What is Not Mine," she portrays a powerful picture of an unequal society, but also says with firmness that despite a woman's oppression, her mind can remain hers. Her penetrating words leave the reader before an immense opening, "Whatever exists is now/ is not mine/The man who is showering/ before he bathes in my body/ is not mine/ ...The house armed with the ordinary and the familiar/ is not mine/ The house framing my imprisonment/ is not mine…" But "The passion of a free horse/ is mine/ …The splendor/ and this universe/ are mine!" The issue of freedom and the journey to freedom continue in the poems of Fawziyya al-Sindi, who is also from Bahrain. She writes, "I wander/ my journey's provision: thirst of the deprived." Al-Sindi travels incessantly—through places, people, poetry—in search of that ultimate door that will allow her to be whole: "Two lonely people on the/ sidewalk of despair and the prickling of writing./ Rain stumbled on the echo of our steps." She leaves us in search of, or in the center of, a vivid awakening waiting to awaken.

The Kuwaiti poet Su'ad al-Mubarak al-Sabah writes about the imperative of freedom as well. Al-Sabah's work also reflects anguish over human rights violations and the necessity for Arab unification. She expresses the despair that Arabs have felt, the pain they have endured, and the profound anger that lives inside of them in the face of war, injustice, and a truly turbulent history. She writes about love, the "only native land," to which she owes "allegiance."

The Kuwaiti poet Sa'adyya Mufarreh carries us to the spell of blazing trees. But though "the spell of the blazing tree" is "flowing/ ebbing/ transforming into a sun…" it does not intend "to set/ for very long." Mufarreh continues her odyssey beyond her tears, her heart, her words, and war, beyond the beauty she finds and the spell she falls into.

The radiance and endlessness of trees continue in the poem of the Qatari poet Zakiyya Malallah, as she writes, "Flap your wings on my bare trees/ teach me/ the little tales." And like Fawziyya al-Sindi, Malallah leaves us with "countless awakenings." Malallah's work reflects a woman and her many minds, thoughts, directions, ways, her social, cultural, religious, and emotional constraints. Her poems demonstrate a woman's moment with herself and the discovery and rediscovery of herself. She swims in her "…own breaths,/ …playing with pens and papers,/ and annihilating…" herself or rather extinguishing everything inside of her that confines and constrains her.

Many vibrant voices are coming from the United Arab Emirates. Dhabya Khamees is a poet confident of her femininity, her identity as a woman. Her work expresses this confidence along with her profound love for freedom. She explores the themes of love, of selfhood, of ambition, and of solitude freely, fearlessly, and boundlessly, and will let nothing stop her. She writes, "I love you when I want/ I love you when you want…" and even if "The sea stares at my dream/(I cannot come to the sea's aid)." Maysoun Saqr al-Qasimi is more experimental but still addresses issues of freedom and the necessity to eliminate the sufferings of women in the face of inequality and subjugation. Al-Qasimi also writes about the many relationships men and women have. Her poetry has a certain sensuality and equally a sense of frustration. She writes, "No shadow in the long hallucination/ Oh, how much I deserved this body." And further along she says with an ounce of sarcasm and irony, "It's fair, that we feel satisfied/ by kisses." Nujoum al-Ghanim's work has elements of Arabic folklore. Her images are full of symbols, transmitting to her reader Arab culture and life. Her poetry is also about Arab women, their agony, and their repression; she writes, "Where is my blemish, if my veil is removed/ and robes sob over my body?"

Yemeni poets have been profoundly affected by and have written profusely about the pre-1962 trauma. Before the 1960s, South Yemen consisted of a number of British protectorates and along with the British-colonized Aden, formed a Federal Union. North Yemen, which included its capital Sanaa, was ruled by the Imams, who were the hereditary rulers. After years of frustration the Yemenis revolted in 1962 against the Imam dictatorship; thus began the Yemeni revolution which was to last until 1969. At this point it became the Yemen Arab Republic, although it is often referred to as North Yemen. South Yemen revolted against the British in 1963, became independent in 1967 and became known as the People's Democratic Republic of Yemen, though it is most often referred to as South Yemen. Although there surely are women writing in Yemen, they are virtually invisible in the literary scene. Nevertheless Huda Ablan manages in her work to portray the dilemmas of women's lives and minds, the struggle between the traditional and the modern role of women, and the difficult conciliation between these roles. Her poetry is ripe and firm with passion. She writes, "No one belongs to the path/ except a pocket/ stuffed with the leaves of night./...When hungry,/ it devours their warm, ripe whispers./ When thirsty,/ it drinks their cries washed with holy water." Like many Arab women poets, Ablan is on a journey, and often finds herself back where she started: "There is no one in the house/ its dozing cracks obscure/ the rounded journey of a small sun."

North Africa

> Ce qui est terrible, c'est que la folie qui me traverse a une réalité.
> —Nabile Farés, *Le Champs des oliviers*

> Personne n'entend plus un peuple qui perd ses mots.
> —François Mitterand

There is a great deal of contemporary literature from North Africa written in both French and Arabic. Both bodies of literature have an important literary history. Albert Memmi expressed with dismay his belief that most likely, literature written in French by Maghrebian writers would fade and Arabic would take over completely. This has not happened; francophone North African literature continues to be dynamic. We must not forget that the older generation of North Africans went to French schools and did not learn classical Arabic: thus, literature up until their countries' independence was mainly written in French. North African poetry written in Arabic, like Arabic poetry generally, followed the same literary evolution from the classical into modernism, and had the same influences such as Nazik al-Malaika, Khalil Gibran, and others. It is also important to mention that besides French and classical Arabic, some writers have also written in colloquial Arabic and Berber. As in the rest of the Arab countries, literature flourished in North Africa in the 1980s, as new voices and works emerged, evolving thematically and stylistically.

North Africa has had a long history of colonization. Algeria was colonized by France in 1830 and became independent on July 3, 1962. Tunisia was a French Protectorate from 1881 until independence on March 20, 1956. Morocco became a French Protectorate in 1912 the same month and year as Tunisia. (Morocco was also occupied by Spain in the early twentieth century.) And both the French and Italians occupied Libya in the early twentieth century. In the Maghreb, French was the dominant language taught in the schools and adopted by the governments (though Italian, and sometimes Turkish, were used as well). Although these countries gained their independence nearly half a century ago, French is still spoken, written, and taught.

North African women throughout their history have been heroes and legends, martyrs and resistance fighters, nationalists, feminists, and writers, participating in all aspects of their civilization historically, culturally, politically, socially, and artistically. Maghrebian women writers who were born in France or lived their entire lives outside of North Africa tend to write about family memories of their country, childhood memories, or impressions gathered during visits. Such experiences are common to poets who have been exiled or who have emigrated, and are common to post-colonial writers. Many North African poets deal with issues of bicultural anxiety, bilingualism, duality, pluralism, exile, emigration (describing life in France as North African immigrants) and conflicting or lost identities. Their works also often interrogate the tension between tradition and modernism, and almost always investigate the deep struggles of women's freedom, equality, and position in society. Algerian women have been more silenced than women from Tunisia and Morocco, but two Algerian women novelists have opened the door to North African women writers. The first is Taos Ambrouche, with the publication of her novel, *Jacinthe noire* (*Black Hyacinth*, 1947), whose theme of biculturalism was to continue in the work of many women writers. The second is Assia Djebar with the publication of her novel, *La Soif* (*The Mischief*, 1957), which also dealt with a theme that would continue be present in North African women writings, that of women's oppression at all levels and the fundamental necessity of women's equality and freedom. Both of these novels were written in French. To my knowledge, although poetry books written in Arabic were published in the 1960s and 1970s, the first novel published in Arabic by a North African woman writer was *Body Memory* (1993) by Ahlem Mosteghanemi, another Algerian. Of the four North African countries, Algeria has produced the most literature in both Arabic and French, by writers of both sexes.

But North African women writers have not yet been able to obliterate their invisibility. The problem must first change within their own countries. Although North Africa considers itself advanced, the position of women remains bound by traditional Muslim dynamics. This conservative approach does not allow favorable reception of women writers, especially when the readers are mostly male and do not always agree with the fact that women have the right to voice their opinion. Women have written about their suppressed and marginalized status, and the necessity for social change; however, their voices and experiences are not heard enough in the Arab world and in the West. One very important setback is that women writers, with the exception of a few, have not really evolved their craft; thus, their poetic and aesthetic flaws have set them aside. The fact that they have not been encouraged to write and voice themselves has contributed to their artistic weakness. Furthermore, censorship has been another problem in the spreading of North African women's writings. The biggest publishing houses are controlled by the state and small publishing houses never last very long. These factors have often discouraged women writers. Although many have published one book, maybe two, and published in journals and magazines—such as *Alif* (Tunis), *Souffles* (Rabat), *Parcours maghrébins* (Algiers), *Dérives* (Montreal), *Horizons Magrébins* (Toulouse), and *Notre Librairie* (Paris), and some of the previously mentioned magazines and journals published in other parts of the Arab world—many did not continue to write and publish.

North African poets, like Arab-American poets, share notions of duality.

But they are perhaps even more multiple in their identities, as their poetry stands on its own as North African poetry (they have strived for this standing), and is also part of Arabic, African, and in the case of those poets writing in French, francophone poetry. Today, although a poet might write in Arabic or in French, both languages are still part of his/her life—this is the case of most, if not all, of the North African poets included in this anthology. Since, in the North African case, language is such an important cultural and social factor, it is imperative to speak about it further. Many North African women poets have emigrated and dealt with issues such as alienation and discrimination, but their issues of duality and bilingualism started in their homeland; the problem stems from colonization. Many North Africans have emigrated to France, and thus, even after their independence they were left with two cultures, two memories, two homes. The theme of emigration is very present in North African literature, especially Algerian literature—the anguish and longing, the double belonging, the feeling of exclusion, the continuous inner and outer struggle of their *twoness* and their profound need to find *oneness*. In France, the children of North African immigrants, known as "beurs," have published many literary oeuvres, but the future of "beurs literature" cannot be determined. Nonetheless, what has already been written and published bears paying attention to not only for its artistic merits but for its social, cultural, and historical *témoignage*.

Despite the independence of North Africa, colonization continues in subtle yet profound ways. Assia Djebar said in her novel *L'Amour, la fantasia* (*Love, the fantasia*, 1985), "Le français m'est marâtre." She says that French, her language of expression, the one she writes in, continues to colonize her even though her country is independent. Jamilah Buhrayd, a legendary Algerian hero of independence, once explained in an interview that Arabic was not her first language, French was. She added, "after that in importance came German, and Italian, and, finally, Arabic. I feel ashamed of myself when I sit down to write a letter to an Arab friend, for, if I tried to write in Algerian dialect, I would have difficulty choosing the letters. So I end up writing in French" (Fernea 252). Buhrayd continues to explain that she grew up being taught that France was her country, the Gauls were her ancestors, that the French flag was her flag, that Algeria did not exist. She says, "It was *French* Algeria. And we carried around our French identity every day in school. It wasn't easy to get rid of that identity; we'd had it all our lives" (Fernea 254–255).

It is a profound conflict since in many ways the writer is not only a victim of colonization, but of her own self-colonization, since her language of expression is in the language of the *other*. Writing in the language of the colonizer can be daunting, can be a deprivation of one's identity, of one's being, and can make one feel like one doesn't exist. It also creates paradoxes and contradictions in an individual's mind and being, as the individual goes from one language to the next, from one world of images, expressions and visions to another, which are in this case completely different, and often even conflict with each other. It is a profoundly complex cultural and psychic conflict. On the other hand, some writers have found that writing in the language of the other is not conflicting but offers a field of more possibilities. Some believe that writing in another language isn't necessarily an exile, nor does it have to surface feelings of dispossession and displacement, but instead should demonstrate the society's multiplicity and the unity of its diversity (linguistic, cultural, and religious). In the case of North African poets, it is not actually writing in another language that is the crux of the problem, but rather, not having the option to do otherwise, since colonization deprived them of their own language.

Furthermore, although linguistic expression should not marginalize writers or leave them confined to the shadows, it often does. Someone like Rawia Morra, who is Palestinian but writes in Swedish, has difficulty finding where to exist as a writer. Writers who are multiple should be included in the different literary spaces they belong in, and their linguistic expression, ethnicity, etc. should not bind them. After all, didn't the Irishman Samuel Beckett, the Romanian Eugène Ionesco, the American Julian Green all write in French, a language other than their language of origin without being marginalized? Thus, language or race shouldn't set aside Arab writers. And hasn't the world become multicultural, aren't we heading more and more toward globalization?

Some writers might write in a language other than their language of origin, but as Hector Bianciotti (an Argentinean writer of French expression) says, even if he writes in another language, his "imagination comes from somewhere else" (Riding 7–8). Therefore, *these* writers should be celebrated for bringing a new dimension to their particular literatures, be it new and/or different metaphors and images, rhythms and symbols, myths, landscapes, new visions and dreams. Maghrebian poets of French expression have brought these elements, have brought a new cultural horizon to French literature, just as Commonwealth writers such as Derek Walcott and Wole Soyinka have brought a new cultural horizon to English literature, and Arab-American poets have brought the same to American literature. And even if what Etel Adnan pointed out regarding francophone literature and the separation it creates between "native" and "foreign" writers holds much truth, a change seems to be slowly taking place. The works of these "foreign" writers of French expression are beginning to be considered French literature, whether voluntarily or by necessity. After all, many of these "foreign" writers are being awarded the most prestigious literary prizes of France, and most reside in France. Some of these well-known writers are: the Moroccan Tahar Ben Jelloun, the Russian-born Andreï Makine, the Spaniard Jorge Semprún, the Cuban Eduardo Manet, and the Canadian Nancy Huston. Then again, some critics are skeptical about prizes: for example, the French critic Angelo Rinaldi believes that these foreign writers have been awarded prizes for their exoticism. Nevertheless, as Manet said, "France is going through an identity crisis" (Riding 7–8). And so are North Africa and the United States.

Indeed, language is a country, but poetry is also a country. Do we really have to classify? Doesn't that put boundaries on our human soul and spirit, on poetry itself? Doesn't it insult poetic integrity to put boundaries on the poet and herself, on the poet and her poetry? Can't poetry exist outside the boundaries of identity and nationality? Mahmoud Darwish has often been bothered by the fact that he has too often been labeled only as a Palestinian poet and never simply as a poet. He believes that by only referring to him as a Palestinian poet this indicates that he is a poet who only writes and represents Palestine and Palestinian themes and issues. But although Palestine might be one of his primary concerns, it is not his only concern. Thus, this focus on labeling puts aside his aesthetic and poetic merits and limits him and his poetic oeuvres. And ultimately, isn't poetry its own language, a universe of its own.

Algeria

Although many contemporary Algerian women poets have written and continue to write poetry, they remain virtually absent in the Arab literary scene. There are very few women poets that have been able to get their works published, and when they do, it has been by secondary publishing houses with very little distribution. Algerian women poets write in Arabic and in French, and numerous poets have published in journals and magazines, but the fact that their works never make it into book form keeps them on the sidewalks, sustaining their invisibility, restraining their literary evolution, certainly discouraging them at the publishing level. Thus, we are left with pieces of their works, one poem from this poet in one magazine, another poem from that poet in another magazine, some poets publishing more poems, but nevertheless, their works dispersed in different journals. At times, women wrote with pen-names or used their initials—for example, Assia Djebar's real name was Fatima-Zohra Imalayene—other times their works were published but the journal did not print their name. It is well-known that many women have manuscripts piled up somewhere in their house or hidden in a drawer; some we might discover, others we might never get a chance to read. Algerian women poets were affected by the Arabic literary renaissance, participated in resistance literature and in nationalist literature after their liberation, and were also open to many different themes. Algerian women are witnesses of the inhumanity inflicted by the colonizer, and Algerian women poets have transmitted those horrors in their works. Their works have been concerned with daily life and its sufferings, with the fight and struggle against colonization, prison experiences, the torture, violence, rape, brutality, and repression women have endured, and the courage they sustained. Their works also reflect their multiple identities, love and passion, nature and dreams, hopes and fears, inner and outer voyages, and solitude. A few lines from one of Annie Steiner's poems seem to echo the experience of Algerian women writers: "She was coming from I don't know where/ She was going I don't know where/ She did not know herself/...It was necessary that we love you" (Achour 221).

The tragedy of Algerian women shares many similarities with that of Palestinian women. Both Algerian and Palestinian women were an important part of their country's resistance. The strong presence of Algerian women during the Algerian war of independence was admired by Arab women and women all over the world. But after Algeria's independence, instead of attaining their long-sought freedom, they fell under the oppressive rule of Islamic conservatives.

Since the late 1960s and especially during the 1980s, many Algerian women contributed to many different literary expressions, from cultural criticism to literary criticism, and in the 1980s and 1990s more Algerian women started to write in Arabic. It is important to mention, once again, that until their independence most Algerian, Tunisian, and Moroccan writers and intellectuals, both men and women, wrote mostly in French. Arabic was absent for such a long period from schools and higher education that many did not have literary knowledge of Arabic. Anna Greki published her first book of poems in a bilingual edition in 1963. Nadia Guendouz published a book in 1968, and Assia Djebar published one in 1969; both authors write in French. Mabrouka Boussaha and Ahlam Mostaghanemi, writing in Arabic, published their first books of poetry in 1970–71. This was the first time women's voices were included in the Algerian literary current. These women poets express their suppressed situation in Algeria and call for liberation. Some of these poets have published some poems in journals or magazines, and other poets have published a book or more, but their work is difficult to find and they are virtually absent from both French and Arabic literary discourse and the literary scene. Some of these poets have been included in anthologies and mentioned in books of criticism of Maghreb literature or francophone literature, but that is still not sufficient, for Algerian women poets remain invisible. Perhaps their contributions were minor, or they did not have an important enough impact on poetics, or perhaps some poets only published a few poems but did not continue to write, or perhaps these poets are marginalized. There is probably some truth in all of these reasons. Furthermore, Algerian women poets are nearly absent in the discourse of most Arab critics and other poets. Here are some of these women poets (some write in Arabic, some in French): Djamila Amrane, Leila Djabali, Malika O'Lahsen, Zhor Zerari, Anissa Boumedienne, Leila Benmansour, Aïcha Bouabaci, Nadia Guendouz, Safia Kettou, Karima Manar, Leila Nekachtali, Taos Sadjine, Louisette Cherifi, Myriam Ben, Zineb Laouedj. Algerian women poets are listed above to demonstrate and emphasize their silencing, since only one poet is represented in this anthology. (This isn't the case for Morocco and Tunisia, which is why a list will not be mentioned for these two countries—although neither country actually has as many poets as Algeria).

From 1963 to 1991, an estimated 48 books of poems by 41 Algerian women poets living in Algeria or France were published, but only 12 or 13 were considered by critics and other poets as having real depth and literary merit (Déjeux 38). There remain more Algerian women poets who write in French than in Arabic. The Algerian poet Habiba Muhammadi, who is included in this anthology, writes in Arabic. She is on a journey of self-discovery and confronts the contradictions inside of her, "The lion of waking roars/ And takes revenge/ On a part of my dreams." She wants to free herself from herself, free herself from all forms of oppression and silencing. She wants to free her life: "I write/ To shout/ To live..." She wants to free her heart, dreams: "I lay my head on the pillow every night/ To sleep/ But you haunt me in my dream/ And reach for the seasons of the woman/ In me." But Muhammadi persists to attain the freedom she seeks, so she tries "to wake up/ Early/ so that the dream/ May not become/ Taller than me..." and searches for the day when she "will rise/ Without a memory" to haunt her and her pillow will have room for her dreams, her freeness, and freedom.

Algeria in the future will hopefully be an open and free society, a society that can eradicate the darknesses of the past and progress freely socially, culturally, and artistically. Maybe then, Algerians will be able to define and redefine themselves, their identity, and their literature will attain its full blossom.

Tunisia

In Tunisia bilingual education continues to exist, and a great number of Tunisian women today are highly educated. Although during the colonial period literature written in French did not have a strong standing, today it has grown. Nevertheless, most of those writing in French live outside of their country. Tunisia has had many influences be they Arabic, Islamic, African, Mediterranean, or Western. Tunisian poets' thematic preoccupations are multiple, displaying different geographical, cultural, and political concerns. Tunisia's continuous opening politically throughout the years has enabled new creative spaces to exist. And it is probably safe to say that Tunisia is the most avant-garde country in the Arab Muslim world. Tunisia supported women very early on, knowing the importance of women's role in society, and knowing that the advancement of women's position was mandatory for the country's evolution. Many laws were passed in favor of women—the right to vote, suppression of polygamy, obligatory education for women etc.—and Tunisia remains an example to the rest of the Arab world. Tahrir Haddad's *Our Women and Islamic Law and Society* (1929) must not be forgotten, as it played a vital role in the emancipation of women.

Tunisian women have always been important to their country's history and heritage, as they have been present in all aspects of society. They have participated in the nationalist movement, have flourished on different literary and artistic levels, including comedy, music, and all forms of writing, and they have been portrayed in literature as modern women with values, as both Muslim and western, vibrant and present in their society and its evolution. But despite Tunisia's advancement, women continue to face marginalization. Nevertheless, Tunisia's rapid development, its proud and ambitious literary heritage, has enabled it to continuously head toward progress. The recent rise of Islamic extremists in the area cannot be avoided, and Tunisian women along with other Arab women must constantly be cautious, and must continue to participate in the fight for Arab women's freedom and equality.

Although women's participation in contemporary Tunisian literature, both in Arabic and French, existed before their independence in 1956, it was after the 1960s that their literary contribution grew, gaining a remarkable energy and dynamism and expanding and evolving rapidly and steadily. And in the creatively abundant 1980s, even more quality poetry surfaced.

Tunisian women first started to publish in journals and magazines and participate in radio programs in the first half of the twentieth century. Despite the many existing women's magazines, it was not until the end of the 1960s that books written by women began to be published. The well known radio program, *Huwât al-adab* (Amateurs of literature), became a real literary institution, and with the help of older generation writers and critics, many young voices were introduced to the public, allowing them to be heard and known (Bekri 43). During that time, Leila Mami published *A Burnt Minaret* (1968), a book of short stories that, like Laila Ba'albaki's novel, helped spread feminism. Mami's book dealt with women's desire, with women's right to liberty and equality, socially, sexually, culturally, and in every other way; and condemned any law or structure that restricts women and does not allow them completeness. Many women writers followed Mami, dealing with similar themes. It was not until 1975, however, that a Tunisian woman writer, Jalila Hafsia, published a novel in French. Hafsia's book, *Ashes at Dawn*, was controversial for it actually was about her life. She described her profound intimacies, a display that is viewed as unethical by men and by North African society in general.

The poet Fadhila Chabbi, who writes in Arabic, emerged with a vigorously political voice. Her works reflect her support for Arab unity and her response to the tragedies that have affected the Arab world, especially the Palestinian calamity. Her poetry also echoes the struggles of Arab women and her anger against women's injustice and inequality; her poetry travels deep into memory, deep into subjective and objective realities, deep into inner and outer realities full of symbolism, deep into the endless landscapes of the imagination. And indeed, she "left nothing behind.../ ...forgot nothing." Chabbi's first book of poetry, published in Beirut in 1973, is called *Odors of the land and of anger.* She is probably the most well-known Tunisian woman poet, although her fame has not blossomed as it should have; according to Chabbi, her poetry has been neglected. She has often said that women's works have been set aside and not considered works of value. With the translation of her work during the 1980s, Chabbi became better known outside of the Arab world, winning literary prizes and invitations to read throughout Europe.

Amina Said is presently one of Tunisia's best known women poets writing in French. Said is part French, part Tunisian, and living in Paris. Said's work has often been said to be Arabic poetry written in French. Her poetry is rhymed, with vivid images reflecting her identity, myths, symbols, and history. She uses no title, punctuation, or capitalization. She believes that titles limit the text, reveal too much, and shatter the continuity that exists from one poem to another. In "I present myself to the world" she writes, "the earth is heavy with humanity/ beings and things which adorn it/ are works of here and of that elsewhere/ the dead fix their eyes on/ here earth and rock are memory/ the saints lie in obscure repose/ promising enchantment/ here even miracles are discreet." She journeys through word after word and never ceases to leave us in a "mysterious continent."

Amal Moussa and Najaat al-Udwany both write in Arabic, both leaving a certain dreaminess on the shoulders of their poems even when they write about disasters. Moussa longs to find herself, her family, to find light, love. She embraces herself, "longing for herself," strolls inside of herself when she is weary of herself, enters a garden "that does not entice [her] against [herself]." She doesn't fear any revelation. She claims the memory of the "old house" where her "grandfather composed his formal poems," where her "first cry echoed," where her "grandmother was throned a bride." The poet claims, as she crosses herself, that she "wears love like a cape," "and the courtyard becomes/ twice its size." Al-Udwany "...rides the poems,/ ...follows the winds." She wants to escape what is behind her, before her, beyond her, but she cannot escape her past, present, future. She writes, "O Mother! extend to me your face/ to swim in it/ ...I am incapable of swimming./ I burned my boats/ and I have not found behind me/ a sea/ nor found/ before me someone to fight!" The poet's work is concerned with the rights of women, with war and its atrocities, with the tragic destiny of children, and people of impoverished and destroyed countries.

Morocco/Libya

Moroccan women, like Algerian and Tunisian women poets, have had similar experiences of colonialism, bilingualism, and biculturalism, and they too participated in the resistance against colonialism. Their presence in the struggle for independence helped change Moroccan consciousness, and the society has gradually moved toward progress. Recently, the government proposed a plan that would grant women more rights, namely, supporting literacy programs for rural women (60 percent are illiterate), eradicating the practice of repudiation, and dividing assets equally during a divorce.

There are fewer Moroccan women poets and even fewer Libyan women poets. Although many Moroccan women poets have published in journals and magazines, Saida Menebhi, who writes in French, was one of the first Moroccan women poets to publish a book. Her book, *Poèmes, lettres et écrits de prison* (Poems, letters and writings from prison), appeared in 1978. But as in the case of Tunisia and Algeria, not many poets have sustained their literary production. They too have faced the setbacks, previously mentioned, that other North African women poets have had to endure.

The Moroccan poet Wafaa' Lamrani writes her femininity, explores her body, her fantasies. She is naked even in her nakedness, "naked except for [her] own nakedness." She rises and "[teaches] the sky to rise, rise." She is openness and delicious sin, and she teaches the sky "openness/ ...[teaches] it sin." She says that she is "taken by tender rapture" and then continues, "O heart spread out/ O eye wander/ And O diamond-like body/ engrave your secret..." Lamrani is limitless, frees herself from her body, her burdens, her limits, her name, her dark shadows. She lets herself be "interpreted" and "embraced." "Everything falls down/ except air..."—and except Lamrani, who flies. On the other hand, al-Zahra al-Mansouri's "dream falls from [her] dozing,/ the sun tumbles from the angles of [her] body." She needs "...huge trees to grow within..." her and "stars to water" her calling. Her past seems to have defeated her, but she tries to revive all that has been killed within her. She searches to find ways to "water the springs of [her] shades." And the Libyan poet Fatima Mahmoud finds "...harmony with the law/ of the tree." She goes beyond harmony, beyond what is not conceivable as she observes great beauty and great darkness standing so close together, and describes the harmony of nature and the destructive nature of man. She remains stunned before "invented" accusations, tortures and what she thought was inconceivable of her country, yet not far "In harmony—a horizon/ of carnations./ A bundle of lavender." Mahmoud's powerful images never cease: "With staring pebbles/ the beautiful children stone them..." And although we are continuously shown or reminded of the "season of fires" and the "ashes/ of the era," never far are the "seasons of desire" and the beauty of irises. She leaves for her country's "seed," her people's "seed," fields of possible harmonies and the "whiteness of the page."

Arab-American / Arab-Canadian Women Poets

> *Know from where you come and where you are going.*
> —Akavya Ben-Mahalalel

> *He who denies his heritage has none.*
> —from *As the Arabs Say*, by Isa Khalil Sabbagh

> *I lost a river, culture, speech, sense of first space*
> *And the right place? Now, Where do you come from?*
> *Strangers ask. Originally? And I hesitate.*
> —Carol Ann Duffy

Arabs started emigrating to the United States (as well as to the Americas, Australia and Africa) around 1875, although some "documentary and archeological evidence proves that Arabs arrived in America many centuries earlier" (Haiek 9). These early immigrants were predominantly Christians (Roman Catholic, Russian Orthodox, Greek Orthodox, British Anglican, American Protestant) from the Province of Greater Syria (incorporating modern day Syria, Iraq, Lebanon, Palestine, and Jordan), which was then under Ottoman rule. By the mid-twentieth century, during the years between the 1940s and the 1967 Arab-Israeli war, more immigrants from the Middle East (particularly the Levant, Egypt and Yemen) came to America. There were more Muslims in this wave and they were much more educated, in contrast to the earlier wave of immigrants.

The early Mahjar poets mentioned before, started to write and publish in English in the beginning of the twentieth century. Poetry written and published in English by Arab-American women poets for the most part only goes back about thirty years; yet in this brief period we can find rapidly growing contributions. A landmark publication for Arab-American women's writing was the 1994 anthology edited by Joanna Kadi, *Food for Our Grandmothers: Writings by Arab American and Arab Canadian Feminists*, including over forty Arab-American and Arab-Canadian women writers. The "community's posture was stimulated by three principle reasons: a substantial influx of new immigrants; reverberations from the Middle Eastern turmoil; increased ethnic identification and community awareness" (Haiek 9). The 1970s and 1980s also saw the emergence of new Arab-American organizations and centers with political and social agendas, which led to a stronger Arab-American lobby in the 1990s. Also, the advancement of technology, namely the internet, gives the West more accessibility to the Arab world and vice versa, and allows more possibilities for interaction and contact. In addition, in terms of literature, numerous Arab-American literary journals and magazines—namely, *Al Jadid, Jusoor*, and *Mizna*—have emerged, Arab-American writers' organizations have been founded, and conferences and events focusing on Arab-American writing have been organized.

But although recently the invisibility of the Arab-American community has begun to be reversed, and Arab-American women poets have been included in certain multicultural and American poetry anthologies, they are still virtually absent in feminist discourse, and in literary criticism in general. Let us go back for a moment and look at the evolution of Arab-American women poets.

The first recorded Arab woman immigrant writer in the United States who published a book was Afifa Karam (1883–1925), a resident of Louisiana who was from Mount Lebanon). Like many of the early Mahjar male poets, she wrote in Arabic and was published by al-Hoda Press in New York City, which also published the writers in the Pen League such as Kahlil Gibran and Amin Rihani. Her first novel, *Badiyah and Fuad* (1906), became very popular in her native Lebanon. Her last book was an autobiography entitled *The Girl from Amshit*, published in 1913. She published her own magazines: *The Syrian Woman*, which eventually led in 1913 to *The New World for Women*, which lasted a few years. In addition, Naoum Mokarzel, owner and editor of *al-Hoda*, made her the first female journalist on his staff and she became the most known woman journalist of her time.

Other women poets/writers who emigrated to the United States but continued to write in Arabic include May Rihani, Mariam Qasem el-Saad and the previously mentioned Lebanese poet Amira el-Zein. Etel Adnan is the first recorded Arab-American woman poet to publish a collection of poetry in English, *Moonshots* (1966). In 1972, D. H. Melhem, a New York born poet and writer of Lebanese parents, published a collection of poetry entitled *Notes on 94th Street*. A third pioneer, Consuelo Saah Baehr, was a Palestinian Christian who was not a poet but a novelist. She published *Report from the Heart* in 1976. Then from the beginning of the 1980s until the present a wave of Arab-American women poets began publishing poetry. This surge in women's publication parallels the surge in publication by Arab poets living in the Arab world.

The concern of these poets in finding a place in their bicultural upbringing, and their search for, struggle for or claim to an Arab identity, has played a significant role in their poetry. Who are these Arab-American women poets? Most of these women poets were born in the United States of Arab descent, or born in the Arab world, usually the Mashriq, and emigrated to the United States. It is estimated that about ninety percent of Arab-Americans originate from the Levant (Orfalea xviii). A large majority of these women do not speak Arabic, some have never been to the Middle East, and many are Christian, although that has changed in the 1990s with the emergence of more Muslim-Arab poets. Some might wonder how these poets claim to be Arab without speaking Arabic. But culture is not only language; different linguistic traditions do not necessarily mean different cultural traditions. Also, not all Arabs are Muslim, and yet shared sociopolitical, historical, and economic experiences form a collective memory that binds the past, present, and future across continents.

Recently, children of Arab Muslim-American immigrants have surfaced in the literary scene. Yvonne Yazbeck Haddad, in "A Century of Islam in America," says that "If the Muslim community continues to grow at the present rate, by the year 2015 Islam will be the second largest religion in the United States" (1). Most of these Muslims are Arab, African-American, Pakistani, and Iranian, and many of them are highly educated. This rise in the Muslim population of America most probably will affect Arab-American literature, its definition, the literary spaces it will occupy, and the direction it will take in this new millennium. The Muslim-American, Syrian-American poet Mohja Kahf, not only considers herself to be Arab-American, but when I interviewed her for *Al Jadid Magazine*, the poet expressed fervently her identity as a Muslim-American. Her poetry draws on Islamic symbolism and culture, and Muslim-American identity and duality.

But as the American anthropologist Sharon Zukin says, "in common American usage, culture is, first of all, "ethnicity…" (Zukin 263). Therefore, in a society like America that forces one to think of color, origin, and religion, one is driven back to his/her culture or "ethnic" group. Apart from this social reality, which, directly or indirectly, forces the notion of ethnicity as a means of self-definition, these poets voluntarily claim their Arab identity. Many arguments could be raised pertaining to the claim of identity through blood identity—accusing the idea as being one of "racist differentiation," but the fact remains that society consciously or subconsciously binds us to our ethnic groups. Arab-Americans ethnically remain Arab. But ultimately it is not language, ethnicity, geographical location, birth, or nationality but one's claim and profound sentiment that creates one's identity. Kanan Makiya, an Iraqi writer asks, "What is the connection between the passport one holds, the views one expresses, the books one writes, and one's innermost emotional and belief system, which is of course what constitutes one's identity?" (Makiya 23). The answer is obvious to him even as he poses it: what one feels inside is ultimately "one's identity." After all, in Lebanon, Lebanese women cannot pass down citizenship to their children, only Lebanese men can, and in the Palestinian case, there is no passport. Actual citizenship or birthplace may be of minimal significance to a certain individual. And take the case of Sargon Boulos: he has American citizenship, but is never referred to as an Arab-American poet. Is it because he writes in Arabic or is it because he never claims to be an Arab-American? Then there is Mona Simpson, who was born in the United States, writes in English of course, and is of Arab descent (her father is Syrian), yet is hardly ever referred to as an Arab-American writer. Is it because her work does not reflect her Arab heritage or is it because she doesn't really present herself as an Arab-American? We can use various facts to define a person's identity, but finally we do not really have that right; an individual's claim is ultimately the most essential and must be respected.

Some scholars, critics, or others might voice the possibility that Arab-Americans, by labeling and hyphenating themselves, risk participating in a form of racism; they might ask whether Arab-Americans do not therefore create their own alienation. But in America nearly every ethnic group hyphenates itself or they are hyphenated by society: African-American, Jewish-American, Latina-American, Irish-American and so forth. Naomi Shihab Nye is a Palestinian-American, an Arab-American, and is also considered one of America's finest and most successful poets. One can belong to a literary ethnic group while still belonging to the "American" literary circle. Anyhow, what is American literature if not an arena of poets of different origins having in common the United States? The philosopher George Santayana, in his book, *Character and Opinion in the United States*, says that even "if there are immense differences between individual Americans... there is a great uniformity in their environment, customs, temper, and thoughts. They have all been uprooted from their several soils and ancestries and plunged together into one vortex, whirling irresistibly in space... To be an American is of itself almost a moral condition, an education, and a career" (quoted in Feinstein 17).

Most, if not all of the Arab-American women poets in this anthology, have gone back to their culture of origin and tried to understand it, be part of it, nourish it and expand it into their lives and beings, while remaining in an American context or background. Indeed, a notion of our origins is a principal element in defining who we are. Often these poets have come to relate to other American writers of ethnic backgrounds, namely Native-American, Latina-American, Asian-American, African-American; writers such as Joy Harjo, Gloria Anzaldua, Maxime Hong Kingston, Rita Dove, June Jordan. The bond Arab-American women poets feel with other ethnic groups can be observed in their works. It is a bridge to help them identify with America, to help them in being and becoming American, by comparing themselves to those *others*. It is a way of reassuring themselves that they are not alone, a way of understanding themselves better by observing others having the same experiences, and a way of stating that America is also about *this diversity*. It is also interesting to note that even if one of these women poets has an Arab father and an American mother, her experiences do not differ much from those poets who have two Arab parents. It is not uncommon that while growing up these poets went through a moment of denial and refusal of their Arab heritage—mainly in order to fit in and/or because they were momentarily spellbound by Arab stereotyping, thus rejecting their Arab association and roots. The Palestinian-American poet Lisa Suhair Majaj responds to her father in a piece entitled, "Family Name": "How could I learn about being Palestinian if he never told me anything? Of course, I wasn't eager to overstress my Arab identity, either." Nevertheless, they have all written about their Arab-American identity—a powerful statement in itself.

Marcus Lee Hansen, in his famous essay, "The Problem of the Third Generation Immigrant," laid the groundwork for numerous debates about immigrant history and being Ethnic-American. He writes, "what the son wishes to forget the grandson wishes to remember." This pattern of behavior explains perhaps why hyphenated Americans are often even more patriotic than their original fellow compatriots—many Armenians might want to have more relations with the Turks but many Armenian-Americans are vehemently against Turkey; similarly, many Jewish-Americans are more extremist in their views on Arabs than many Israelis. Most Arab-American women poets (and male poets), have written about Palestine, and are still active in the cause and in the search for a just peace. Arab-American poets write about the Arab-Israeli conflict despite the enormous pressure they are under, thus solidifying their alignment with Arabs and the Arab world. Such efforts must not be taken for granted, for "for an Arab-American poet to criticize his country's [the United States] stance in anything but the most veiled terms is risky. He had no legs to stand on, political or literary, in the halls of power" (Orfalea xxiv). The Lebanese War also played an important role in solidifying Arab-American identity. D.H. Melhem said, in an interview I published in *Al Jadid Magazine,* that it was during this war that she realized she was Lebanese, Arab, Arab-American.

But the Gulf War played perhaps an even greater role in terms of identity construction and reformulation, particularly for younger writers. During this devastating time in history, Arab-Americans solemnly questioned their Arab identity. It was a moment of profound self-revelation—they took a position against the United States's political stance. They felt betrayed by many of their fellow Americans, Majaj wrote in an essay entitled, "Boundaries: Arab/American." She describes a radio commentator's proclamation that, "in war there are no hyphenated Americans, just Americans and non-Americans" (Kadi 82). Therefore, what would that make them, the non-Americans? It is difficult to belong to a country with a politics that discriminates against your country of origin. Often these poets are put in the position of having to choose—and they almost always speak on behalf of the Arabs. Their voices persist as they remind Americans of the aftermath of the Gulf War, its calamities and trepidations, and as they protest against the sanctions in Iraq. Thus, political concerns are an important theme for Arab-American women poets. They have been affected by all the major historical and political events that have happened in the Arab world. Through their work they voice their opinions against injustices and stereotypes, against the often unfavorable stance the United States takes vis-à-vis the Arab world. By voicing themselves through literature, they are not only demonstrating unity and solidifying their Arab-American identity, but they are also consolidating their national presence. They write the past, bewail their tragedies and losses, long for their ancestral land. Describing the land is a way to express where their roots rest, especially among the Palestinian and Palestinian-American women poets; and it is a way to demonstrate love of their country or express resistance. They describe the land and its elements and while doing so assert their belonging. Their poetry is filled with dates, oranges, lemons, figs, almonds, and olives, and their beautiful trees.

Food is one of the most important themes in Arab-American literature. It provides an emblem of their history and culture, their Arab life away from home and their national identity. It is not a surprise that the two pioneering anthologies of Arab-American literature have in their titles the indication of food—*Grapeleaves: A Century of Arab-American Poetry* edited by Gregory Orfalea and Sharif Elmusa, and *Food for Our Grandmothers*, edited by Joanna Kadi—suggesting how olives, bread, thyme, yogurt, grapeleaves, and mint become emblems of Arab life that recur in Arab-American experience. In the United States, Arab food has found a place, and is probably one of the most authentic aspects of Arabic culture found in America today. And as Kadi says, and most Arabs and Arab-Americans believe, "We owe it to ourselves, our ancestors, and the ones who come after us to celebrate our wonderful culture, whether we find it in the *laban* we eat or the stories we read" (237).

Family is another strong source of identity and, Orfalea and Elmusa argue "one might not be exaggerating to say that for poets of Arab heritage, family *is* self" (xix). Family is at the heart of what these writers write. Family is a representation of themselves, their tradition, their culture. They describe their grandparents and parents, and feel part of the Arab world through the memory of their forefathers. Memory is thus a vital vehicle in the construction and affirmation of selfhood and culture. Much of these poets' heritage is acquired through oral tradition, passed on from one generation to the other. The self-reflection and powerful images of the relationship between these women poets and different family members play an important role in their work. After all, "the family is the basic unit of social organization in traditional and contemporary Arab [and Arab-American] society" (Barakat 97). The religion of their ancestors is omnipresent, especially among the ones of Muslim faith. There is the importance of their names, and of *asl* (ancestry), the blood of ancestry. As Lila Abu-Lughod says, blood "links people to the past and binds them to the present." And she continues, "As a link to the past, through genealogy, blood is essential to the definition of cultural identity" (41). One can change virtually everything from name to legal status but not one's blood.

Arab-Americans investigate their doubleness and cultural in-betweenesses in their writing. They experience an on-going negotiation of self as they explore their many experiences, visions, and heritages, and bring wholeness to their multiplicity. They affirm their ethnicity, their Arab and American identities, their national and religious identities. Apart from the conflicts and complexities often attached to multiple identities and contexts; apart from politics and socio-cultural dynamics and turmoil; apart from crossing the boundaries of their identity and demonstrating alliances and parallelisms with other ethnic groups; apart from demonstrating experiences of discrimination and marginalization, Arab-American women poets are also engaging in self-criticism and bringing to surface subjects that are considered taboo in Arab-American society. This is of extreme significance because it demonstrates a widening and expansion of the society, a willingness to break societal boundaries to promote change and advancement. Some Arab-American women poets have also been responsible for important feminist writings and literary criticism. The Palestinian-American poet Lisa Suhair Majaj deserves recognition for her important and pioneering contributions to Arab-American literary criticism. She constantly reminds Arab-American, Ethnic-American, and American critics and writers of the invisibility of Arab-American literature in their critical discourses, and emphasizes to Arab-Americans the importance of writing more criticism on Arab-American literature. As Majaj points out, literary criticism helps to create a positive context of reception for these works, and helps to situate Arab-American literature for Arabs and for readers in general. And she adds, it has a "crucial role to play in highlighting… the cultural and sociological,… [and] the literary dimension of our writing, reminding us that we are, first and foremost, writers" (Jusoor 72). Majaj has helped lessen the exclusion of Arab-American literature in feminist discourse and literary criticism generally. She has helped place Arab-American literature in a wider, more global context by the publication of her papers, studies, and criticism of Arab-American literature in Ethnic-American and American journals, anthologies, and books of criticism. Joanna Kadi, another poet whose aforementioned anthology helped launch Arab-American women writings, has also made important contributions to feminist thought and discourse. In her book of essays, *Thinking Class: Reflections of a Cultural Worker*, Kadi raises issues of class, race, ethnicity, exclusion, and marginalization through critical analysis, using a feminist approach. Arab-American women poets are helping to eradicate stereotypes of Arabs, of Arab women, and are partaking in the transformation, expansion, and evolution of their literature, identities, and selves. They are creating new spaces, new breaths.

～

Etel Adnan remains the poet with the most numerous identities—she stands at a crossroad between East and West, Arab and European, Muslim and Christian, Lebanese, French, and American. Her work, as previously discussed, reflects this multitude of identities, mirroring influences from the works of Arab poets such as Khalil Hawi to that of the American Beat generation. D.H. Melhem, unlike Adnan, was born in the United States, in Brooklyn in 1926. Her work is American in essence, and her themes universal. She has written numerous books, including *Blight*, a novel, and several books of criticism, including *Gwendolyn Brooks: Poetry and the Heroic Voice* (1987) and *The New Black Poetry: Introductions and Interviews* (1990), which won the American Book Award. But one of Melhem's most powerful and complete works remains *Rest In Love*, published in 1975. It is a long poem tracing her mother's life and emigration from Lebanon to the United States. In Melhem's latest book of poetry, *Country*, many of the themes common throughout her work are present. Melhem is continuously in search of herself and the self, in search of *country*, which is the world, and all of its elements—the earth of heavens and heaven's earth, stars of words and a word's star, the map of dreams and a map's dream. She saves everything in her mind and tries to give a voice to everything that exists. She travels through all of the United States, physically or mentally, through its mountains, valleys, rivers, hopes, dreams, fears, its people, poets. She observes all of the gestures of her neighborhood (New York's Upper West Side), breathes all of its breaths, listens to all of its voices, secrets, silences, screams of joy and of pain, and understands it all even when she doesn't. Her work goes back to the past without inhibition, searches the present intensely, and awaits the future. Melhem is full of complexities and so is her poetry as she closes "...name/ into angles of initials [puts] away/ vowels [rounds] sonorities/ into pages." She is full of discoveries as she travels through the ambiguities of her identity, as her mother and later herself are asked, "syrian?/ what's/ that?" She writes of the fear and internal conflict over identity many Lebanese experience: Melhem's mother tells her: "*say french*: who knows what lebanese is?/ or syrian?...people don't mean/ to be mean/ nevertheless/ better say/ french." Melhem says, "to write the country/ as a poem/ incomplete/ is the truth/ of geography." Incomplete is also the truth of poetry to Melhem.

Along with family there is a connection to the *beit* or family house/home, which also an expression of a profound alliance with the country or land of origin. This is present in the important semi-biographical novel, *Children of the Roojme*, by Lebanese-American Elmaz Abi-Nader. The *roojme* is a stone terrace situated at the conjunction of the homes of the Abi-Naders in Abdelli, in the mountains of Lebanon. Abi-Nader fictionalizes or uses some fictional techniques to tell her story. Her use of the semi-fictional is different from, yet parallels in many ways, what the Lebanese-American novelist Vance Bourjaily did in his semi-autobiographical novel, *Confessions of a Spent Youth*, in which Quincy (Bourjaily's alter ego) goes back to his father's mountain village in Lebanon. Abi-Nader makes yet another voyage back to her ancestral roots in her recent play, *Country of Origin*. The play is about (Lebanese/ Lebanese-American) women and immigration, their identities and cultural multiplicity.

In Abi-Nader's poetry one feels that she is at peace with her heritage. There doesn't seem to be any conflict vis-à-vis her Arab identity, only affirmation. Whatever sense of distance she might integrate in her work, it is to express her individuality, and not to demonstrate a division between herself and the Arab world. She sees the hyphen in-between Arab-American as a bridge, not a separation. She writes about history and immigration, about having more than one home, about belonging to more than one country but being from Lebanon—her "country of origin" following her everywhere she goes, leaving its marks in her features and her soul. She often makes reference to the "Arabness" of her physical appearance; she conveys in her work that she looks like an Arab woman and is proud of this inheritance. Abi-Nader's poem, "Letters from Home," is a perfect example of her relationship with Lebanon. In this poem, *home* is Lebanon. And as Abi-Nader observes her father reading a letter from Lebanon, she obviously feels his pain and anguish, his longing. She discovers her ancestors through him and allows herself to identify with them as naturally as her father does. She says, "Every time you weep, I feel the surface of a river/ somewhere on Earth is breaking. " As the poem continues, family unity is depicted. If she doesn't understand the Arabic language, she feels it; as she says, "Your brother and sisters have gathered/ around you. I don't understand/ the language but feel a single breath/ of grief holding this room." She also refers to the devastating realities of the war and the diaspora. She writes, "Your own children/ seem like nomads. They sit in scattered apartments/ where you can't see your three daughters/ gazing from their windows or your three sons/ pacing the old wood of their rooms." Although Abi-Nader feels part of Lebanese history and heritage, she wants her belonging to be complete, and thus expresses her need and desire to learn Arabic (and perhaps French, for as we have seen, French is an important language in Lebanon). Thus, she writes, "…when the letters come,/ I run my fingers across the pages./ I hope I can learn the languages/ you have come to know." The poet leaves us constantly at the edge of beauty and wholeness, at the edge of *waiting*, although waiting doesn't really exist for her; she transcends it. Her visions are wholesome, uninterrupted, enlightening: "I wait/ because I can see from the edge of this earth/ to the next, sun set and moon rise/ in one breath."

Abi-Nader and Naomi Shihab Nye really rose in the 1980s. Nye has published numerous books and is presently the most well known Arab-American poet. Nye never forgets to capture the details along her journey. The politics of detail have always preoccupied the poet, and her prose, like her poetry, is filled with moments when she is observing the tiniest details. There is an intimacy between her and those things we forget exist; and she is capable of finding the most fragile human sentiment or characteristics through an "ordinary" object. Her preoccupation with details goes beyond marginalized objects such as a yellow glove, an onion, or a buttonhole, for she is also concerned with marginalized motions, characters, and feelings, such as the gestures and necessities used to wash dishes, and with becoming intimate with her own name. She takes us to the "small life/ thread,/ fragment,/ breath." She takes us inside the "smaller petal/ perfectly arranged inside the larger petal."

Nye is not in a hurry, though her life seems to hurry. What more could be expected from a poet who has a Palestinian father from Jerusalem, who spent most of her childhood in Missouri, who lived in Jerusalem before going to Texas where she now resides (and of course, we mustn't forget those stops on the side, such as India and Hawaii). Amazingly enough, even her religious background is multiple, for she had a "non-practicing Muslim" Palestinian father and a "non-practicing Lutheran" American mother, was raised as a Hindu from the Vedanta Society in St. Louis, and later studied at the Armenian School in Jerusalem. Her traveling, though, goes beyond the physical world as she never ceases to travel inside, never ceases to need "the birds worse & worse as [she gets] older," never ceases to realize that although "The shape of talk would sag/ …the birds be brighter than ever."

Her work explores exile, Palestinian identity, the mysteries of childhood, heritage, motherhood, human relationships, and places. She understands her Arabness, understands pain, even if an Arab man in her poem, "Arabic," tells her that until she speaks Arabic she "will not understand pain." Nye celebrates her Arab, American and ethnic heritages, and she naturally unifies human instincts, minds, hearts; and so naturally gathers all worlds, external and internal. Her work is sensitive to ethnic cultures and/or those considered as *other*. Her accessible style and her intensely universal approach dominate her writings. When she is expressing a personal experience that involves her otherness, she doesn't confine it to a Palestinian experience but places it in a larger context. Among Arab-American and especially Palestinian-American poets and writers, the journey toward cultural identification has been a persisting theme. They have to deal with being hyphenated and/or often suffer from a double-consciousness, and in most cases, the negotiation seems never to cease. Nye, on the other hand, seems in harmony with this duality. She doesn't feel marginalized; nor does she suffer from bicultural crisis. Instead, she finds her differences grounding. The poet is at peace with her two halves and has achieved a wholeness rare among Arab-American, ethnic or other poets and writers who find themselves in such a state of in-betweenness. Nye has found, despite the complexities of her diversity, her "whole self." Nye gets tired when she thinks "of the long history of the self/ on its journey to becoming the whole self…" But as she says, it's the "kind of trip you keep making." And she keeps *dancing* toward wholeness, dancing in her whole self. In her hauntingly beautiful poem, "The Small Vases from Hebron," Nye leaves us in a place many of her poems leave us, in the splendor of a pause in an echoing word. She leaves us with the small vases from Hebron tipping "their mouths open to the sky." She leaves us with "'Ya' Allah!" and its endlessness.

Another important voice among Palestinian-American, Arab-American poets is that of Lisa Suhair Majaj, whose criticism I have already mentioned. Majaj's words are breathlessly breathing all the scents of the seasons of her worlds. Majaj's work weaves melancholy, longing, and pain together in a lyrical manner that intrigues and transports the reader. Why such depth of suffering? Are these her experiences or are they experiences of her family members or is it her Palestinian soul pulsing in the fields of her words? With Majaj it is probably all of the above. She argues against war: "consider the infinite fragility of an infant's skull,/ how the bones lie soft and open/ only time knitting them shut." She describes the empty space that grows wider inside of her, as she realizes her father's absence, as she describes herself, her heritage so intensely embroidered with that of her Palestinian father: "My father knew the weight of words/ in balance, stones in a weathered wall./ ...Today his words surround me with the quiet intensity of growing things,/ roots planted a long time ago/ lacing the distances of my heart." Majaj's relationship with her father is portrayed with immenseness in many of her poems; this also demonstrates the intense emotions and relationship she has with her ancestral land. The poet claims her Palestinian identity but still resides in-between, in a place she is constantly negotiating. Majaj analyzes her entirety and all the spaces she occupies. She demonstrates the complexities of being a minority at many levels—as a woman, as a Christian Palestinian who grew up in the Arab world but who doesn't speak Arabic, and as a hyphenated American. But Majaj never stops at any defeat, she expands her marginalization until it is no longer marginalized, she examines her contradictions until she understands them. Although her double consciousness torments her and she struggles to settle her identity, this state of duality also allows her to exist in places she wants to exist in. Majaj writes, "Between dreams and day an immense distance/ fills my throat. Who could speak across such spaces?" Majaj speaks "across such spaces." Everything exists in Majaj's in-betweennesses. And she knows it. And her poetry shows it as her "Words flow through [her fingers and our consciousness] like stars..."

Palestine is present in the works of most, if not all, Palestinian-American women poets. Everything associated with being Palestinian seems to surface in their works, such as feelings of invisibility, being oppressed, longing for a homeland, etc. The Palestinian experience is diverse and singular simultaneously, in that all Palestinians share "Palestinianness" and all that this identity encompasses, yet their diasporic history has also led them to diversified cultural spheres. For example, Doris Safie's Palestinian-American identity extends itself, as she was born in El Salvador to Palestinian parents and moved when she was very young to Brooklyn and then to Rye, New York. She also extends the "gloomy day" of rain to the "sound of soldiers," extends making copy after copy and seeing "dead paper" fly to dead bodies "like dry tongues." Safie's xerox machine copies war, even recites war's sounds. The image penetrates the mind of the reader as we visualize and hear horror in an ordinary object. But Safie continues to hope, continues to look for the emergence of beauty, for a possible peace amidst a disturbing reality. She writes, "I keep trying/ and trying to find/ the jewel in the machine in this room/ that tolls the music of dead/ masters, lost in the whirr of the machine/ that blurs the tender craft of those/ who see, as I copy and copy and copy…"

Suheir Hammad adds another dimension to her identity, as the title of her poetry book, *born Palestinian, born Black*, suggests. The title is taken from one of the poems of African-American poet June Jordan, in which Jordan, responding to the massacre of Palestinians in Lebanon in the refugee camps of Sabra and Shatila after the 1982 Israeli invasion, wrote, "I was born a Black woman/ and now/ I am become Palestinian…" Hammad was born in Jordan of Palestinian refugee parents, moved to Beirut, then to Brooklyn. Since she grew up in Brooklyn with so many different ethnic groups—Puerto Ricans, Haitians, Jamaicans and so forth—her identity expanded from a Palestinian-American, Arab-American identity to a more ethnic one. Hammad seeks to erase the borders that exist between ethnic groups and demonstrates the diversity of the Palestinian, Palestinian-American experience and identity. Hammad uses Black to make a political statement, to eradicate the negativity associated with Black and to show the similarities between being black and being Palestinian. Although she demonstrates the commonalties among ethnic groups and aligns their experiences as minorities, Hammad still celebrates their differences. Palestine does not only represent her heritage; it is also a political symbol for her. She writes about Palestine to participate in the fight for Palestine and Palestinian recognition.

The poet has a powerful voice, which at times speaks from the heart, at times from the streets of her heart, other times from the groves of her heart, and other times, from the angry sidewalks of her heart. She writes about the Beirut war: "no mistakes made here/ these murders are precise/ mathematical/ these people blown apart burned alive/ flesh and blood all mixed together/ a sight no human being can take." She writes about her struggle for freedom from a family with conservative traditions, her fight for selfhood, womanhood, for her right to be a poet. She writes after being obliged to leave her family in order to be who she is, "missing my family/ who couldn't understand/ …we struggling to understand/ we were where we needed to be/we are who we have to be." She unveils the violence and denial that exist in Arab families and society, and hopes and fights for change, by voicing herself, by exposing violent realities: "her father lit the match   brothers poured the flammable/ the women they watched   the women they tucked/ their sex away under/ skirts under secrets/ in this world of/ men and molotovs/ ...they beat you blue/ ripped each hair out your head/ each one by one in the name/ of good and land   spit on you and/ cursed the evil that is/ woman."

Hammad's portrayal of brutal behavior in Arab society is not directed as an attack on Arab culture but as a reality that exists in Arab society, as it does in every society, but one that must be acknowledged by Arabs and that must change. Hammad is the "girl of riot and a poet" continuously contributing something new and participating in positive change.

Micheala Raen adds yet another element to her identity, for she is a lesbian Palestinian-American, which marginalizes her within an already marginalized Arab-American identity and even more alienated Palestinian-American identity. But by voicing her difference, as Joanna Kadi does, Raen participates in something that is essential to the evolution of Arab society: acceptance of difference and acknowledgement of the existence of a gay Arab community. Raen's work also contributes to the unsilencing of gay people around the globe. A predominant part of her journey is focused on understanding herself, her heritage, her femininity, and her sexuality, and like Hammad and many other Arab-American women poets, she aligns herself with other ethnic groups. Raen's usage of Spanish words and sentences is just one way to demonstrate that alignment. Raen writes, "I,/ white skinned opinionated queer girl,/ am valueless to men./ I,/ lesbian (of color if only deep inside),/ am to them a freak./ I want to know/ the women in my blood./ I need to know/ the entirety of what it is I have chosen to rebel against./ can I hide my "lesbian-ness"/ my love for todas las mujeres."

The following Palestinian-American poets, whether they were born in Palestine or lived there for a moment, often transmit their direct experiences or memories of the land and of the people. S.V. Atallah writes, "Once a year up the long road from Jericho. Hot summer. Mothballs in knots of tulle,/ lavender sachets. Suitcases dragged down from the attic, their locks sprung open./ ...In each suitcase a sachet of sorrow never unpacked." Atallah powerfully describes the meaning of being part of a diaspora in her poem, "Diaspora," in which she writes, "Mother/ so many pins/ and every day your smooth hair/ holding them all together." Then there is the more radical voice of Lorene Zarou-Zouzounis, who was born in Ramallah, and whose poetry is rooted in the Palestinian struggle both politically and socially. She weaves Arabic culture into her life, her being:

"Arabic tapestry embroidered/ into my soul/ is my memory/ of home."
She praises Palestinian women for their pride and strength. She writes, "A
woman refugee arms herself with pride and faith/ generation after
generation/ occupation after occupation/ still thriving, giving birth and
love/ fights for her right/ with all her might." She continues praising their
determination and courage, saying, "A Palestinian woman has a heart that
bleeds rose petals/ in a bloodstream of tainted water/ and sweats the colors
black, green, white and red/ through a granite skin that stretches/ but
never breaks." There is also Nadia Hazboun Reimer, who was born in
Jordan and who continually looks eastward. In her poem entitled, "The
Middle East," she praises the beauty and endlessness of the Middle East
while demonstrating the sad hypocrisy often planted in the lives and ways
of Middle East peoples. She writes:

no, it is not only the date clusters
in the palm trees
but also the oil, the phosphate,
the potassium, the olives, the citrus,
the salt,
the milk and honey,
and the manna that falls from heaven.

People kill to share this land,
while the verse on their holiday letter
their holiday letter
reads:
"Peace on Earth!"

Annemarie Jacir takes Palestine with her everywhere she goes, takes her
Arabness with her through her journeys and intrigues. She never ceases to
deepen her connection with her origins, never ceases to understand her
people, their ways, their past and history. She bathes "in olive oil" and sits
"On the sidewalks/ of Jerusalem eating/ Pistachio ice-cream/ with the old
man/ whose ancient face tried/ to explain to [her] that we fought/ with our
hearts and/ not with our heads—therefore/ we would not win." Deema
Shehabi mesmerizes us with her image of Palestine. Her lyricism resonates
with the lyricism of Arabic verses. Shehabi's poetic style and her thematic
concerns are profoundly rooted in Palestine and the Palestinians, and
Palestinian and Arabic poetry. She writes, "You come to me from rows and
rows of orange trees/ rows and rows of lemon trees/rows and rows of olive

trees…And I can't say I love my people/and I can't tell my love how to leave our land without weeping/ and I can't always love this land…[but] some yearn for years." She questions, wonders incessantly. In "The Cemetery at Petit Saconnex," a poem dedicated to her father, she says: "I wonder if you think of exile,/ and how this land now fills our blood/ with roots of belonging." She continues to wonder in "The Glistening": "Where is the mountain of fire/ the prophet prayed for/ to separate Mecca from its enemies." Her powerful voice and poetic images leave the reader in a haunting breath of beauty, leave the reader looking for the "…bald beautiful mountain,/ …glistening darkly/ in silence."

A very different poet is Mohja Kahf, who was born in Syria and came to the United States when she was young. She experiments with language and breaks boundaries. Kahf often uses a language rooted in the American culture, and in a witty manner sarcastically depicts that same culture's distorted views vis-à-vis Arabs. She depicts stereotypes toward Muslim women and mocks an America so "knowledgeable" yet so profoundly "ignorant" of other cultures. She speaks of how Muslim traditions are viewed as repressive, and explains the difficulty the West has in comprehending Islamic traditions. She conveys the fact that a woman wearing a *hijab* (veil) doesn't mean that she is not modern or that she is repressed, and that some women have chosen to wear the *hijab.* She tries to show multiple sides of Arab and Muslim culture and traditions.

In her poem, "The Roc," she describes the Arab immigrant experience, from her family leaving Syria, "…mom and dad leaving/ all familiar signposts: Damascus, the street they knew,/ measurements of time in mosque sounds…" to her family "…crossing the world…" and then arriving in the United States. She writes: "The time is March/ 1971./ They know nothing/ about America: how to grocery/ shop, how to open a bank account…" Kahf questions if east and west will ever understand each other, transcend their barriers. Kahf introduces an important Islamic element to Arab-American literature, the way Hammad introduces a politicized embrace between Arabs and people of color and finds junctions between these two ethnic groups, or as Nye does when she writes about Mexican-Americans and Latina-Americans.

As said before, many of these Arab-American women writers find a cultural and psychological connection with other ethnic groups, since these groups share similar feelings of marginality and alienation. The experience of alienation often begins from childhood. Lebanese-American Joanna Kadi describes growing up feeling misunderstood and set aside, for the Arab community was almost non-existent in her white, working-class neighborhood. She had no support, no point of referral or place to go to or return to. She describes being *other*, describes discovering her *otherness*, describes being Arab: "Finding stories translates/ into feeling a broken tongue./ Feeling a broken tongue/ equals residing with bodily harm./ Residing with bodily harm,/ is the life of an Arab transplant." She then questions, "Who can bear it?/ Who can live/ with a heart wide open?" But Kadi has "always known the life/ of an Arab transplant." Her poems are powerful pauses in the life of an Arab, the life of a working-class Arab, the life of an immigrant, of a minority, the life of a marginalized soul. Kadi's work also vividly protests against the Gulf War, the Palestinian plight, against the injustices committed against the Arab world and people by the United States, by the West. She says, it is "A brutal ambush/ by white hands." Kadi's poignant words continue: "When Arab babies die/ no one speaks,/ but their names live/ in my bones." And this solidarity of pain travels in the works of most of these Arab-American women poets, just like these poets' insistence on celebrating their Arabness, remembering their country of origin, their people.

From Egyptian-American poet Pauline Kaldas come descriptions of Arab greetings, "*Sabah el kheir/ sabah el fol/* morning of luck/ Morning of jasmine" and feelings of homesickness, as she remembers and longs for her Cairo: "streets/ filthy with the litter/ of people,/ …bare feet and galabiyas…/ sidewalk cafes with overgrown men/ heavy suited, play backgammon/ …sweetshops/ …baklava and basboosa/ women, hair and hands henna red/ their eyes, khol-lined and daring." Kaldas realizes that although she is away from her country, when she flies across and lands, her hands press "into rooted earth."

Jordanian-American poet Laila Halaby catches "handfuls of wind/ At 120 kilometers per hour/ In Amman;" she folds herself and sends herself in place of a "crinkled letter," or so she imagined, to fill the voids of long distances. And she thinks of a Palestinian refugee, and writes, "The lungs of the wrinkled gray-eyed man/ bellow with love/ for a dusty quarter/ of land/ that lies a stone's throw/ from the rock/ where he sits everyday/ and watches /his neighbor,/ his fields." The refugee "bleeds/ a river/ to take him home;" Halaby bleeds a word to take her home. And Syrian-American poet, Mona Fayad, takes us to a whisper, providing us an "access into/ boundless caverns/ echoing [her self]." Echoing is the voice of "Salma in Wonderland." In this poem Fayad portrays discriminating forces that can destroy and distort even one's image of oneself, as "Alice with her blue eyes/ Steps firmly into the mirror/ Knowing she will find/ Her image." But for Salma (the Arab girl), "the mirror only/ Shimmers and dissolves."

Not far from Fayad's words are Dima Hilal's, as she describes Lebanese women wishing their "hair blonde," their "eyes and skin light." Hilal goes on to describe a familiar Arab immigrant experience: "we come to america where they call our land/ the East meaning different/ dark/ dirty." But as in D. H. Melhem's experience, one common among the Lebanese, Hilal explains that the Lebanese think speaking French makes them "sophisticated" so they "greet each other with bonjour instead of salaam/ proud of [their] colonizer's tongue/ [and they] forget the Qur'an sings in arabic." She continues to portray the sad hypocrisies of her society, of the Lebanese: "we stared at pictures of our children/ eye sockets carved out by rubber bullets/ ...we turn away from bruises and broken bones/ ...we forget we once stood on the same ground/ they die on/ we look for the arabia packaged by the west/ we escape into clubs/ ...and tell each other/ how much we miss our home." Hilal's honest and important portrayal and criticism of her people, along with her deep insight into their defects and complexity, is a vital step for change. Ultimately, fundamental change cannot take place without an honest eye into one's society and culture.

Hilal was born in Beirut and then came to the United States. Each of the following Lebanese-American poets live on one of the American coasts and wherever they are, Lebanon is not too far, the Arab world not too far, yet not too far also are endless other themes. From the West Coast, Hilal expresses her agony and frustration of the war in the Arab world, expresses the misunderstanding the West has of Arabs. She writes, "My hands turn to claws, tear/ newspapers declare war/ the West erupts against/ those backward Arabs/ my throat bubbles, chokes with acid hate/ rage..." Hilal's voice never ceases to perforate the pages of our minds. Then from the East Coast emerges the voice of Sekeena Shaben. She was born in Canada of Lebanese parents (like Joanna Kadi), and currently lives in New York. Shaben takes her reader into the tempest of the page, of the mind, of the heart. Sometimes "there is little inspiration," sometimes New York passes by like the winds that pass "like good-bye kisses." Sometimes in New York, "love...is occasional" and all that is "certain is time spirals." Shaben's poetry has a particular lightness, like a breeze that seldom flows through our beings. Her words delicately caress the surface of the page, passing smoothly through us and leaving us with "love composed on [our] foreheads" reminding us "of beautiful things/ things we crave/ things that leave us in shadows." The Lebanese-American Brenda Moossy stands in the shadows of the South, in "a notion of grace." The song in each one of her words presses, transporting us elsewhere, where "a great bird lifts us/ at the nape and holds us fast." Her words transport us to where we realize that there "is so much/ to regret" but "We are willing victims swept/ up in the great wide wings of want.../ ...In vain, we want." And thus, we "...fail to see/ light prism off the shirred and feathers tip,/ hear the song of Heaven's aching silence,/ feel the embrace of air in our descent." Indeed, her inner voyage, through even the cracks of self, is intensely beautiful and forcefully honest. Moossy's work can portray what happens "when fat women fear famine" to what happens when civilians are oppressed, tortured in the Arab world, as she writes about her "muse" who "was imprisoned.../ ...six months encased in stone/ outside of Hebron./ ...[who] learned to sleep through torture,/ to smile as they split her tongue." Moossy takes us far away and close by. So too does Adele Ne Jame. Ne Jame's lyricism elevates and flows line after line, taking the reader from the sunsets of Hawaii, where she resides, to the sunrise in the memory of her father's Lebanon. From a feast of Arabic food, "...roasted lamb and eggplant,/ fish baked with tahini and lemon..." to her life and moments with love in Hawaii, "I will build you a house of windows to let/ the light in, to see the ocean, even the rain/ each time you raise your eyes no matter where./ There will be no dry kiawe,/ sun-bleached taro, no dark song." The poet understands the intricateness of passion, love, of the heart, of men, understands the foreverness of a moment, as well as its short moment. Ne Jame's poetry allows us to see "stars,/ common as breathing."

As we have seen, Arab-American women are affirming their Arab identity and memory, challenging negative perceptions and stereotypes, and participating in the construction and solidification of Arab-American culture, history, identity, and literature. They understand the boundaries of their societies and strive to transcend these and to arrive at self-actualization, while nonetheless remaining participants in their societies.

Although Arab-American women poets are abundant, to my knowledge there are no published Anglo-Arab women poets, only novelists such as Ahdaf Souief. This is very interesting since there is such a large Arab community in England. Perhaps, that could be explained by the fact that they are mainly first generation Arabs, and thus write in Arabic. It is equally interesting to note the absence of Latina-Arab women poets, if we consider the extremely large Arab communities (mainly immigrants from the Levant) that exist in Latin and South America. Perhaps that could be explained by the fact that Latina-Arabs have assimilated so well in the Latin world that they write as Latinas. I do believe that these women poets will emerge in the twenty-first century. We will come across them, whatever identity they might claim.

Arab women poets have gone a long way from those isolated early years, but they still need to attain more recognition and inclusion among writers and critics globally, and especially among other Arab writers and critics, and their voices still need to be taken more seriously. They should not have to face inclusion or exclusion according to their thematic concerns, whether or not their writing is in accordance with what is accepted and/or considered important to Arabs—for example, politics vs. women's issues. The struggle continues, for, as Adnan says, "....Arab writers, with very, very few exceptions, do not acknowledge the existence of an Arab literature written by women, even when it is written in Arabic" (Shimon 61). Yet isn't this anthology a confirmation of the existence of Arab women's poetry, of its diverse breaths and breathings?

Arab women poets have struggled for freedom, for an enlightened Arab world, for universal recognition, peace, and equality. Arab women poets have encouraged a look toward the future rather than the past, while still holding onto the richness of past literary manifestations. They have gone toward an international tradition, and have interacted with the West—the United States, Europe, and the world over. Their spirit is a force of change in an unstable Arab world. Their experimentation with poetry has been a way to express their realities; it has been a self-exploration, an interrogation into their relationship with inner and outer worlds, and a vehicle for revolution and evolution, even as it has been a way to work on their craft linguistically and poetically. In the past fifty years, their development thematically and stylistically, the development of their technique and form, has only but evolved. Although they are relatively at the beginning stages, it is most definitely a rapid and forceful departure.

The introduction has thus far demonstrated, and the rest of the anthology will further present, the unity of the Arab feminine spirit and of Arab culture, the shared failures and dreams of these poets, and the individual characteristics in the poetry of each Arab country and in the work of each Arab woman poet. Poetry written by Arab women poets is finally beginning to travel beyond its first breaths.

Works Cited

Abramson, Harold J. "Ethnic Pluralism in the Central City." *Ethnic Groups in the City: Culture, Institutions and Power.* Ed. Otto Feinstein. Lexington: Heath Lexington Books, 1971.

Abu-Lughod, Lila. *Veiled Sentiments: Honor and Poetry in a Bedouin Society.* Berkeley: University of California Press, 1986.

Achour, Christiane. *Diwan D'inquietude et D'espoir (La littérature féminine Algérienne de langue Française).* Algiers: ENAG/Editions, 1991.

Akash, Munir and Khaled Mattawa, eds. *Jusoor 11/12: Post Gibran: An Anthology of New Arab American Writing.* Bethesda, Maryland: Jusoor Books, 1999.

Alcalay, Ammiel. *After Jews and Arabs: Remaking Levantine Culture.* Minneapolis: University of Minnesota Press, 1993.

Altoma, Salih J. "Nazik al-Mala'ika's Poetry and its Critical Reception in the West." *Arab Studies Quarterly* 19:4 (Fall 1997): 7–20.

Arebi, Saddeka. *Women & Words in Saudi Arabia: The Politics of Literary Discourse.* New York: Columbia University Press, 1994.

Badawi, M.M. *A Critical Introduction to Modern Arabic Poetry.* Cambridge: Cambridge University Press, 1975.

_____. *Modern Arabic Literature.* Cambridge: Cambridge University Press, 1992.

Badran, Margot and Miriam Cooke, eds. *Opening the Gates: A Century of Arab Feminist Writing.* London: Virago Press Limited, 1990.

Barakat, Halim. *The Arab World: Society, Culture, and State.* Berkeley: University of California Press, 1993.

Berg, Nancy E. *Exile from Exile: Israeli Writers from Iraq.* Albany: State University of New York Press, 1996.

Bekri, Tahar. *Littératures de Tunisie et du Maghreb.* Paris: éditions L'Harmattan, 1994.

Boullata, Issa J., ed. *Critical Perspectives on Modern Arabic Literature.* Washington, D.C.: Three Continents Press, Inc., 1980.

Boullata, Issa J. *Trends and Issues in Contemporary Arab Thought.* Albany: State University of New York Press, 1990.

Cooke, Miriam. "Arab Women Writers." *Modern Arabic Literature.* Ed. M.M. Badawi. Cambridge: Cambridge University Press, 1992.

Cooke, Miriam. *War's Other Voices: Women Writers on the Lebanese Civil War.* Syracuse, New York: Syracuse University Press, 1996.

Déjeux, Jean. *La littérature féminine de langue française au Maghreb.* Paris: Éditions Karthala, 1994.

Fernea, Elizabeth Warnock and Basima Qattan Bezirgan, eds. *Middle Eastern Muslim Women Speak.* Austin: University of Texas Press, 1994.

Gerson, Louis. *The Hyphenate in Recent American Politics and Diplomacy.* Lawrence: The University of Kansas Press, 1964.

Haddad, Yvonne Y. "A Century of Islam in America." The Muslim World Today (Occasional Paper No.4), American Institute for Islamic Affairs, School of International Service, The American University: Washington, D.C., 1986.

Haddad, Yvonne Yazbeck and Jane Idleman Smith, eds. *Muslim Communities in North America.* Albany: State University of New York Press, 1994.

Haiek, Joseph R, ed. *Arab American Almanac.* Glendale: The News Circle Publishing Co., 1984.

Hafez, Sabry. *The Genesis of Arabic Narrative Discourse.* London: Saqi Books, 1993.

Hourani, Albert. *A History of the Arab Peoples.* New York: Warner Books, 1991.

Jayyusi, Salma Khadra, ed. *Anthology of Modern Palestinian Literature.* New York: Columbia University Press, 1992.

_____, ed. *The Literature of Modern Arabia.* Austin: University of Texas Press, 1990.

_____, ed. *Modern Arabic Poetry, An Anthology.* New York: Columbia University Press, 1987.

_____. "Modernist Poetry in Arabic." *Modern Arabic Literature.* Ed. M.M. Badawi. Cambridge: Cambridge University Press, 1992.

Kadi, Joanna, ed. *Food For Our Grandmothers: Writings by Arab-American and Arab-Canadian Feminists.* Boston: South End Press, 1994.

Khouri, Manah A. "The Prose Poem as a New Form in Modern Arabic Poetry." *Studies in Contemporary Arabic Poetry and Criticism.* Piedmont, CA: Jahnn Books Co, 1987.

Majaj, Lisa Suhair. "Boundaries: Arab/American." *Food For Our Grandmothers: Writings by Arab-American and Arab-Canadian Feminists.* Ed. Joanna Kadi, Boston: South End Press, 1994.

Makiya, Kanan. *Cruelty and Silence: War, Tyranny, Uprising and The Arab World.* New York: Penquin Books, 1994.

Orfalea, Gregory and Sharif Elmusa, eds. *Grapeleaves: A Century of Arab-American Poetry.* 1988. Northampton, Mass: Interlink Books, 1999.

Parmenter, Barbara McKean. *Giving Voice to Stones: Place and Identity in Palestinian Literature.* Austin: University of Texas Press, 1994.

Riding, Alan. "Neocolonialists Seize French Language." *The New York Times.* 8 October 1997: 7–8.

Shimon, Samuel. "Private Syntheses and Multiple Identities: An Interview with Etel Adnan." *Banipal* 2 (June 1998): 59–61.

Sulaiman, Khalid A. *Palestine and Modern Arab Poetry.* London: Zed Books, 1984.

Tadie, Arlette. "L'Univers des Romancières Égyptiennes." *Etudes sur la Littérature Égyptienne, Peuples Méditerranéens* 77 (Octobre-Décembre 1996):47–94.

Al-Tami, Ahmed. "Arabic 'Free Verse': The Problem of Terminology." *Journal of Arabic Literature* XXIV (July 1993). E. J. Brill, The Netherlands: 185–198.

Tomiche, Nada. *La Littérature Arabe Contemporaine.* Paris: Éditions Maisonneuve & Larose, 1993.

Tucker, Judith E., ed. *Arab Women: Old Boundaries/New Frontiers.* Bloomington: Indiana University Press, 1993.

Al-Udhari, Abdullah, trans. and ed. *Modern Poetry of the Arab World.* New York: Penguin Books, 1986.

_____. *Classical Poems by Arab Women.* London: Saqi Books, 1999.

Zeidan, Joseph T. *Arab Women Novelists: The Formative Years and Beyond.* Albany: State University of New York Press.

Zukin, Sharon. *The Cultures of Cities.* Cambridge, Massachusetts: Blackwell Publishers, 1995.

THE POETRY OF
ARAB WOMEN

❦ Elmaz Abi-Nader ❧

Although the Sky...

reaches down like a hood
and meets the horizon on my left and right,
although the shades are pulled
and the windows are shut
to paper, weed, wind blowing
passed the house—
although the solid blue sky
is the slate on which each mountain
and hill are drawn in exactness,
I wait. I have driven straight
on a road that does not end,
put my hand out the window to the pronghorns,
white and golden, to the single boy
sliding his sneakers across a shiny rail
where like the cottonwood, cedar,
he rises alone on the horizon.
I have stood beside the truck
on a hill, I didn't expect it to climb
because I wanted the one eagle
on the far-off post in my palm.

Although the wind pitches like a madness
in a family, a private language, a gesture,
a wink, I wait—inside the dropped eyelid
of the sky, the wind trembling sage and prairie grass,
atop the snow hidden under the trees
on Happy Jack. I wait
because I have inhabited this place
before, stood on its lunar landscape
away from homes, schools, and the car that floats
across the highway, silent. I wait
because I can see from the edge of this earth
to the next, sun set and moon rise
in one breath.

New Year's Morning

You don't have to be awake
    to feel the night change:
        the old air—
        dry now—rises
to the gray of a dark morning
        then settles
        between mountains
        outlined with light.
Slippers shuffle across a room.
A vast history, an unknown life
begins. What swells before us
is not the persistence of memory
the past and its perfection. Stars
              are unnamed;
              steady, not lost
              in mythology.
A large hand folds over a smaller one.

I look into this mirror and see
a thousand mirrors behind me:
        My mother's face,
        between bright curtains,
        watches the damp garden.
        My father sits
        under a lamp
        with his eyes closed.

In this accordion of memory,
        I do not see my own face,
        fanning in and out.
I cannot begin.
  The dark dreams of silence blanket
        the gray distance between rising
                    and living;
        between speech and breath.
We listen while forgetting.

What We Leave Behind

Winter pushes into my room. I waken
      And walk to the porch. Windows rattle
Threats of falling. Fragments of glass,
      Veins of dark wood.
I hold the windowsill, watch the trees
      Struggle in the cold. Winter mists
From my mouth. Invisible fire.

Cold flattens against our cheeks, faces us
      Steals the warmth from the goblets
Cupped in our hands. The sun cannot
      Sink into tops of our shoulders.
We do not walk the field from end to end.
      A name you hear makes you shiver.
The pages I am writing mark my day.

When I place my hand upon the glass,
      The print released is no longer mine.
I do not want to be alone. Without amber.
      Without the steam rising on a city street.
Back in my room is a whirlpool of light
      I leave thumbprint and palm, and the map
to my destiny in their stead.

Letters from Home

To my father

Every time you weep, I feel the surface of a river
somewhere on Earth is breaking.
You wipe your eyes as you read
aloud a letter from the old country.
From the floor, I watch the curls of the words
through the sheer pages.
Your brother and sisters have gathered
around you. I don't understand

the language but feel a single breath
of grief holding this room.

Your mother writes of her weakening body.
She walks to church but cannot leave
the village. When you sat with her,
You wanted her forgiveness for your absence
but did not ask. She took you to her closet
to show you the linens she had gathered
which have already yellowed. Her hands
seemed small through the lace. You kissed
her palms, smelling your own fragrance on her skin.

She tells you of the refuge people have found
in the village. Others have gone to Paris.
You have a niece who is a doctor,
a nephew, an architect. Your own children
seem like nomads. They sit in scattered apartments
where you can't see your three daughters
gazing from their windows or your three sons
pacing the old wood of their rooms.
Yet you write to your mother,
they still pray.

You visit your mother now when you can.
Each summer you cross the Mediterranean;
each summer you stand behind her house
looking into the sea hoping she will not die,
this time. And when these letters come,
I run my finger across the pages.
I hope I can learn the languages
you have come to know.

❧ Huda Ablan ❧

Strangers

1.

No one belongs to the path
except a pocket
stuffed with the leaves of night.
It keeps steps in stock
from a shop at the crossroads of the will,
patched with the skin of an old dream.
When yawning,
it invites them to a dance
with few feet and much madness.
When hungry,
it devours their warm, ripe whispers.
When thirsty,
it drinks their cries washed with holy water.
When lonely,
it forsakes its length and shrinks
to a remote corner of the heart
leafing through pictures of those
who have passed away
ensnaring with their song…
It will cast glances,
and tremble with the silence.

2.

No one belongs to the rose
except its melting
in the hand of a sad lover
who plucks it from slumber
every morning
and plants it in the vase of a tear
overflowing with pain.
He teaches how love sings
and how to breathe the secret

hiding behind the eyes
so it may reveal itself
without words.

3.
No one belongs to the heart.
Immersed in opening its chambers—
Shut tight with red forgetfulness—
It stirs the beats of a love
over which a curtain has been drawn
for a thousand nights,
and shakes a cup of blood
freezing as it faces circulation.
It alone
stabs the rug of the wound
made ready for crying
and prays
facing death.

4.
There is no one in the house
its dozing cracks obscure
the rounded journey of a small sun.
In the enclosure of the spirit
its walls bend in the face
of blows from the winds.
Its warmth ages and shrinks
in the coldness of waiting.
With the eyes of the absent
it soaks up warm places that flow
at the very edge of the passage
and melts in the shudder
of an endless beckoning.

Translated by Ibrahim Muhawi, with Nathalie Handal

❧ Fawziyya Abu-Khalid ❧

Two Little Girls

To Nour
My mother, the poet whose poems I have appropriated

I hang on to the hem of her dress like a child hanging
on to the string of an immovable kite

I climb her braid like a squirrel climbing a hazelnut tree

In the late afternoons we jump from one world to another
we play in the wind
like sparrows that opened the door to the cage

We move from game to game

She teaches me the names of the flowers
the seasons of the rain
the love of the homeland
and I teach her obstinacy and mischief

We share one apple and innumerable dreams

We paint a paradise of questions on the face of the desert

We spray each other with the water of the mirage
accompany a fleeing doe

Sunset surprises us in the thick of dusk

Who can solve the riddle:
which is the mother,
which the daughter?

Translated by Farouk Mustafa

A Country

Her hair is long, very, very long
She wraps its ends around her feet as she stands

Her fingers are long, very, very long
She can pick the fruit from the lotus tree as she sits in her boudoir

She bathes in rain gushing forth from her lap
And she dreams.

Translated by Farouk Mustafa

To Enjoy the Horror

There was a common wall between the fence of our Elementary School
    Number Five
and the cemetery of al-Ruways neighborhood, north of the sea in Jeddah.

During recess we would push the fence
in alarm and recklessness, fear and levity
as if lifting a stage curtain.
Unveiling the mystery of being.
Muffling the laughter of a little girl in the sleeves of our school uniforms,
we watch, in happiness that we hide, the panic in the eyes of the
    teachers.
We rush between the nether and the upper worlds.
Snatching stories that sadden the living and disturb the dead.

Before the last school bell, we'd set the swallows free
and stuff our school bags with ghosts and bats
which we carry with us to the neighborhood
to continue the game after the mid afternoon prayers
and to enjoy the horror.

Translated by Farouk Mustafa

Geometry of the Soul
To Mona Saudi

You trick your thorny rope with little joys
just as a woman tricks her maiden heart
with a passing ecstasy or a long rope.

You bend tenderly over the desolate sculpture
you turn embers into spirit
and the spirit into a wing,
that the wall strikes...
The distances fill with feathers
the waves shame the sea
you hover around the impossible
like a moth hovering toward its death
celebrating suicide.

You draw near like an offering moving toward
the altar with pubescent zeal
you draw nearer, nearer,
the iron is welded with the spirit.

You move away, farther and farther away
like a sparrow sensing a hunter.

Your shape sensing a hunter.

You shape geometries of mysterious voids
and masses that form in contrary directions.

You weave dreams and stone
and keep moving farther and farther into quicksand
as if both of us were in the same place
as if our identity were the same abyss
as if the only thing we had in common
was the shroud.

Translated by Farouk Mustafa

❧ Zulaykha Abu-Risha ❧

Marble

Marble on the milk of this night
an opening blocking our door
why when we hunger
don't we find
what buries
our aches
alive?

Translated by Clarissa Burt

Khobayza

Our kisses are mountain mallow
our kisses are the writhing pain
we long for.
and our longing is
....
....

　　　our death.

Translated by Clarissa Burt, with Nathalie Handal

Note: *Khobayza* means geranium.

Tree

O Little Brother
Come let's dream together of journeying far
Come, let's not go back

when the homeland expels us
and there remains nothing but our tree
alone
in the swamp.

Translated by Clarissa Burt

Mewl

When we were by ourselves
harassed by capricious cats
the birds were the last to come
and the first to leave this warm room
because they
             as my mother told me
are busy painting the high points outside their nests
                          with a new dawn.
When we're alone, we stifle the traitorous giggle:
.....
We had two faces
             one for water
             another for annoyance
even though we—usually—are the last one to break
yet the air which stews its froth on
                          morning's curves
went by hastily
went by hastily
And after it, there remained nothing
.....
....
                          but the color of gasping breath.

Translated by Clarissa Burt

ࣷ ETEL ADNAN ࣸ

From The Spring Flowers Own

A butterfly came to die
between two stones
at the foot of the Mountain
the mountain shed shadows
over it
to cover the secret of
death.

From The Indian Never Had a Horse

There is a word that never
makes it.
It slides and breaks against
the inner walls of one's
teeth
it fizzles and flattens...
that word is *death*.

From There

There

In the green escape of my palace, over a bridge, under a
canopy of opalescent light, through there, between dark
branches and their shivering leaves, I'm lost in the scent of
yellow roses, arrested by the range's filtering light.

Are you counting the years of my absence, remembering
a first encounter, a place, an hour? Were we already enemies
or did that happen later, not here, no, but at some point in

the past, inside a room with closed shutters, and where has all
this gone?

You were a boy on a bicycle, riding across an alley of icons,
and I don't know why you were talking to no one but me.

When the weather becomes the whole of one's identity, light-
ning becomes speech and thunder residence. You're sitting on
your house's stone floor watching the season's flow.

Where, here, on this earth, with the trains missing and the
siege, I shall find out who's bringing me death, in this tunnel
longer than the night.

Here

What is *here?*: a place or an idea, a circle focused in God's eye,
a cosmic wave's frozen frame, transient, doomed?

Here, where the heat mollifies, when the body surrenders
before solicitations could reach it, and there, where the
temperature boils the mind and makes it explode into sudden
action; here is the point of no return . . .

There

There, in the wastes of the soul, within its repetitions, where
we wonder if there are differences between the mind's
inner chambers and the imagination's outer realms, lies the
confrontation between the self and itself.

Where territory is pure memory, rarefied air, where a line
is thinner than the horizon. I encounter the demands of
definitions, the pressure of realities which I thought weren't
my own anymore.

Listen, we have to call you, bring back your attention to this
particular place; we can abolish time, yet it doesn't seem
capable to surmount spatiality, we cannot betray matter, win
where the gods tried and failed.

There are stones in Greece, there's white marble in one's
sleep there, where things move, where one can experience
stirrings of freedom, you, a night visitor with infrared gear
can see me while I can't see you, so the fight has no honor,
what has to be killed is already dead, let's not waste the time
left for those angels who want to mingle with humans;
we scared them off, the land being poor and the imagination
lacking, the gods won't punish us, we're of little importance.

We cannot confuse the signs, no, we can't, they will outlast
us. Their nature requires that they remain clear, like the sky
today, unbearably clear, creation occurs every morning, the
signs are distributed over the horizons.

Moral impotence makes us successful. War is raw. Clearly
so. It intensifies desire, the ultimate one, the one meant to
annihilate what is and make happen what was not to be, turn
the metaphysical enterprise of love into hate.

War is our dialogue. It brings explosions at home, debris of
human limbs, booby-trapped love letters. We're sorrow's old
veterans, having written lamentations on too many bones.
Always the writing, that recorded silent voice which jumps
generations to claim eternity for blood.

So what brings you back from over mountains, in July's
aridity, under the sun's dominance, missing parents, divinities
that we share, where is blind energy coming from, the earth,
the sky, the void?

There

From the primeval waters we arose—you and I, from the
beginning we went on a search and when the gardens grew
we looked together for a shade, didn't we?

From the desire to live we arose and built nations, didn't we?

Then we were visited by a creature not named by any of
the gods and we called it Death, and it took power over us,
and autumn on its first day started to shed yellowish leaves on
our beds; then the trees stared at their own bareness and we
didn't come to their aid, did we?

⚜ LAILA 'ALLUSH ⚜

The Path of Affection

Along the amazing road drawn from the throat of recent dates…
Along the amazing road drawn from my old Jerusalem,
And despite the hybrid signs, shops, and cemeteries,
My fragmented self drew together to meet the kin of New Haifa…
The earth remained unchanged as of old,
With all its mortgaged trees dotting the hills,
And all the green clouds and the plants
Fertilized with fresh fertilizers,
And efficient sprinklers…
In the earth there was an apology for my father's wounds,
And all along the bridges was my Arab countenance,
In the tall poplars,
In the trains and windows,
In the smoke rings.
Everything is Arab despite the change of tongue,
Despite the trucks, the cars, and the car lights…

All the poplars and my ancestor's solemn orchards
Were, I swear, smiling at me with Arab affection.
Despite all that had been eliminated and coordinated and the
    "modern" sounds...
Despite the seas of light and technology...
O my grandparents, the rich soil was bright with Arab reserve,
And it sang out, believe me, with affection.

Translated by Abdelwahab M. Elmessiri

⚜ LAMEA ABBAS AMARA ⚜

San Diego (On a rainy day)

The light rain makes me long for you
and autumn sheds all of my leaves...
My footsteps winged,
the wind my path,
your face my *Qibla*
I pass solemnly along the shore
as if you are the frightening Pacific.
I wander in my reverie
there
lost in song
some wondrous cottage
snug in a shady thicket,
I wish we could live there
but time and exile
separate us.

Has spring been forgotten in San Diego?
Has it stayed behind with no season to follow?
Alone in the green hills—like a child—
spoiled by relatives and visitors.

The beauty of San Diego
reminds me of Lebanon
if only the bleeding would stop.
It reminds me of Kurdistan at festive times
celebrating with flutes and tambourines.
And the wrested homeland
—how much we have lost—
how much noble Jerusalem means to us.

The beauty of San Diego tortures me.
The silver clouds slaughter me.
How can I live comfortably in a country
where swords are sharpened for our people?

Translated by Mike Maggio, with Nathalie Handal

Note: *Qibla* is a sacred place a prayer faces when praying.

The Commandments

All *no*'s become *yes*'s under the law.
Don't lie.
Lie!
But insist on it
record it
make it grow limbs and eyes.
Don't steal.
Steal, but be clever
and donate openly
to the poor.
Don't commit adultery.
Marry, divorce, marry, etc.
Be careful of social diseases.
Blame it all on the devil and self-weakness.
Don't kill.
Kill, but with no witnesses.
Or wage war,

for murder on the glorious battlefield is eternal.
Don't bear false witness.
Do so!
Don't rob.
Rob, plunder, murder
as long as there are lawyers.
Excuse me.
This is unjust.
We defend justice through the law.
Justice?!!
Where is justice
when each case has two attorneys?
And each coin two sides
and so justice
and so freedom.

Translated by Mike Maggio

ঙ 'AISHA ARNAOUT ঙ

Orbits

I

Shapeless, the waves rise toward their elements, where the foam of
time swells in the cells. We will not need bridges. In the dream, the
bridges move. Our own liquids augment the surfaces of streams,
moving into chaos. The cracked soul desert the gleaming body.

Absolute nonlogic. Proof of the indefinite. Categories of disbelief.
Withdrawing finger-prints from the corners of accuracy.

Probabilities that groan madly: how can you and I conclude a maze
of directions which are impossible to measure?

Fabric of the moment: how can I appear in the silence of thunder?

How can I exchange my trenches for speculations of radiance?

I sip what remains of chaos. I clothe the texture of the heart, hiding its resemblance to the invisible. I hinder the crushing of time and the tread of distances. I seal off the gleam of mirrors and complete the face of my substitute.

Some day maybe I will overcome my certainty
where spaces zoom by
and time repositions itself.

Translated by Mona Fayad

Spinal Cord

In your sight
I swallow mercury
I drink ink through my pores
until my body splinters
I gulp down water
shear off the down
of spiders
I forgive the papers
for being white
and the corners
for turning.

In you I want to hide
my racing spirit
to make my dreams snuggle up
like fractions among the stars
of the heart
I have not yet learned
how to separate my body
from its shadow
how to propagate in stones

how to erupt in cherished fluids
how to sprout myself.

In your sight
wings are flooded
with a light
that congeals them.

2

I find you inside me
where springs unleash
my fluids. I miss you in the
interrogation of a spear,
in the space of conjecture,
at the suture of a wound
the division of a circumference.
I saddle you with coral
with the fusion of writing
I find you inside me
when alphabets are drowning
in suspicion
and the brightness of labor pains.

With you
I double up on
myself
your secrets touching my surface
like a swarm of light
particles

I encounter you
at the moment of growth
as my body becomes familiar
and I am alone in my nakedness.
Our motion together is like
a statement crumpled into
the square of doing

and the circle of silence.
Our skin is like a planet
that dictates its commandments
in the memory of the protoplasm
where directions have a dual taste
and ash has senses.

We go together
our eyes barefoot
solidifying in the
bastion of love
the climax of death
the stuttering of birth.

Translated by Mona Fayad

⸙ S.V. ATALLA ⸙

Diaspora

After so long
to stand at your dresser
hairpins
in the dusty cup

Unfamiliar
bright black
new

In place of the ones
that loosened themselves
and slid away like days
to lie wherever you lost them
stray time
in their teeth
I wish I could find them

pry open
those long wiry jaws
retrieve your fragile face
from their greedy grip

But you
are new
collected
in the cup

Mother
so many pins
and every day your smooth hair
holding them all together

Visiting the West Bank

Once a year up the long road from Jericho. Hot summer. Mothballs
in knots of tulle, lavender sachets. Suitcases dragged down from the
attic, their locks sprung open. Elaborate embroidery explained,
unfolded. Beautiful handknit sweater for trying on.

Every time we arrive this unloading begins. From freezer and pantry
the delicacies of each season: vine leaves wrapped in April, winter's
marmalade, quince jelly; zaatar dried in June. As though life when we
leave stops passing, starts piling up, packing itself neatly into shoebox
and suitcase, preserving itself in the pantry with pickles and jam.
Even the gossip postponed, each anecdote sealed away, saved to be
savored at this annual sharing.

Daily, at the windowsill, chickenwire, loudspeakers.

In each suitcase a sachet of sorrow never unpacked.

❧ THÉRÈSE 'AWWAD ❧

My loneliness
ages like wine.

I arrest it
between parentheses
bridle it
together with the tumult
paste doubt to it,
question marks…
Meanwhile,
leaning against the pulsing surge
        of the rain
I make love
to that hunger
deep within.

Translated by Kamal Boullata

I undressed myself
of my crust
and wore you:
A nightgown of Love
I buried my eyes
under the marble of your reign
split a crevice
to the light
a road into your flesh.

Translated by Kamal Boullata

I found one word
secluded myself
by my own hand froze.
    I hung it.
from the ceiling and hugged
the heat of the sun.
An umbrella floated
between
two gods.

My body my witness
alone it feels the sequences.
Over my skin
the echoes of famine
persist.

Translated by Kamal Boullata

❧ Fadhila Chabbi ❧

The Blind Goddess

And the blind goddess, when we touched her
like a twinkling of the eye.
On the dry shore her hurried gait…
And in her face when sun and moon quarreled,
and in her step when the sea pecked a drop of life
the water receded—having become pregnant—for a time.
How can the letter be Seeing, Omnipotent,
a peer to the belated, jealous god.
And in the blind goddess when she dimmed
and the earth came to be
and it was the insolence of the ages.

Translated by Yaseen Noorani

Engraving Twenty-Nine

I left nothing behind me
No, I forgot nothing.
The words were thrown in the trash
and the expanse of whiteness.
The wolf is kind to the lamb…
That sentence I tore to shreds.
No eye-witness besides a fly rubbing its wings
beneath the autumn sun
and the heavy silence of a dying century,
to be born wrapped in waters of ferocity after ten meters deep
the sea snake slithers from one culture to another…

Translated by Yaseen Noorani

❧ ANDRÉE CHEDID ❧

Full face

Sometimes   I lie in wait
for the death I will be

from out there
the plain does not need another builder
nor time another clock

the call to arms falls silent
rumors scatter
the face emerges complete

Then suddenly I turn and resume
my stretch of life

Translated from the French by Lucy McNair

Going Forth

You come from the ages' origin

Each birth elects you
Each fear cuts you to the quick

you resurrect
from hope

you recognize as heritage
breath   ember
and movement

the heart's shelter
the brief passage
death held in reserve

and Song!

Translated from the French by Lucy McNair

Turn

Build cities
for time and time's seeds
for the heart and for the eye
for age and for the infant

Tear open the husk—then!

Suspend yourself
upon borderless winds

Succumb to every sea, retrieve life
from every shore

Scale that dune whose only offspring
is silence

Then   again
return to those cities
where events await you.

Translated from the French by Lucy McNair

Renegade

I saw your gaping eyes
where sight had ended

The bluish marks on your temples
betrayed your thoughts

Your lips had clotted
on the words held back

Under your blind skin
blood had lost its melody

It's then that loving you
more than any dead

I dug you out of your lapsed body
to plant you in the heart of mine

Translated from the French by Lucy McNair

❧ SIHAM DA'OUD ❧

I Love in White Ink

I Love in White Ink
at evening, who knows what day or time
from my brow bursts a memory
smuggled from jail to jail
scattered like my land's windwisps
my breath under my embroidered scarf
fleeing in white ink
in smuggled folksongs
of his color—don't ask—like grapes, like wine
and when snow fell from my face
I wanted to tell him good-bye.
I searched, aspired to his height
took a walk to dry
the storm in my throat

all my words have been detained
maybe written in white ink

I reviewed Arab history
found no dream to borrow
again shook myself all over:
how do you keep turning into a lie
so that my throat remains detained
in the airports of the universe
I long for my land's windwisps—
always departing, I leave love at addresses
that can't even be looked for
and in your beautiful eyes
and again
I wanted to draw the disfigured faces
you bear
the tortured homeland infiltrated me
between wisps
and birdwings
but I—I have only my skin
and a dream in white ink
and eyes as big as Mt. Carmel

all that was between us—
my full height
and days passing
on Palestine time—
maybe in your true form you are beautiful
maybe
but I'm just a tear, wet
on my mother's scarf, fed up with its color
its noncolor
a dried tear on the scarf
so I'm telling you all
I'm giving myself up to fruiting and multiplying
I know the truth
and love the words stitched on my old scarf
ready to pounce day and night

and love my land's windwisps
and babies in Beirut and Sakhnin
and I love my storm birthing
and the pomegranate bursting

Written in Arabic, translated from Hebrew by Helen Knox and Smadar Lavie

SAFAA FATHY

The Sailor

Because the question was, "Where am I?"
Strangers lay down across the thresholds of homes
so the sailor would stumble over them and curse the finite horizon
without the slightest conviction.
That's why I decided to turn to books in search of misfortune
while the strangers were pulling the covers of what was to come
    over their heads,
so as to ignore the drunken sailor,
as he ran down the streets of the expiring century
in pursuit of the wayward sea bird
which landed one day on a sail sketched by the artist's fingers.
So I stopped at the grocer's to buy you some fruit
you'll relish come winter.
Then you'll have the consolation of a moment of truth,
which is the absence of colors.
I shall also procure for you a bedouin tent,
to carry when you visit the drowned of the deep.
As she sits in the café pitying the passers-by
the stubborn sea birds will tuck themselves away
and refrain from consuming your sacrifices
despite their past addiction.

The abstract paintings got ready to scurry along with the hasty
    procession,

and you alongside, waving your arms to make way.
There were many ruins, so I took you to her home to show you
    the rooms,
and I started to clean up,
and pile the trash in little piles,
so the archaeologists could search for small valuables
and preserve the papers dripping with fog.
As if it were an ancient sanctity.
Or as if it were a modern outrage.

She sits there now, at a café at the crossroads,
watching the birds and the passers-by,
facing the waiting phone booth
as a spring day dawns,
on a shore that contains them as they gaze into infinity.
Will their gazes consume the ending?
Or will they become
pearls of the deep in oceans
that will obstruct the way to the heart of the courtyard?
There we will see you, Jonah the Wise,
or maybe we'll see that drunken sailor
buffeted by the wind,
giving up diving into the deep.

Translated by S.V. Atalla

Seasons

There was a month I called May. When I buried it in papers, passion
    streamed down,
flooding the tiles of the rooms.
Herds of gazelles searching for mercy lap it up . . . and I wander
    about in search of a
knife
to sharpen against my cheekbones, as I turn the pages of these moments.
You are a stranger to me, and your eyes are the foam of distances
    running like rivers

between us.
Don't ask me about my evaporating grief; perhaps it has become salt
    with which to
doctor wounds,
or maybe seeds I can scatter across the floor, to absorb the words that
    creep there in
search of a story.
Perhaps my sorrow was a bedsheet that couldn't cover its old bed.
Its only pretext was to gaze at the sky and snatch up stars.
Thus, with no trace of treason.

We were sitting on the couch casting glances into the horizon, arrows
    of light years.
Waiting, we defied the hours.
Our revolt . . . ashamed to wear a mask, its savage visage.
Our feet stalked insects to crush them, while they flaunted themselves
    like naked words
Determined to gasp their last breaths in our sight.
Between us there are also silken buds, fluttering spring butterflies.
Their clusters are like the sun's bashfulness when it gathers the girls'
    milk teeth,
causing the seasons, and among them you, cunning Spring.
Is what's between us the empire of Ahmad Taha?
Or those gleaming golden circles, panting behind steely eyes?
I wish I were a leaf, with cells in rows.
My splendor, seasons borne by sailboats.
My ending the winter, when geckos hide away to dream of new
    plants growing.
From your bandaged wounds, in salt and fog,
soaring across riverbanks the morning of erupting promises,
running from shore to quay like a short story collapsing breathless on
    the streets.
Does anyone forbid fabrication?

Or might those cities that swallow fog conjure the word away too?
The same palm outstretched to God,
the same bare feet.
The same eyes, sparkling with poetry's delight.

Is this why you tremble, dreading the city's pages?
Is this why you left the streets, to seek refuge in the nightmares of years?
Will you take comfort in the disgrace of seasons,
and the vagrancy of lone words
on the sidewalks of meaninglessness?

Translated by S. V. Atalla

Notes: When Egyptian girls lose their milk teeth, they throw them to the sun with a little song that asks the sun to take their donkey teeth and give them gazelle teeth, take their buffalo teeth and give them bride's teeth.
Ahmad Taha is the Egyptian poet who wrote *Empire of Walls* in the early 1990s.

❦ MONA FAYAD ❧

Whisper

A whisper is a sibilant thing
Sliding from the throat
Straight to the ear
an intimate thing
I'd say to a sister.
A whisper provides
An access into
boundless caverns
echoing myself.
A whisper breaks
Narcissus' reflection
of himself. A whisper
is Echo's words.
This time, they are heard.

Note: In the Greek myth, Echo tries to say her own name, but can only repeat Narcissus'.

Salma in Wonderland

She eyes herself in the mirror
Black kohl of a *houri*
Drawing a circle to mark her limits
A circle the mirror
Cannot reflect backwards
Or turn into magic.
Wonderland outside
Forms a steady pattern of snow
The imprint of a white winter
Railing against her glass.
The rings around her eyes
Shift in the mirror
To two melted pools

Hiding shades of darkness
Baffled beyond the surface.
Alice with her blue eyes
Steps firmly into the mirror
Knowing she will find
Her image inside.

For Salma the mirror only
Shimmers and dissolves
Uncertain waves lapping
At her irises, draining them
Of all things but the black
Contours of kohl
Where her eyes used to be.

Notes: *Kohl* is a black paste traditionally worn as eyeliner (around the eye or just inside the eyelid). *Houri* is an idealized beautiful woman generally associated with paradise.

❧ CLAIRE GEBEYLI ❧

A Man is Dead

Sunburned eyes
Carved in figure
Nothing ahead
But a cry
At the heart of his darkness

A man has died
His time sinks
A foliage
Drops its leaves letter by letter
And walks on dates
Across mirrors
To re-enact his life

A child runs down like rain
A shadow under the arcade
"Your veil little girl
To dry up your smell"

Led ahead
By a spider's voice
He walks
And walks
Towards thoughts which split up
Eyes like sponges
"Your song desert girl
Dark eyed girl"

A roe-deer wakes up
A crack in the rock
A far away surge
Echoed like a salute

A man has died

Thursday showers its bread
And the anise valley
Watches for this new thorn

Nothing but one more instant…
Names carried away
Cities
Lived moments climbing
On unhinged doors
Cubes of years
Piling up all around.
The sleepy tune
Of a subdued flute

Nothing ahead
But a cry…

An hour
A god
A woman
All eaten up by this instant

When a greedy sleep
Fulfills its schedule

Its paths thin out
The summers rot
A skin warily spreads out
To prolong its body

A man is dead

With his bones
With his fists
With his waist
I trace my way

A humming-bird by an abyss
All the steps
On the sword edge
White, broken down
The same cry reveals me

This noon in the sun
Women
Sweet to watch
Close to singing children

Translated from the French by Mona Takyeddine Amyuni

Beirut

For Beirut I write...

Like veiled women, years listen at doors, seasons close their eyelids, softly touch her broken fragments, and the burned soutane of her walls. The wind alone enters into rooms and murmurs softly. No one interrupts its monologue.

For Beirut I write...

The chalky side of the empty market, the barbed wire planted in the blood stained quarters of the latest battles, the black opening of galleries on dark cliffs.

Signs engraved in passage ways, carved within buildings, the gray dust which speaks for the anger of fire.

Behind a shutter two tearless eyes. A far away voice recites prayers. A worried cat removes a bit of its prey.

For Beirut I write...

How trivial it would be for old crews to fix their silks over this city
sunk in her misery. Let memory manage its gold over splinters, make
wounds guilty, humiliate the kidnapped Capital, and burden her
with regrets.

For Beirut I write...

To call again, to love in vain, to lose one's self and sleep in this ship
betrayed by its song and its lust for life.

For Beirut I write...

Her dress made of a thousand alliances, her checkered fabric, her
dark arteries, her orders at night, and her stones reddened each day
by her light.

For Beirut I write...

So that I watch her as she comes back to life, as she attends to her
chores with time, with death, with the denial of absence. I watch her
as she invents this sand which puffs and covers up with the same
whiteness the tombstones and the cornfields.

Translated from the French by Mona Takyeddine Amyuni

⚜ NUJOUM AL-GHANIM ⚜

Sand in Flames

I put my cameleer off two thousand and one times
Proximity forgave not my compassion for my orphans—
those are the worshippers of darknesses
spitting forth fires on the horizon.
      O star,
my grief is for you, swinging in the void like a skeleton

calcifying before its feet can walk
in that the cutters of death stand their arrows on end to throw at you—
Is it conceivable, this stricken one in my folks' house?
While I'm the radiant virgin
whose face the rivers unrolled for me.
I am led into captivity,
my states are plundered,
my companions are exiled.
I greet a hill to which repair untouchables
and bereft mothers
while my sons—moons in whose presence
shooting stars hang themselves,
are guarded by the unclean.
Where is my blemish, if my veil is removed
and robes sob over my body?
And what is my failing if I receive dust on the part of my hair
with honor
and every day men wound a heart for me.
Return me to my stall
Shackle the *zajals* on the tongue which mourns with them,
Cauterize the eyes
Hunt down sighs
        hunt down
the questions between you and me.

Footfalls deafen the ears
The girl cameleer comes out of hiding split-pocketed,
her hair fly away behind her
her hands above her belt unsheathe her dagger
but mothers weep crying for help
ah! unto the heavens
The girl cameleer
stabs the air
as if the pattering of rain showers did not reach the tribe.
Any captivating appearance,
tongues smack their lips in lust
while the walls crack, the rooms collapse,
        dreams die

blood spurts from everywhere, a wail,
bodies float by... the city drowns
in blood.

Translated by Clarissa Burt

Note: *Zajals* are folk songs.

From Trespasses

I don't know how I lost my amulets
and my absolute certainties revert to despair at the peak
of their pulsation.
Here I am winning and losing
mostly I lose my gardens from the first round.
Here's Night coming overcast with its angels
and Babels crowding about.
Description is not what you fear
but the crash of the penetrator into them;
they yell back and forth
bird.

By the Bird:

Water with which to calm your winds, O cameleer
is a citadel for tremblers,
poetry for your bewildered sadness.
I will run away from my ravens,
descendants of despised prophecies.

And when you exchange the pavilion
I'll be frittered away pound by pound
because I am a magician with no spells
or pages,

so darkness won't discern me.

Now in order to recite my homelessness to you,
witness my ruse to myself, so you can stone me
if I allow paradise to be my refuge.
Rising in the roving around as the scream of dew,
and like the wavering of an echo in a well
waves follow one after another inside my body
a prisoner to all parts
a rebel against the elements.

Believe that angels' wings grow tender
when ideas wear thin,
that the shriveled are healed in hands
while the murmuring of homes play with your hearing.

You don't know how they aim their cracks
but they make them the places your heart settles,
by themselves the parlors realize why windows are wary
before the convulsions of dawn
and the blue is broken at any turn unto death.
By itself the sky
shies away
whenever paths surrender to their evacuation
while
like an old shelf
you await a hand to remove the dust
squatting, intimate with isolation
divulging your hidden secrets to the empty chairs.

The house is an ailing old man
the corridors are covered like a wounded tent
like a stranger in a town unappealing to you…

Translated by Clarissa Burt

❧ Nada el-Hage ❧

Follow me

Sir, How much do you need
of laughter and tears
of heart-throbs and shivers
to improve?
Shall I raise you as prayers and incense
melt you as candles
pick you as stars
render you ink on paper
and transform you into a saint, a prophet, a god
in the hymns and myths of passion?

~

Listen to my voice when I'm silent
see my silhouette when I move away
follow me to the place I succeed or fail to reach
from the deepest love to the most extreme
follow me to I don't know where
just follow me!
Let the pearls of rain wash you
and my God protect you!
Follow me and look deep in yourself,
I'll disappear from here,
I'll appear again as a shooting star there.

~

I call upon all poetry of the earth
I draw you on the pages of passion
a lord,
I shield you...
For you, I create dreams
I paint you, unimaginable colors

I attract fairies and gods of all tales
to sprinkle their fabled glow on you.
I erase you with a warm tear or a mocking laugh
to sow you again, spikes of wheat in my hands.

~

Live in me
breathe life into my soul
wrap me up in a moon cradle
and utter sea pearls in my heart.
The sea is no more alone to seduce me
the sky no more my only haven
passion for melodies not my sole confidence
nothing, nothing more
than to write you
in the size of my love!

Translated by Nathalie el-Hani

A Land Stretching up to the Sky

The time of loving and fluttering has not yet come
for I've grown into the land stretching up to the sky
I've absorbed rebellion and appealed to God
for I am the cloud, alone, I turn to myself
for I refuse to love and leave
and I've grown into the land stretching up to the sky

I've embraced the twilight
and God blessed
my love
my bliss
my faithfulness
my pain
for my life merged with God

For I've slipped away, no trace at all
I could seize the moment that quenches my soul
floods it, calls up my craving,
I recoil and leave
For I refuse to believe
any grain of feelings could save mine
could overshadow my Love
For now, I do not pray without being granted,
I compose and leave...

I unfold bliss
scatter it in the wilderness
drink my ethereal being
and just leave...

Translated by Nathalie el-Hani

Overflow

A word
A tear
And the universe was filled

Translated by Nathalie el-Hani

The Journey of the Shadow

By the light of the night
in the midst of life
I continue
Between the leaves of the heart
in the outcry of silence
I continue
From the utmost futility
to the essence of faith
From the kiln of flames

to the frost of the soul
I continue
Holding on to my shadow
detached and away
even from my nakedness

Body and soul united
I continue
I do not know where
I do not mind but
I continue
What remains of my life
overflowing as water
quavering as the voice of God
roaming the wind's surface
isolated in the moon's eternity

~

Let my eyes fill up with trees
before my departure
Let my lungs fill with air
before the sky embraces me
And there, I will not long for a tree
I will not be short of air
I will be the sea
my eyes two trees
my arms two blossoming branches
and my body the world
I will not be short of anything
I will penetrate the shadow
I will reach light
with the faces of the ones I've loved
with them, I will cross the Secret

Translated by Nathalie el-Hani

❧ LAILA HALABY ❧

Handfuls of Wind

This summer I caught handfuls of wind
At 65 miles per hour
In Kentucky
And imagined
That the air in my hand
Was laced with orange blossom,
That the billboards were not in English
And that you were next to me.

Your memories are piles of silk:
Colorful and unraveled
In a heap
Like your promises
I keep in a mother-of-pearl box
With the turquoise earrings
You gave me at birth
To ward off evil.

One summer I caught handfuls of wind
At 120 kilometers per hour
In Amman
And imagined
That you were not taking me
To the airport so late in a night
That tasted of whiskey
And that you would be next to me.

Your memories are photographs:
Black and white
On my desk
Like my stories
That I carry with me everyday
With the turquoise ring

You gave me at birth
To ward off evil.

Refugee

For Saad Abu-Saud

The lungs of the wrinkled gray-eyed man
bellow with love
for a dusty quarter
of land
that lies a stone's throw
from the rock
where he sits everyday
and watches
his neighbor,
his fields.

The path leading up there is beaten
with his dreams
mixed in the lonely dust.
Everyday
you will find him there
with tears
racing down his cheeks
as he bleeds
a river
to take him home.

Long Distance

I folded myself and sent me to you
in place of the usual crinkled letters,
or so I imagined. What would you do
if it was me in your postbox, not pictures?

Would you read me over one hundred times
the way I do with each smile you send
long distance? Would you break the pantomimes
the oceans made me think would never end?

I know what you'd do: iron the folds out,
pin me to the wall in your living room
where I could hear your voice of exile shout
in person, and let me study your gloom,

from which you seek refuge in the caress
of a young girl who can't pronounce your name.
You sing ghazals to her with bold finesse
but she dances on your grave just the same.

Some would say your exile is not so bad
and that you are living well in freedom,
but all I see inside your eyes is sad
stories of a king without his kingdom.

⚜ SUHEIR HAMMAD ⚜

manifest destiny

we four
sitting nursing
plates of rice and beans in a cuban diner
we all should have been other people
with other people

one
who should've been a neo-nazi aryan baby breeder
or a machete wielding man hating dyke
was a lover of both men and women   girl of riot   and a poet

another
who should've been a witness of jehovah knocking down doors
or a gyrating video hoochie
was a scholar of african glory   lover of knowledge   and a poet

the other
should've been a cold landowning elitist
or a rich corporate robot
was a fighter for independence   lover of an island   and a poet

and me
who should've been a doctor of western medicine
or married   at least engaged   but always obedient
me   searcher of truth   lover of humanity   and a poet

missing my family
who couldn't understand
we four all missing family who wouldn't understand
creating a family
we struggling to understand
we were where we needed to be
we are who we have to be

broken and beirut

no mistakes made here
these murders are precise
mathematical
these people blown apart   burned alive
flesh and blood all mixed together
a sight no human being can take

and yet we take and take
desensitized to the sacred defamed
witness youth strap 40 lbs of
dynamite to sore bodies 'cause
we always return to what we know

and if that's war
we return over and over to it
sit at its feet to
remove stone shoes   bones and blues

don't know what to do with visions
of blown up babies   so we
lamé nails and lame tongues
which should protest
love those who cannot
love us   hate ourselves   and become
obsessed with puzzles

shifting through rubble   we ask
where is the head that goes with this 7-year-old shoulder
shattered   this leg looks like it fits with this hip
this dead with that dead   cause they wear twin rings
on bloated purple hands

tired of taking fear and calling it life
being strong and getting
over shit   to prepare for more shit

(when my heart was broken i turned to the only dynamic i knew
more hurtful   my father)

we return to what we know
it's 1996 and beirut all over again
this time the murdered are those who survived the last time
and this time's survivors are preparing for the next time
when fire will rain down on heads bowed in prayer

i want to go home
not only to mama and baba
i want to go home to before me and
pain   bombs and war   before
loveless sex   poetry   and chocolate

i want to remember what i've never lived
a home within me   within us
where honey is offered from my belly
to sweeten babies' breath   make boys moral
and girls strong

want to return to the belly of my honey
and feed myself earth
before 1996   1982   '73   and '48
before tv   race   marriage   and meat

return to what we've forgotten
what hunger has faked
return to the whiteness of black
to the drum   the hum   the sum of my parts
to god   the boiling in my belly
touch it taste   name it and
come back to here

come back   and make no mistake
be precise   get back to work
shifting through the rubble   mathematically
building a new   day
with offerings of honey and memory

never forgetting
where we come from
where we've been
and how sweet honey
on the lips of survivors

of woman torn

did her skin smell
of *zaatar* her hair of
exploded almonds

between the olive trees
her father lit the match   brothers poured the flammable
the women they watched   the women they tucked
their sex away under
skirts under secrets

in this world of
men and molotovs

family pride laid
between her thighs
honor in her panties
and no oslo accord
or camp david signing
could free her sex
from its binding

i can only pray light
a candle and hope
you were not raped
he was not rough
a relative   a drunk stranger

i can only hope you were
loved once   in his
arms that he touched you right
where you needed
often as you
wanted whispered loving
i hope he was sincere

where is he now

where was he when they found the swelling
of your belly   proof of humanity
where was he when they stuck fists up
inside you to prove you loose

when they beat you blue
ripped each hair out your head
each one by one in the name
of god and land   spit on you and
cursed the evil that is
woman

palestine's daughter
love making can be as dangerous
as curfews broken
guerillas hidden

you join now those   who won't leave
the earth   haunt my
sleep   who watch my
back whenever i lay
the forced suicides the
dowry deaths and

nora
decapitated by
her father on her forbidden
honeymoon   he paraded
her head through
cairo to prove his
manhood   this is 1997

and i can only hope
you had a special song a
poem memorized a secret
that made you smile

this is a love
poem cause i love
you now woman
who lived tried to
love in this world of
machetes and sin

i smell your ashes
of *zaatar* and almonds
under my skin
i carry your bones

Note: *Zaatar* is a mixture of the powdered leaves of thyme, which grows on the mountain slopes of the Levant, and other ingredients such as *summaq* and roasted sesame seeds.

ᛘ NATHALIE HANDAL ᛊ

Goran's Whispers

travel through evenings without memories with memories
of choking riverbanks and dying lime trees,
memories of soldiers who look past each other
for they have forgotten their own faces, memories of death
and broken hourglasses lost amidst the scars of war
Goran's whispers whisper, "why must we witness
the fate of small things as they vanish in screaming
grounds, witness their speech before their end"
they cry out, "*klaonica*" and they repeat "*klaonica*"
repeat "*klaonica*" repeat and repeat "*klaonica*"
as if it was the only word they could remember, their only testament,
then their words like their bodies become ashes
in a graveyard behind the broken streets, broken houses,
broken hospitals, behind the empty stores, empty fields,
empty voices, behind the terrified children and their
terrifying games terrified of the terror inside of them
and the entire world seem to have lost Goran's whispers
somewhere in their memory of yesterday, now all seem
to exist in bruised skies, in conversations people have of the past
except for those without a house, without clothes, without silence
except for those souls still screaming beneath the grounds,
afraid that they will be killed over and over again

Note: *Klaonica* in Serbo-Croatian means slaughterhouse, butchery

Forgetting, Love

I am not afraid of loving, I am afraid of forgetting I loved
and so I leave my naked body to the evenings, to the
breeze of a September night not too far way from winter
leave my kisses to the yellow and red butterflies
to allow them to fly in my absence
leave my passionate poems to the rivers
so that they could recite them to passers-by
leave my scent to my old lovers
leave my fantasies to those I saw once
leave my secrets in between the pages of books
leave the pavilions of laughter
and weeping pavilions side by side
leave all the blooming trees to my dreams
so that they can remember that happiness
is in the legs of nature, that silence can be as painful
as love, that love smiles but is never satisfied,
is happy but never for too long, like the stranger
in your bed who speaks to you as if he knew you, loved you
knowing he will never see you
and who are we after lovemaking, after every lover?
Are we still afraid of what love might mean to us?
I speak of we for those who feel the way I do
I do believe I must leave everything of me to someone, to someplace
so that they could remember for me

The Sigh

The sea sighs, thieves fly
fleeing the suburbs of gloomy dreams—
and sorrow
wanders in the motions of a farmer
as he ploughs his life
in slender pieces—
like bits of wind under the fingernails of childhood…

Why does the darkness invite beggars?
Does treachery lie between
a bird and a butterfly,
between the legs of fear—
dreaming
a strange dream—
that the sea sighed and the
quiet steps of light
held terror in their throats—
nothing crowds us but to see and the sea
as it sighs and sighs in the mouth of will...

◊ DIMA HILAL ◊

ghaflah–the sin of forgetfulness

born by the mediterranean
our mothers bathe us in orange-blossom water
olive trees and cedars
strain to give us shade
we come to america where they call our land
the East   meaning different/dark/dirty
we soon forget
our grandmothers combed hair like ours
we wish our hair blonde   our eyes and skin light
we know barbie
looks better than scheherazade
we think french makes us sophisticated so
we greet each other with bonjour instead of salaam
proud of our colonizer's tongue
we forget the Qur'an sings in arabic

when we arrived
our fingernails pierced the palms of our hands
we stared at pictures of our children

eye sockets carved out by rubber bullets
on the 10 o'clock news
our brothers and sisters spit up blood and teeth
and CBS declares them "terrorists"

now we turn away from bruises and broken bones
body counts and funerals
we know we cannot help   anyway
we forget we once stood on the same ground
they die on
we look for the arabia packaged by the west
we escape into clubs to watch
blonde belly
dancers named jasmine
sashay almost naked
we eat pasty hummous at eight dollars a plate
and tell each other
how much we miss our home

A Different Morning Altogether

1.
The rain thunders on the roof
the balcony railing
and umbrellas of kids
in uniforms heading to school
the rain slams to the earth
flattens the soccer field
rushes through trees
while the asphalt darkens
on a two-lane-by-way

In bed
I listen to the water crashing
sheets crumpled at my feet
I listen and believe the sky
wishes to pound

the curves of Costa Rica
flat

2.
I lean against the balcony railing
studying the view
we paid two extra dollars to see

My skin unfamiliar
with the weight of air
will soon forget being
without its constant touch
heavy and humid

Time moves slower here
I watch men in shorts
sit beneath an awning across the street
drinking beer
but I only hear the rush of rain

Bedouin Eyes

My hands turn to claws, tear
newspapers declare war
the West erupts against
those backward Arabs
my throat bubbles, chokes with acid hate
rage and saltwater form cesspools
in my Bedouin eyes and blind me
my breathing shallow
mind numb and calculated

The gardenia scent of my country
has never seemed farther away
I see your guns aimed in the name of justice;
tearing flesh, stopping a breath
in mid-exhale, a heart

in the second half of its beat
when you scream terrorists
I hear the prayer of my family
a tight canopy against the falling sky
while you count mortalities, I see faces
that look like mine

Now my lips will not form the words of Allah
as I feel our city shudder, then
break and collapse onto itself
my lungs save their wind for curses
as my people, bruised, cannot rise
and I welcome
the nausea which overtakes
weakens
forces my body to sink to the floor

❧ HODA HUSSEIN ❧

A Room of One's Own

One day
I will have a room of my own,
fix on its walls
well-chosen clippings,
surround them with question and exclamation marks.

Intense moments will flash
in the thread of a reflected electric light,
as a ball of clay I made
earning my mother's reprimand
as it had left me with dirty hands

like a bird I will peck at the soil
next to one of the pillars

we have been familiar with
at open-air metro stations.

I will press my bag to my chest
a worn-out smile will appear
behind your glasses covering two thirds of your face,
I will draw your attention
when the remaining third radiates
to the fact that my blouse is décolleté.

One day
I will have a room of my own
and remember the grief we had
when we were homeless.

Translated by Cornelia al-Khaled

Male Grownups

I know
that I do not understand what
male grownups mean by
homeland, love and liberty—
making a toast to the great centers of civilization—
royal hats taken off to honor the epitome of knowledge.
I know, when these hats knock
my small head,
showering down morsels of wisdom,
I have to feed on them with pleasure:
savoring knowledge should appear delightful
in the eyes of others.

Translated by Cornelia al-Khaled

Childhood

I want to make a toast to some victory,
to blow up something of great authenticity,
to collapse now.
Perhaps belief in annihilation
will fill me with rage to face what is happening.
A child will crawl under my feet
I myself will crawl to steal her childhood away.
I will try to logically persuade her
that losing early things is simple
as a vaccination.
I might even dare,
if she ignores me, awe-struck by the
enormity surrounding her,
to burst a strongly worded laughing balloon
with the tip of a thermometer
up her bottom.

Translated by Cornelia al-Khaled

ᦥ Donia el–Amal Ismail ᦥ

A Moment of Mourning

Gaza, creeps
with cold hands and feet
like my life in this hot-city
of sins.

Boiling before me
like a fit of pain,
its body flapping,
the body that had kept elegance
for twenty-three years, passed...

Now professionally practicing whoredom
over traditions of Revolution, fashioning red neckties
over newspapers in a cloudy morning.

The city which I dreamed in her love,
throughout all the stages of pains that I passed
or those that grow in me insistently,
exceeding the limits through her lust, giving birth to principles,
never idealistic—
now sinks in her blood
licking the past that will never return
trying to believe herself
the lovely belly dancer...
too proud, too deceived by this praise.

For two years the sky has never rained,
the Griffin has sold its immortality
for whoever grants her a temporary lust,

a lust that has evaporated
with a time
of organised crime.
Now she is enjoying her luxurious pains
like an old woman complaining about her teeth falling...

The sea that kept its color
through years of sadness and sufferings
has been polluted by capturing
the dreams of the exhausted in exile—
the holy sands falling from their shoes.
Shall it capture their sins in oblivion?

This time is a space
with no good prospect.
The Beach camp which has agreed it will never be a city
sinks in its winter reflections.
In its summer dreams that never come true,
its pains are groaning, overflowing

despite the balloons of celebration
spreading in the sky.
Are there any feelings
other than grief and defeat
in this city which eats her children?

Deprivation is saturated by its greed
and exchanges what remains from the country with decorated greed...
While the wire, separating dream from reality,
blows a trumpet for help...
with each dawn, pours its labour
and buses carrying faces crowded with defeat,
submit to the needs of the time.

Seeing everything from far away,
very close, touching the pupils of my eyes.

More sad
more tired
more pale, more and more
more defeated, more and more and more
witnessing its death, that will never be beautiful,
while an old OLIVE TREE insists on the change
and gambles on its FACT.

Translated by Atef Abu-Seif, with Nathalie Handal

Notes: The Griffin is the Canaanite symbol of Gaza City.
The Beach camp referred to is actually a refugee camp on the beach of Gaza City.

❧ 'Enayat Jaber ❧

1. Solitude

The boxes,
having waited so long,
and the letters,
which make my presence felt,
are either sick or absent.

The ominous knocking
and rapping,
on the closed doors of the evening,
in the brimming loneliness,
changed my colors;
I now resemble
alley cats;
too miserable to miaow,
too gray,
to cross the street with care,
or heed the evils of bad company.

2. Clarity

My desire is
to open the door,
even when the knock is faint—
to know who's there.
But the room is the same—
it tightens when we blossom,
roses, asking.
The softness of the scattering clouds
does not accompany
your biting inattentiveness.
This rose is red:
say it is a rose,
and is red.

And I want it:
it broke.
If you wished, you would have caught up with me,
with exacting weight,
when you say you love me.
A moment is not moments,
or a place to let go.

3. Smell

Small but splendid is,
the disappearing vision,
the image of my grandmother, the veins on her hands,
her tired dress,
with the smell of her age,
so faint, and it soon dispersed,
as did the rose season;
why the trail when it did not lead to a path?
The school,
friends' homes,
are no longer there, and would not come back.
Time, it left;
why the heavens, when they show no mercy,
caving in,
from the weight of birds?
And my maturity;
why the ribbons when they kill my poetry?

4. Circle

He breathed deeply,
when the street awoke,
with the very features of yesterday.
He was not ready yet
to deal with the morning.
In her first absence,
what worries him

is not this morning,
he can make it through another morning.
What really worries him
is the mornings after,
his sitting absentmindedly,
suffocated by air,
counting the seconds
and the movements of emptiness.
One little kick will do,
in his tremulous freedom,
to put love in order again,
and to calm the quivering world.
Just one little kick,
for the sake of bliss, which
overflows from her hands, roaming
on his back.

Translated by Wen Chen Ouyang

◈ ANNEMARIE JACIR ◈

Pistachio Ice Cream

They told me the
Arabs named the stars
algol, sirius, aldebaran...
My mother's olive-shaped eyes
sandaled feet
led me into centuries
of vast empires
forgotten treasures
Now, only ruins remain.

This was the summer
i bathed in olive oil

and sat on the sidewalks
of Jerusalem eating
pistachio ice-cream
with the old man
whose ancient face tried
to explain to me that we fought
with our hearts and
not our heads—therefore
we would never win.

i am dead to my tribe
i will never learn all
its salty secrets
So tonight I want to sleep
with *vega, deneb, altair...*
because they will disappear
with the morning sun,
and only ruins remain.

❧ SALMA KHADRA JAYYUSI ❧

Dearest Love

Dearest love, listen:
after the cave where death's artillery blazed in the mind,
where bullets are fields, houses chimneys,
the dead heaped like frozen waves,
when at flood tide the Bedouin wind raged through the camps,
their deadly steeds galloping to triumph—
after terror,
after my heart was torn out,
after the knock-out,
we woke up to live again.

Forgive one who came back from the dead,
who saw what he saw,
who saved himself in time.
From the black cloud I saved myself
but when new life came my way,
I walked proudly
in the dusty graveyards of our dead.
But ah, love of my life,
you weren't there, and so
I married my cousin after all.

Translated by Charles Doria

In the Casbah

I thought the war was...
here we died, Mai and I,
flattened by armored wheels
while you were fooling around
                in the Casbah...

I found my children's broken bodies
lying in the streets and picked them up,
I swam over my head in nightmare,
then yanked off my skin,
hung it over the flame to dry
and once more I almost drowned
                in their dream.
I flew, crawled, hid—
I heard the wind crying:
                "Salma... Salma
they've bought and sold you"
thousand snakes—a blazing coil
                around my heart.
And you were fooling around
                in the Casbah,
                weren't you,

when our nation became
war's killing ground?

Translated by Charles Doria

The Sunken Ship

My ship is sinking.
I don't save it.
Night frost gathers snow in it.

Don't come closer:
I'm the Death that covers
the summit of the depth.
Don't come closer!

I'm the Death that frightens you,
I'm the ancient sorrow,
I'm the trembling fear-and-shame.
Haven't you heard of me?

Night frost has taken root in me,
nestling in my heart.
Who'll save you from my blast?

Do I love you?
Yesterday we were lovers,
sharing madness and warmth,
venturing,
nurturing our love;
But when the sea-storm came
I was alone.

My ship is drowning,
clothed in sea-and-mountain-frost.
I don't call it back.

I've fought nagging yearnings
to bury my embers in it.
Are you trying to light dead embers?
Haven't you heard of me?
I'm Death on the summit
                          and in the pit
washing off the slap of shame.
I'm the Death I love.
There are ghosts in the streets and cafes,
I'm the only one alive.
The winds enfold me from the feverish world,
the purity of snow has torn me to tatters.
Haven't you heard of me?

I'm the only one alive,
I died just yesterday.
Night frost wraps my head with silence.
An ocean of forgetfulness engulfs me,
curing the mute wound in my heart.

Growing in purity with Death!
Haven't you heard of me?
I'm a mother,
a woman without love;
yesterday I died in shame,
without a heart, without a country,
without a home.

Leave me to my shutters.
Dare you touch the depths of exile?
Beware!
Beware the unraveling of my secrets!
You'll see your suppressed terror…
in my heart.

Translated by Suneet Chopra, with the author

❧ AMAL AL-JUBURI ❧

Enheduanna and Goethe

We are both different:
you thought and spoke your verses,
I gave my poems birth,
then conceived my thought.
Why do you blame me when I gather
the tribes of lovers and the exiled
into the days' cemetery?
You have awakened women whom I imprisoned in the dungeons of hell.
O West, I am hurtful...
There is no piety in my heart
but I am the priestess of the great suffering,
I drag your land from the webs of words
while you drag me to your "West-East Divan."
We both balance on the same rope
though we part walking toward two abysses.

I open the windows of your words,
I find my coffin in your elegies,
exiled, abandoned by a distant East.
My years are horses wounded with your lances...
they never cease neighing.
A stranger in your home
but in my home
I am the mistress of lamentation.
O East, what have you done to me?
I loved you but you brought me shame.
You disfigured me like a herd of blind Scheherazades,
you exceeded all bounds in dancing over my body,
you have fed me the lust of the stars
in the fleeting moments of lightning—
but all of that from behind a veil.

Translated by Salih J. Altoma

Note: Enheduanna: The translator Salih J. Altoma writes: "The earliest known author in world literature, Enheduanna (c. 2300 bc) was a Sumerian princess (the daughter of King Sargon 2334–2279 bc), a high priestess of the moongod of Ur and a poet specially noted for her cycle of hymns to the goddess Inanna. Apart from their religious overtones, Enheduanna's hymns reflect her own personal tribulations, her banishment (exile) from Ur, the political turmoil of her time and highly intimate subjects. Al-Juburi's attempt to incorporate some of Enheduanna's poetic elements represents a growing literary use of Enheduanna as indicated in recent adaptations or works by mostly women writers."

Protest

Why did you reproach him
and turn him away?
Then curse him?
It is not honorable for Adam to kneel.

Adam, you who have ruined my life...
Listen: the Lord will one day revoke
His decision,
in regret.
How did He make you the caretaker
the prophet
the murderer
the commander
the master and slave
the father and son?
And you,
you are nothing but
a pair of flawed boots.

Translated by Salih J. Altoma

❧ JOANNA KADI ❧

Looking Back

You drifted lazily from the sky,
touched down
in that loneliest of organs.
We probed through scarred hearts,
thickened from the war years.

For the first time,
I didn't finish my sentences.
You spoke my secret language
of east moved to west
stopped at factory door.

Only a week
and you drifted again,
no piece of anchor handed over.

Later,
another scar formed
on my left ventricle
as your tongue
made a wide detour
around my name.
No surprises for me;
I've spent too many years
on the front line.

Look all ways,
dart into that
one patch of open space,
grab these five long minutes
before the bombs plummet again.
Make the connection. Run.
Leave no trace

of this furtive meeting
under the night sky.

Our parents wanted faces kept forward.
They leapt from the east
landed clumsily in the west
your mama sprawling face down
my father on his back.

They warned us:
Looking back means remembering.
Remembering guarantees
finding stories.
Finding stories translates
into feeling a broken tongue.
Feeling a broken tongue
equals residing with bodily harm.
Residing with bodily harm
is the life of an Arab transplant.

Who can bear it?
Who can live
with a heart wide open?
Surely not us,
our marked hunks
of gnarled muscle
beating slowly.

When the shelling ceased
you opened for one brief moment,
let the sun from my twisted tongue
warm you,
then you left.

Not me.
I look back.
I see you.
I remember.

Your face in my dream.
I find your story.
    Buried deep in desert sand.
I feel your broken tongue.
    Kiss my purple lips.
I live with bodily harm.
    You'll never look back.

I've always known the life
of an Arab transplant.
The heart is a lonely organ.

ArabInnocents

I

Tuesday, torrential downpours blackened
every corner of the sky,
by Thursday morning
the topsoil brimmed to saturation,
next day, rivulets edged
into the bedrock,
Sunday, surface puddles gathered.

No one ever explained
sadness can haunt every space,
loss can be heaped
bail upon bail.
When the little ones got away,
I invented a new equation:
losing two babies means
losing two futures.

As watery grief streamed from
the pores of my tired breasts,
my ears could distinguish

only the special words reserved
for dead white babies:
innocent, pure, angel.
When Arab babies die
no one speaks,
but their names live
in my bones.

II

Over centuries,
'Arab' and 'innocents'
twisted comfortably together
among jasmine.
A brutal ambush
by white hands
forced a rock wedge between them,
bludgeoned the connection.

I'm bent on talking
about ArabInnocents,
big and small,
dead and alive.
Failure doesn't worry me,
the stars offered reassurance.

"Crazy girl. Stars don't talk."
But for years
I strained my neck,
walked with head back,
listened carefully.

Late one night
a burnished glint
murmured my name.
'Joanna Kadi,' it entreated,
voice equal parts
French accent

flirtatious hussy
water vein sliding through desert.

The deluge continues,
I re-channel
this elemental power.
Each morning I guide silver wetness
on a new course.
The force of dripping water
hides inside tear-shaped drops.
Touch down on granite
soften a groove
open a hole
dissolve the rock.

❧ Mohja Kahf ❧

The First Thing

I am Hajar the immigrant

There came to me the revelation
of the water

I left the world of Abraham,
jugs sealed with cork,
cooking-grease jars,
Sarah's careful kitchen fires

The horizon is a razor
I moved over, severing
slates of earth,
sediment of ancient seas,

to stand alone, migrant, here,

where the shape of the cup of morning is strange,
where dome of sky, mat of earth have shifted
where God does not have a house yet
and the times for prayer have not been appointed,

where the only water is buried deep
under hard ground and I must find it
or my unborn people die within me
The first thing
the founder does
is look for water

I am Hajar, mother
of a people
I stand here straddling
the end and the beginning
Each rock cuts into the heel like God
Each step is blood, is risk:

is prayer

The Roc

Here's my mom and dad leaving
all familiar signposts: Damascus, the streets they knew,
measurement of time in mosque sounds,
the regular scrape of heavy wooden shutters,
the daily boiling and cooling of fresh milk.
Anyone back home who had no phone fell off
the disc of their new world: tomato-cart man,
schoolchildren in skittish flocks. Crazy Fat'na
the Goatwoman, all the newly married cousins,
the porter at the door
they left behind

Here they are crossing the world,
hoisting up all they know like a sail,

landing in Utah. The time is March
1971. They know nothing
about America: how to grocery
shop, how to open a bank account,
how the milk comes, thin glass bottles
on tin chinking them awake,
what "you bet" or "sure thing" meant
in real spoken English, outside
the London-grammar books so creased,
so carefully underlined. It was,
my mother said, as if a monstrous bird
had seized them up and dropped
them in a fantastic terrain

      Here's my mother studying
the instructions on the coin-
box of a laundry machine,
enrolling us in kindergarten,
tape-recording her college lectures so
that she could play, replay, decode
the stream of alien phonemes into words
That's her refolding foil, stretching
the little budge over the month, making
the ten-cent toys
our treasures of Sinbad

      Here's my father staking
his life's savings on one semester
He works hard and at the end of the term,
on the day before the last dollar
of the life savings is gone,
he walks into the Chair's office
and the Chair gives him a job teaching
Other friendly natives explain
subsidized student housing,
coupons, and the good places to find
bargain basement merchandise

The pilgrims were so happy
at being shown how to survive here
after the first long winter,
they had a feast. That's mom
laughing at the strange loaf of the bread
There's dad holding up the new world coffee
in its funny striped boxes. That's us,
small, weightless, wobbly
with the vertigo of the newly landed
voyager

Here they are, mom and dad,
telephoning back home, where the folks
gather around the transmission
as if it was from the moon
The phone call to Syria was
for epic events only. The line pulsates
as if with the beating of enormous wings.
They shout and shout into the receiver
as if the other end were ages
and ages away. Spiny talon
digs into rock.

On the Death of Nizar Qabbani

I will never be this beautiful again
My body will never be like light across a fountain
My breasts will never be this full and tipped with milk
I'd finally learned to own myself
I'd finally learned to give myself
because of you and now you're gone
Nobody talk to me about accepting
You're the one who taught me to say no

No: I refuse to be a sheep and acquiesce,
even in weeping for you

No: I refuse to murmur the pious formula
The tape will not rewind
The sea will not flow backward
The sprigs of March will not begin again
So nobody talk to me about returning,
especially not you who police the gates
of turning and returning

No: I refuse to mutter eulogy clichés
I never wanted to hang your image
in a gilt frame over my bed
I wanted to roll with you on the page
in the sweat and muck of writing
Every morning I wanted to see
how you would tug the rope of writing
this way, yanking me suddenly into the mud
or that way, into the brilliant sea
and I, resistant, yanking back

I refuse to make flowered poetry like wreaths,
to lay pretty metaphors on my head
and skip through your books like a gazelle
Because you taught me to be savage,
I wanted to be a claw and tear your cheek
I wanted to write like the claw of a cougar
How can I be the claw when the cougar is gone?
So nobody talk to me anymore about poetry,
especially you who guard the gates of Arabic
and slam it against us who stand outside

I will never be this beautiful again
On the day you left I saw on my face
the first lines of ugliness beginning
I saw my skeleton, I saw my white death
So nobody talk to me about poetry or beauty
Spring, the April sea, our language, nothing
will ever be this beautiful again

❦ PAULINE KALDAS ❧

Morning
For Chiji Akoma

as if words could shed their skin
left bare skimming the air with "good morning"
between me and another walker
cold air striking our faces

entangled in other greetings:

Sabah el kheir
 Sabah el fol
Morning of luck
 Morning of jasmine

Sabah el noor
 Sabah el eshta
Morning of light
 Morning of cream

call and response
syllables carried bring jasmine to my breath
 the voweling of light pulling me to the day

here, the winter language
disconnects bare trees, morning air
and a deer's staring

mumbled so the "good" disappears
only "morning" left
as if to assure ourselves that
this is where we are

not even a mouthful of sounds
stopping me long enough

Home

The world map
colored yellow and green
draws a straight line from Massachusetts to Egypt.

Homesick for the streets
filthy with the litter
of people, overfilled so you must
look to put your next step down;
bare feet and galabiyas pinch
you into a spot tighter
than a net full of fish,

drivers bound out
of their hit cars
to battle in the streets
and cause a jam as mysterious
as the building of the pyramids,

sidewalk cafes with overgrown men
heavy suited, play backgammon
and bet salaries from absent jobs,

gypsies lead their carts
with chanting voices,
tempting with the smell of crisp fried falafel
and cumin spiced fava beans,

sweetshops
display their baklava and basboosa
glistening with syrup
browned like the people who make them,

women, hair and hands henna red
their eyes, khol-lined and daring.

The storms gather from the ground

dust and dirt mixed into the sand,
a whirlwind flung into my eyes,

I fly across
and land—
hands pressing into rooted earth.

Landscapes

Caught caterpillar
in spot of grass

Out of socket
cat limps
manhole fluttering wrappers
unkempt streets dispose crowds in resewn shoes
flaps cut edged around
thread needled in to confuse

What am I doing here
full of autumn's blood red foliage
fading to a vague impression of itself

I elbow the air
no hand crashes my thigh
or foot trips me into a skip step
camouflage the desert with city's hindstep into crowds of human sweat
to divulge the secret of this magnet that draws us to nearness
till we tumble into ourselves turned in

❧ FATMA KANDIL ❧

Thorny Gaps Suddenly Moving

The keys that open doors
are the keys that close them,
and the keys strangled in chains
have nothing but the drama of tinkling.
But the key that dies in my pocket
reminds me it is time
that I became a reasonable woman
who lives in a house
without keys, without doors.

∼

A new comet disappears
before we notice its features,
before we realize
that it is the same old comet.

∼

All I saw in my heart afterward
was a deep footprint
where blood could not trace its path.

∼

How did I love a man like a black star
who strips me of all the men I loved,
and who leaves me nothing
except an orphan's joy.

∼

Darkness devours a full moon;
and shaking, it raises
a sickle of defeat.

⁓

Why do you walk into the family scene
like water falling from the sides of a jug.

⁓

I say "Ziyad, I am your mother
          and you shall not be."
I say "Ziyad, my womb is made of shrapnel,
          how can I house you there?"

⁓

Every day
while I am on the express metro
a rundown house flashes by,
a wooden ladder leaning against it,
and a corrugated iron door,
always open.
Every day—
until it became my home.

Translated by Khaled Mattawa

Emaciated Teeth

Where do these trees come from
like a volcano pressing on the window,
and why do I have to
open their dusty curtains
every morning.

I see them
flinging their heavy branches
on the lung of emptiness
cluttered with yellow leaves.
 How can they
catch the wind in their nets
and injure the sparrows?
 How can I
close the window on the stolen light
before it slides on their trunks?
 How can the air reach me
without being poked by their knives?

Every day
they display their colorful innards
as an offering to autumn
and in winter they remain naked
glaring at their own shadows.

An octopus devours the crevices
while the leaves dance a Pharaonic dance.
Emaciated teeth had fallen on them.
And even the Nile
has crammed its body in a tube and insisted
on being present.
They guffawed while leaning on buildings,
and my heart, teeming with cuttlefish,
searched for the slipknot of water
 and hedgerows of birds.

(2)

The scrolls were lifted off
the spearheads of boughs.

Translated by Khaled Mattawa

Veins All Dried Up

Like any seagull in old tales I left... alone... while friends clung to
my punctured boat, their hands appearing like suspended pigeons...
alone... like a piece of ice, its veins all dried up... I promised them
dead fish... and the water swerved its sonorities around the belly of
my oar... I was not taken by the hues of colorful fish and I crossed
savage trees with impulsive blood... There was an island I named
Water's Gaze where I could see distant shores slip into shells... oysters
raise their heavy lids and pearls hide their private parts... I crossed
from foam to the yawning of rooftops... I could lean against the sea's
boulevards and fill the soul in a bottle... The steps of the horizon's
staircase appeared low... I bathed in a language I did not
understand... It took shelter with me and I made a bed for it under
my breast, away from the heart... This is how I unloosened fog and
donned it with wings where the seas rocked it between its shores...
and when my boat sank I was leaning against the sidewalks of the
surf. I was alone... dragging the threads of the horizon from my
memory and weaving a wide net where
human pictures fell, and little by little the water's gaze widened
and widened...

Translated by Khaled Mattawa

❧ DHABYA KHAMEES ❧

Short poems
To the Jamaican poet Benjamin Zephaniah

(1)

Letter

What is it that love said when it spoke?
It said many things
It said that in its isolation it was
      "Pure, chaste
          and sweet
and it is the unadulterated secret of the universe."

(2)

Glance

You walk on air...
enraptured inside,
your heart flying in all directions.
Wherever you look, things turn into
         a big miracle
and faces into mad prophets
with the secret beauty... in the faces of other human beings.

(3)

Standing Worship

I said *bismillah* in your name, Singer,
I patched the weave of my transparent silk—
the silk was in shreds....
its threads more delicate than a spider's web,

The taste of bitterness is colored by
ambergris, musk
and sugar cane.

The bridge of flame stretches long
a "loop" of colors—kinds of people
Bare feet...
        dance the "samba"
on friends' dead bodies...

The face says many things,
expressions dialoguing with the universe...
fists in the face of the—human—universe
eyes slap eyes
a cruelty boils in the whole city's innards.
Mercy kills, standing in the face of cruelty.
Innocence cries out to be saved...
Innocence finds no one...

(4)

Loneliness

The sun pours over me
Inside is a pool of silver embroidered with feelings—
there are no limits to beauty...
The "Voice" reminds me of the world's crimes,
        and of the ugliness of what happens under the sun.

I decorate the daily hurts with henna,
        massage them with the scent of musk and ambergris.

I love you when I want
I love you when you want
I will bend over your wound
        like the dignity of mankind...

I will chuckle with you, as you invite others

to dance, to the tune of your words
painted with blood's pleas for help
poured out every day.

Alone... lonely
but not when I'm with you.

(5)

Gulf

The sea stares at my dream
(I cannot come to the sea's aid).
The sea kills me little by little.... (with its demise).
Death is a fountain never losing its passion
its spray buffets
(all desires).
Devoid of many things
and of humans (ablaze with the heat
of my sun).

Translated by Clarissa Burt

Note: *Bismillah:* Utterance of the invocation: "In the name of God the Beneficent, the Merciful."

♔ HAMDA KHAMEES ♕

What is Not Mine

Whatever exists is now
is not mine
The man who is showering
before he bathes in my body
is not mine

The man who is exhausted
running in my labyrinths
is not mine
The polished man who
files his nails
before scratching my monotony
is not mine
The man who feeds everything around me
and forgets my hunger
is not mine.

~

These polished walls
are not mine
The house armed with the ordinary and the familiar
is not mine
The house framing my imprisonment
is not mine
The horse beautified with bridle and saddle
is not mine.

~

The open country
is mine
The dawn of pasture
is mine
The passion of a free horse
is mine
And the pride of stags
is mine
The splendor
and this universe
are mine!

Translated by Joseph T. Zeidan

Time for Dejection

Forever
it dwells in the windows and doors
and when I slip through its fingers
like a water drop
I hasten into the valleys of ink and notebooks
to fall
on the chest of an exhausted poem.

~

This evening is heavy
I pulled its curtains away
but I did not rise!

~

The stoves throw out their flame
to the corners of the house
and in the corners of the soul
loneliness sends its frost and cold.

~

The wind
hooooowls
and the body
is thrown against the open air's shoulder
and no one!

~

There is no fire in these poems
there is no warmth in this place!

Translated by Joseph T. Zeidan

Time to Shine

Go away a bit my sadness
I'll open my notebooks
and draw the heart's gardens.

∼

Wail, wind
I will not share with you
my crying!

∼

Set up your tents, darkness
and stick the claws of your terror
in our necks.
Let the uproar of the wind
extinguish all the lamps in the streets and houses.
I burn with love
and poems
My heart
is
armed with the morning.

Translated by Joseph T. Zeidan

❧ NIDAA KHOURY ❧

The Last Bullet

In my chest a cave
a gun and a man of storm
I am safe

In my chest an orphan
naked child
in my chest, hope

If I burst and fall slain
I'll gather my body anew
I'll fire my last shot

Translated by Linda Zisquit and Roger Tavor

People of Fire

Burn the generations.
Burn the olive leaves
offer incense.
Burn their fingertips.
Smoke.
Burn the dictionary of embracement
depart.
Burn the cook books
burn the kindling
boil their wit
and spread it
on the rooftops.
They burn the remains of the candle
illumine the shameful graves.
Wear ash and die as embers.

Translated by Linda Zisquit

People of Grapes

Unripe grapes
hang on the fences of morning
and departure.
My soul craves
the sour taste of childhood
but the sun
swiftly grabs me
and hides my shadow
in its shade
and my story ends...

Translated by Linda Zisquit

❧ VÉNUS KHOURY-GHATA ❧

Because they hesitated between roses and darkness
Because they loaded their rifles with rain

they died from indifference

Only the gullible die
who harbor foreign clouds under their roofs
who print their face upon the cities' mud
clutching cannons to avoid the grip of loneliness

Only the naive die
the frail on their stems
who bleed in the unison of poppies
They die when the hours line up
when they draw a blade in the mouth of a sundial

Translated from the French by Lucy McNair

It was a season tattooed on the forehead of the earth

The flight of migrating birds froze in full sky
Only the houses kept going

The coffins threw anchor at our doors
and on our roofs the dead dried their rusty fingers

Only the houses kept going

The men in ragged clothes clutched at dolls
the women dilated their bodies right to the docks
the paper children clipped themselves onto schoolhouse walls

Only the houses kept going

Translated from the French by Lucy McNair

Humbly, he speaks to his tools:

"Bone driller of every abscess
clay in lieu of womb
roots required to hang laundry from the flesh"

Cut off from lunar months
on the margin of marshlands
only the rumors of coal mines reach him
Neither brace nor leadline
to measure the angle of time
to verify the verticality of darkness
Not a single utensil
to make the surrounding chill come to a boil
and serve him his plate of earth

No key to open these stones
and cry on his house's shoulder

Translated from the French by Lucy McNair

They

They bubble up to the surface of our memory
seep into the walls during lunar months
to cut the water's throat and dismantle the pendulums

They scamper up the roots
hurtle down the ramp of the rains
drink the vapors of our wells
swallowing in a single gulp our flooding rivers

They straddle the roofs
bend the post
rouse the children up asleep in their lashes
to listen to the drumbeat of their fingers

They eat the flesh of the jujube tree
tie up the arms of the cypress
and teach it to behave like a candle

They float on the air of cemeteries
turn up tombs
emptying their contents in the potholes of paths

They snow immobile flakes
blow in inert packs
we gather them along the edges of our hips
we macerate them in our sweat
we wring out their tears and suspend them
on lines strung under soil

They saddle our dreams
harness our night
They mount us from the forgetful side of the heart

They force the latches of December
twist the fists of the chestnut trees
pierce the dormer window's eye

then sign our mirrors with mist

They get between the shell and the walnut
trample their effigies of fired clay
our dogs recognize their silhouettes of smoke
and bark as if to crack the moon

They disappear into their bodies
crouch down in their ankles
bent under their measure of earth, they cry from the groin

Their passage sends the clipped-winged beetles
into vertical flight
that's all that's left of them once they've trespassed
the double doors of the earth

Industrious, these dead
how they crawl under our prairies
to fetch the nuts summer didn't want
shaking them like children's rattles.

Translated from the French by Lucy McNair

⚜ WAFAA' LAMRANI ⚜

Dispensing with homelands does not stir me ...
Returning to a country from whence I traveled
                              —al-Mutanabi

The Wail of Heights

I ride the heathen sea to my ache crouching in the heights; some of
my living organs left me, and all of a sudden the disgraceful secret
vibrates, striking my remaining intractable parts ...

Naked except for my own nakedness
I plow the waves of night which hollowed out my certainty
and a moon rested on my orphan ship...
Naked except for my own nakedness
I teach the sky to rise, rise
It neighs near my desolate dawn
I teach it openness
I teach it sin
Naked except for my own nakedness
the palm trees seek refuge with me
the sun invokes me
and I am the frost yearning for its warmth
I am the spring of deaths—
        the deity's revelry—
        the prostitutes' penitence ...
Whenever I weave destruction around me,
I seek shade in its shells
I become enlightened with its appetites
Yes, Gilgamesh moves within me—
        In all the channels
I condensed passion, death,
Travel, ruin, sleeplessness
I destroyed my children's peace
and made of my wounds a wedding feast
        For all youths...
Nothing exists of me but dry stalks
they are alone with resurrection
they enter the halls of intimacy
Choicest wines appear on the forehead of
              exploration
The lady of the moons was crowned—
the princess of grace— the grandeur of rejection—
the sap of magnificence—the prophecy of inquiry
and part of me still defies part of me...
Then this desirable departure—I race with it
my time had lost me, so other times befriended me
whose temptation I delayed until after the killing—
Captivity, and everything you like of the whoredom of ages.

Gradually,
the dawn drags its robe
I write the disappointments of distances
and the lamentation of shoe soles
while engrossed in my blood.
I place myself to be hunted by a train of arrows...
Oh,
My face has exhausted the treachery of day ...

Translated by Tahia Abdel Nasser, with Richard McKane

I am Consecrated to the Coming One

Dawn comes out of its vast silence
crowned by the whispers of the valley
a gate opens on suspicion
and this pulsating is weaker than the most delicate flower
                          in the blowing of the wind
I settle into another day
and age becomes a fruit about to ripen
a tunnel
pavilions
incantations
and footsteps singing the hymn of spilling.
A star for this infinity
                          I do not wish to be obstinate
But I am taken by tender rapture
O heart spread out
O eye wander
And O diamond-like body
engrave your secret on the evanescence.

I nearly destroy you O rock of forbearance
O grass-covered light in the pores
O momentous formulation for eternity
and I suffer a lifetime
I cover myself with burdens

opposites accompany me...
We ascend the cloud of embers
And my woes are the sea
Oh!
Who will wash the sea from the sea?
I have the thirst of ages
but I am like water
always overflowing
I explore between the folds of difficult choices
tame them
and for a time, there is what cannot be remedied
                    or ... even remain
The path
the stepping
and the companion
deviate from me...
I am clamored with incandescence
as if none but God has pulsated me in this overflow
It is a state of fusion
announcing me
I am consecrated to the coming one
                    to the vigilance of exiles
                         to the beginnings of thirst
And in order for the earth to teach me its seduction
I endure the mire's insolence
and my wager, always, is the most beautiful possibility...
For a confused wisdom
for the beginning of the sun
I lit the sap of things
I bestowed them upon barefootedness
and before the journey handed me its new waves
I was transformed into a ray of affliction
                    which rejects fickleness in death
                    or shortness of memory
Sometimes no body, no burden, no limit
                    no name, no shadow

Crossing-point
and this self is the sunrise of horizons
So shed your soul's love
for the velvet of the heart is sheer and clean
less solid than time
more fragile than whiteness
more faithful than the wound of an abandoned lover...

Interpret me, embrace me
O letter, rare like the year's rain
O clear serene namesake
burning freshness
the anticipated release
O perplexity!
Spring leaps now
to embroider the sides of future days
The heart is not embroidered
fertile with all joy
provisions
projecting light
impossible for the eye to tire from greenery
as the heartbeat from love

Everything falls down
except air
... it never becomes lighter!

Translated by Tahia Abdel Nasser, with Richard McKane

❧ Fatima Mahmoud ❧

What Was Not Conceivable

In harmony
we entered the climate of water
in harmony with the law
of the tree.
In harmony
we pronounced grass, recited hedges.
In harmony—a horizon
        of carnations.
A bundle of lavender.
        We tapped on the silence
            of abandoned gardens,
walked—
the road massaging its back
with the sun's ointment
and staring at the choked
        sidewalks.
        The patrolman
        inhabits
        the first line,
        sucks out the blood of language,
        strips the alphabet
        of its dots
        and tears out
            the plumes of speech.
He confiscates the states of narcissus.
He muffles
the coronets of the flowers,
buries alive the jasmine leaning out
        of the gardens
        of the gaze.
The fence is the noose of geography
around the waist of drowsy grass.
And time... wilts.

In the first clarity
of an approaching poem
the boy
washes
from his chaotic face—
the dust of starved herds
    led by hollowed men
    to the official stable.

~

With staring pebbles
the beautiful children stone them,
and the math lesson embalmed
in the teacher's throat
emaciates the leap year.
The patrolman prepares
shackles
for the window
a lock
for the wind
and for the rest of eternity "invents"
    an accusation
    a torturer
    and a scaffold.

~

I climb the thickets of laughter.
I return
to the branch its features
to the wind its shape
to the hedge
    its pebbles.
We glare
at the frontiers of NO,
and our loud singing
flashes.

We adjust our watches
to the patrolman's
                           pulse rate.
Our country   two embers away
was
an oven.

~

Carnations
        lean closer—
                the glass expands
                the forest widens.
Carnations write their crimson
autobiographies.
I read—
                what was tenable
                of the water's
                verse
                and what was inconceivable
                        of your face and my country

~

        I leave for your seed
my fields
and the whiteness of the page.
I search for your hand,
a sentence
in active voice
in the season of fires—
                I smear the whiteness
                with the ashes
                of the era...
and search
for your hands...
        an iris of ecstasy
        in
        the season of desires

~

Carnations
    flee
Carnations
    spill their crimson autobiographies
I said:
    the ember is the master of fire
    the ember
    is its dust...
    Then I became confounded...
    what
    to offer...
    the master's repulsive...
        and delicious mouth
I am singed with happiness
endowed
with the stamps of hollowness
lips
dipped in counterfeit songs
a scented
morning and our faces...
    are spat out
    in handsome
    editions...
    What
        to offer
           the master's repulsive
           delicious mouth

~

I tossed
my heart to him
my hands to him

~

170

The land
is only two wheat spikes away
—and now—
an iris.
Carnations... draw us
in blood
spilled on
the patrolman's uniform.
      He rolls us
into clusters
in the imagination's vineyard.
Blood is
our secret ink,
blood
our aged fire.

Translated by Khaled Mattawa

⊰ LISA SUHAIR MAJAJ ⊱

Jerusalem Song

Your walls fold gently,
a wingspan
embracing the dreaming city.

Your air drifts with the odor of incense,
women's voices floating upwards,
a twist of prayer toward heaven's ear.

I hold your name beneath our tongue
like a seed
slipped into the mouth for safekeeping.

Jerusalem, fold me like a handkerchief
into your bosom. I am
one word in a lover's letter,

a chip of blue tile in your sky.
Even those who have never seen you
walk your streets at night.

We wipe your dust from our feet
each morning, rise from our beds wearied
by the long distances

we have traveled to reach you.
See how we save even the broken bits of pottery,
fitting fragments together

along jagged lines to remember you.
Jerusalem, we are fledglings
crying for a nest!

In Season

My father knew the weight of words
in balance, stones in a weathered wall.

He counseled patience
though, dying, refused his own advice.

Today his words surround me
with the quiet intensity of growing things,

roots planted a long time ago
lacing the distances of my heart.

What he didn't say is sprouting too,
a surprise, like the *eskidinya* tree

that sprang from the smooth brown pit
I tossed off the porch as a child.

Years now I've longed to pick that fruit
—remembering how he'd sit

spitting seeds in a stream to the ground—
but I know it's not yet ripe.

So I think instead of the lemon tree
in my uncle's yard. When it died,

no one could bear to cut it down.
They lopped off the branches,

but kept the dead trunk, stumps
of arms upraised—each bearing,

like bird's nests, a potted plant.
Out of habit, they still water the trunk,

and as if in return, each branch sparks green—
though every heart's separate, now,

not like the lemons that used to cluster
like triple suns. Did my parents know

that what they planted,
roots against the drought,

would survive? Today,
I'm a stump of a branch.

But on my tongue a seed
lies dormant, dense with life.

Unspoken years
fill my mouth like citrus

in winter—sharp promise
of sun. Outside, *eskidinya*

hang heavy as memory,
orange flash from dusty leaves,

their season still ripening.

First Light

Between dreams and day an immense distance
fills my throat. Who could speak across such space?

Who could imagine their lives are real,
wear shoes?

Words flow through my fingers like stars,
pattern the sea. Vowels swim like fish.

Each dawn I cast my net,
reel in silver coils,

rinse the brine from my name.

Arguments

consider the infinite fragility of an infant's skull,
how the bones lie soft and open
only time knitting them shut

consider a delicate porcelain bowl
how it crushes under a single blow—
in one moment whole years disappear

consider: beneath the din of explosions
no voice can be heard
no cry

consider your own sky on fire
your name erased
your children's lives "a price worth paying"

consider the faces you do not see
the eyes you refuse to meet
"collateral damage"

how in these words
the world
cracks open

NAZIK AL-MALAIKA

Cholera

It is night.
Listen to the echoing wails
rising above the silence in the dark,
to the mystifying cries over the dead,
the agonized, overflowing grief
clashing with the wails.
In every heart there is fire,
in every silent hut, sorrow,
and everywhere, a soul crying in the dark.
A voice cries in every place:
this is what death has destroyed,
Death, death, death.
O lament of the Nile this is what death has done.

It is dawn.
Listen to the footsteps of the passerby,
in the silence of dawn.
Listen, look at the mourning processions,
ten, twenty, no... countless.
Listen to the mourners,
to the pitiful child.
They are dead, dead, dead,
without number, without future.
Everywhere lies a corpse, mourned
without a eulogy or moment of silence.
This is what the hand of death has done,
Death, death, death.
Humanity protests against the crimes of death.

Cholera,
in the cave of corpses and terror,
in the cruel silence of eternity,
in which death is a cure,
cholera has raised its head,

vengeance, descending
on the radiant, cheerful valley,
screaming in madness,
deaf to those who cry.
Its claws have left their traces everywhere;
in the hut of the peasant woman
echo only the cries of death,
Death, death, death.
Cholera is the vengeance of death.

The silence is bitter,
except for echoes glorifying God.
Even the gravedigger has succumbed,
the muezzin is dead,
and who will eulogize the dead?
There are only laments and sighs,
and children without fathers or mothers
crying with anguished hearts,
certain to be plucked by the evil disease.

~

O cholera, death's phantom,
You have left nothing but the sorrows of death,
Death, death, death.
O Egypt, my heart is torn by the ravages of death.

Translated by Husain Haddawy, with Nathalie Handal

Five Hymns to Pain

1

It gives our nights sorrow and pain;
it fills our eyes with sleeplessness.

We found it on our way,
one rainy morning
and gave it, out of love,
a stroke of pity and a little corner
in our throbbing heart.

~

It never left or vanished from our way,
stalking us to the corners of the world.
If only we gave it no drop to drink,
that sad morning!

It gives our night sorrow and pain;
it fills our eyes with sleeplessness.

2

Why does this pain come to us?
Where does it come from?
From old it has dwelled in our dreams
and nurtured our rhymes.
For we are a thirsting mouth
by which, thriving, we are satisfied.

~

At last, we dragged it to the lake,
shattered it and scattered it to the waves,
leaving neither a sigh nor a tear,
thinking it would no longer afflict our smiles with grief
or hide the bitter wails behind our songs.

~

Then we received a lovely scented rose,
sent by loved ones from across the seas.

What were we expecting from it?
Joy and happy contentment.
But it shook and began to flow with tears
over our sad-tuned fingers.
O pain, we love you!

⁓

Why does this pain come to us?
Where does it come from?
From old it has dwelled in our dreams
and nurtured our rhymes.
For we are a thirsting mouth
by which, thriving, we are satisfied.

3

Can we not conquer pain,
postpone it to another day,
keep it busy one evening,
divert it with a game, a song,
a forgotten ancient tale?

⁓

What can it be, this pain?
A tender, little child with searching eyes,
quietened by a gentle, kind touch
and put to sleep with a smile and a lullaby.

⁓

O you who gave us our regrets and tears,
who else but you closed his heart to our grief
then came to us in tears, asking for refuge,
who but you bestowed the wounds with smiles?

~

Child, most innocent of tyrants,
loving foe or mortal friend,
a stab asking us to offer our cheeks,
without a qualm and without a pang of pain.

~

Child, we have forgiven that hand and mouth
that dig trenches for tears in our eyes
and reopen the wound...
Yes, we have forgiven the sin, the damage, long ago.

4

How do we forget pain,
how do we forget pain?
Who will light for us
the night of its memory?

We shall eat it, we shall drink it,
we shall pursue it with songs,
and if we sleep, its shape
will be the last thing we see.

~

And in the morning, its face
will be the first thing we discern,
and we shall bear it with us
wherever our desires and wounds take us.

~

We shall allow it to raise walls
between our longing and the moon,
our anguish and the cooling stream,
our eyes and our sight.

~

We shall allow it to afflict our eyes
with sorrow and distress,
and we shall shelter it
among the ribs of our joyful songs.

~

At last, it will be swept down the river,
and will be buried under the cactus,
and forgetfulness will descend on our valley.
Good evening, sadness!

~

We shall forget pain,
we shall forget it,
having nurtured it with satisfaction.

~

Beloved pain,
we deified you in the drowsiness of dawn
bowed our heads at your silvery altar
burned the seeds of sesame and flax
offered sacrifices
sang verses to Babylonian tunes.

~

We built for you a temple with strange walls
and anointed the ground with oil, pure wine,
and burning tears.
We burned for you fires with leaves of palm
and stalks of wheat and our grief,
with closed lips, on a long night.

~

We sang and called and made our offerings:
dates from intoxicated Babylon
and bread and wine
and cheerful roses.
Then we prayed to your eyes
and offered a sacrifice,
and we gathered the bitter teardrops
and made a rosary.

~

O you who bestow on us our music and our songs,
O tears that lead to wisdom,
O fountain of all thought, fertile abundance,
O cruel tenderness, merciful punishment,
we have hidden you in our dreams,
in every note of our sad songs.

Translated by Husain Haddawy

❧ ZAKIYYA MALALLAH ❧

Little Tales

Flap your wings on my bare trees,
teach me
the little tales...

∼

There was once a lady in love
who hid her bags
and fell asleep in the hair strands of noon.
She roamed my body,
bared herself in my soul
and fluttered her wings, a prisoner of my heart.
I housed her in my Gardens of Eden;
bitter poetry
trickled through her silent lips.

∼

I know her.
She came to me every evening, bearing her tremor,
her eyes sunk in the edges of the robe tied around her body,
her hands are oars,
wrestling with the waves of defeat in the bottom of her chest,
breathlessly,
left behind by the footsteps of destiny,
strewing around the passion she has been carrying between her teeth
and asking for forgiveness between my hands.

∼

When she came to me
I was radiant,

my face almost glowing with the magnanimity of a prophet
and the blood of saints quivering in my eyes;
I became frightened,
apprehensive,
kindling my fire.
The smoke was circles of silence
and my burning was my lifeboat.

～

She said: you have it so pure—
turns her face towards the cities,
gathers tulips,
pulls out thorns from palms,
brings green back to eyes,
unravels locks of desire.

～

She said:
my awakenings are countless.

One
She comes when the horizon turns cloudy,
when the stars of slumber roam about,
when the moon shines
wearing a robe the color of wheat
and spilling roses,
leaning on a cane of light
while the dusk follows you,
parting the darkness to make a path for you!

Two
Your sky is filled with fragrance.
Your cloud
is a loaded scripture
that rained
seasons of shadows,
and sprouts of fertility and growth.

Three
You know me as a gypsy river,
washing in the sun's volcano,
bestowing the honor that is Isis on me.
Your doors are closed
and your walls silenced
but you slip away through a crack or cavern.

Four
Sleepless in your night,
aflame by your embers;
I emit fire
and the fire spits me out,
it chatters on your cloak,
getting undressed,
seeking cover in snow flurries.

Five
Acacia branches stretched in your limbs
and trees of pebble grew.

⁓

She quarreled with me and said,
"whether we make up or not,
I have made up my mind to leave, to go to a faraway place;
and going away will
dowse the fire of passion;
and perhaps thorns will grow between fingers,
and sprout from bleeding lips."
So let us go our separate ways;
and between you and me, may a lifetime weave its web,
may a cloud hover.

⁓

And one day she came upon me:
"I will bid you farewell.
I have not risen to your heavens,
I have not tasted your evening.
May alienation prevail in your life,
may you not sip the fleeting moment from our cup!"
I twisted upon my trunk,
and curled my branches around me.
If only she had warned me,
I would have let warmth flow with the tears of my eyes
and she would have napped between my ribs,
like a rebellious cat, my rebellious cat.

Translated by Wen Chin Ouyang

Women

(1)

She picks me
and reconstitutes my colors.
Two bloated hands,
a shirt undone at the seams.
And a spot of blood
hides me in your footsteps
as I step towards a heaven
that will shield me from the pus of the earth.

(2)

I confided in my coffin on the river,
taking a night journey:
Cut whatever limb you wish and prune me,
I know where the waves recede
and where more branches will grow in the body.

(3)

A woman to undo you,
to dig for your crystals,
a woman to speak of you.

(4)

Full of sickles
and bunches of dry dates
and wheat;
You treasure me on your lips,
I burst like a swing
and dangle like fragrance.

(5)

She grows in the ashes of the heart,
impregnated by voices and lights.
She brushes my limbs extending into your yard
and stretches me like a wave in the very sea.

(6)

He let down his curtains on the night
and enveloped me.
I held in my heart the first glass of wine.
He said, your wine is more desirable.
I said, fill your departure with death
and consume me.

(7)

I am in the throes of the waves, gathering my blue ribbons,
and swimming in my own breaths,
sneaking in your drizzle,
playing with pens and papers,
and annihilating myself.

(8)

Clouds are ours
when we curl up in the armpit of the sun,
they erect a trellis on fingertips.
Dwarfs on the two shoulders
are sewing together the arms.
Do not give birth today;
sterility is becoming such a giant.

Translated by Wen Chin Ouyang

⚜ THURAYYA MALHAS ⚜

An Orphan

I am an orphan
if I walk,
I trip on stones.
I am an orphan
if I tell,
I choke with letters.
I am an orphan
if my fingertips move the strings,
the clouds would weep
and surround the passion of the guitar.
Is it you, Moon, my guide?
Or is it you, Stars?
You, Sky?
Or you, Universe?
Where is my way?
Where is my poem?
Where is my guitar?

I am an orphan
my steps
chains,
my tongue, knots
Oh God,
when
when will you come back to me?

Translated by Nasser Farghaly

False... False

False... False
everything is false
under the sun
above the sun
and around
everything is false

I asked about yesterday
about tomorrow
I neglected the present
my dawn got tired
my bones collapsed on me

I knelt on my land
praying:
false... false
everything is false
under the sun
above the sun
and around

I lied in the present
racing the wind
thundering and flashing
dragging my ink

from the source of my atom
I shall not eat
I shall not complain
my pen was broken
and the ink dried out
tears covered my neck
I prayed:
false…false
everything is false
under the sun
above the sun
and around

I walked in my paths
I rolled
searched in the depths
I tripped
my brothers tripped with me
and we vanished
no matter what we were
what our existence was

What is life for?
What is praying for?
A poor poor one
who sees
a meaning in the paths

False… false
everything is false
under the sun
above the sun
and around

Translated by Nassar Farghaly

◈ AL-ZAHRA AL-MANSOURI ◈

The Secrecy of Mirrors

"I need huge trees to grow within me,
stars to water my calling
I need the abysses to return
ripeness to my dream, and dry my bones
from the weight of Commandments."
Like a black autumn, night drops
and the sea claims the salt and fire it promised me
and my narration ripped in the fracture of skies…
O face emerging from the defeats of years
coming from your ruins
and from my loss—
how can I revive the things killed within me?
How can I water the springs of my shade?

~

I dream of a cactus, of a sorrowful bird
and then the universe
and the sea were butterflies.
When the dream dries up
I divide it,
collect the universe in a cigarette box
to make its arrangement easier.

~

Like a quivering rag I collect the sky
to expose faded birds hanging,
the scent of ships the sea forgot in my echo,
sleeping winds
and cloud-corpses enveloping me.
I transform my body into a grave to enter my whiteness
and create suns with fragile irises.

~

The places that once submerged me with their clouds
have become an orphanage.
I watched your water coming from my legends.
I sculpted a twilight from my blood
and whenever the distances sold me
I remembered it
and borrowed drops of its sap,
so the dead would not remove the curtains from my nakedness
and a body whose details I forgot in fugitive skies.

~

The moon must now open, announce the death of my seas.
The moon must grant me the madness of blackness,
to announce my death when trees,
whose rustling I do not hear, pass me by...
Then the wind reveals the graveyards of my suns
the siege of whiteness,
wave arranging its fragility,
and as the dream falls from my dozing,
the sun tumbles from the angles of my body.

Translated by Tahia A. Nasser, with Richard McKane and Nathalie Handal

Abandonment

To the spirit of Salwa, the unforgotten child whom the water
one day loved, and thus drew into its depths

Like an extinguished star,
in the sea's bed she sleeps...
The *lablab*'s branches
and the travelers' shadows
plow through the water's ribs...
her dreams rise to the surface
her paper games

and a school song, beautiful with mistakes.
The images of seaweed float
her discord,
and the throbbing of creeping plants trace the breaking of the sunset.

Salwa,
a moon the depths sheltered,
wrapped its rustling and painted
a weed which the water broke,
a marine butterfly competing with my tiredness
and the call of fatigued flowers—
and where the swallows came, I see her blood ripe,
see a night that sipped her stealthily from me…

Salwa,
She sprouts in the water's roots,
in her face, the algae flower
and the water stops its hemorrhage without me
so that I retreat to her thrones like a restored lily
and weave out the first song of the clouds.

~

Death, lofty trees playing with the roots of night
so that its leaves dim.
Death, a featureless body,
smoke that sends its yearning for an uncanny extinguishing…
you draw your footsteps on its shadows,
and you conceal rain in a crushed heart.
The path of passersby wilts to your step.

And Salwa,
a night tattooed with palm trees' whisperings,
wilted algae in the play of light sleeps.

Salwa, the remnants of grief...

Translated by Tahia Abdel Nasser, with Richard McKane
Note: *Lablab* is Ivy.

❧ MARAM MASRI ❧

Untitled

You who
often go
to disappear for long
indifferent
to the depressed evenings of my heart.
You
who glance with a skill
that brings out tears
the tears of my salt-filled eyes
to erase the fine lines of your face
and to lock
with a sudden frown
your cruel eyebrows.
With a fearful heart I know
that winter is inevitably coming
and to meet it I only have
five
damp
match sticks…

Winter came
and brought with it
only cold and storms
and all of you—
forgave it.
But I
who carried for you my heart
as an open rose
or perhaps
as a broken rose
you did not think of anything except to ask me
where I picked it up…

The earth stole me from
the sea
this is why you see my lips are sand
my words grassy rocks.

The earth stole me from the sea
this is why you see my eyes are two fish
my looks silent
and though my pupils are not blue
my tears are still salty...

The sea called me
to dream with it
so I went before the appointed time
for fear that its dreams would begin
without me.

The dreams of the sea
are wide and mysterious
—and you are my dream—
making it
bluer and more mysterious...

On the shore
I left
my shoes.

In vain in vain I wait
he will not come
an old fisherman
in whose clothes
a prince is hiding...

I planted yesterday
in the sea's evening
one of my dreams
and in the morning
the people found

a small sail boat
wrecked on the shore…

All the words my love
are ropes
and all the smiles
are masks.

Except my words about you
and my smile to you—
the first is Arabian jasmine and pennyroyal and jasmine
and the second
a smile…

Two years and some months ago
I sent you my imagination
for two years and some months ago
my imagination has been spying on you.

Two years and months have passed
with no news of my imagination
As if it was lost in you
or perhaps
made you
its homeland…

God created earth in six days
and on the seventh
He rested
and when He was about to create you
He needed thousands of years
and millions of men and women.

God created earth in six days
I don't know what He did
on the seventh day
but when He was about to create me
He badly needed
a man like you…

On Judgment day God asks
someone about the best
of his youth   how he used it
and his wealth how he gained it
and how he spent it
and his learning and what he did with it
and his body and what he inflicted it with
and when I am present between his hands
Glory to Him
He will ask me only
about you...

You ask me if I love you
I discover you love questions
and love me
I answer I love you
so don't ask me more
for I don't want to discover that you love questions
only...

Translated by Amal Amireh

Small Sins

Tell the wind
to calm down
for I do not like the wind
like a jealous woman
it may mess up my hair
on my way to meet him
who is waiting for me.

Tell the rain
to stop
for I do not like the rain
like a jealous husband
it may wet my clothes

and my new shoes
while I wait for him
who will not come.

~

Remember
I opened my door for you
without you knocking at it...

I was foolish
and thought you didn't steal
anything but cigarettes and books.

~

—Where do you take me?
To a café?
For a woman like me,
cafés mean freedom.
—Where do you take me?
To a garden?
I have one
but everything assumes a different color
with you.

—Where do you take me?
I love to wander with you in no specific direction
and all directions with you are specific.

—Hold my hand
and take me to the heart
for I prefer your home,
oh poetry.

~

My rival in winter
Damascus
and in summer
the sea.

I dreamed yesterday
that I kicked the sea
on its bottom
and pulled Damascus by her hair
from the map.

~

I was walking
on the straight and narrow
when you obstructed my way...
I lost my balance
but I did
not fall.

Translated by Amal Amireh

❧ D.H. Melhem ❧

From Rest in Love

say french:
who knows what lebanese is?
or syrian? (serbian? siberian?)
protectorate is close to
protector

of course there's your culture
a tradition of teachers and doctors
an elegant descent
from phoenicians

but
the immigration officials
and neighbors
employers
perplexed by exotics
non-anglo-saxon
non-westeuropean-nontoxic
attest
the best are
types here
longer

the immigration official
said to me,
syrian?
what's
that?

(and sallow
with a menacing
guttural tongue)

your teacher accused
arabic spoken
at home:
"you have an accent"

though fearing strangers
and the foreign school
I went
showed myself
clean   educated
stopped her

still she detested
your rivaling
the girl on her lap
whose braids she caressed

before the class

people don't mean
to be mean
nevertheless
better say
french

～

clattering like dice
anticipations
fall
to the grasses
of night
where death
accepts them
in silent weeds

～

death

even when you leave
you're on your way

what have I done

～

indeed beautiful the everlasting snow
come suddenly before spring   a shoot
from my mind that collects
its fallen petals as if the snow crystals
could be pressed in volumes   as if
your voice might open to my name

I have closed that name
into angles of initials   put away
vowels   round sonorities
into pages

in your multitudinous self
there was no self
but the poet composed
for others

From Country

16.

to write the country
as a poem
incomplete
is the truth
of geography

37.

Person   place   thing   tree
each in its living space

I learned from my grandmother
to save the string that ties
the past into epiphany
and sets it down to die by fire

On the sixth of January
one returns to a new year—
familiar rooms that house
a self unwieldy
strung with parcels

the sacks and suitcases
of tarnished ornaments
a self   difficult to manage
with grace   stumbling fallible   myopic
retaining the once-dazzled vision
as a portable lost occasion

Boy in a Hospital

Boy in a hospital
lying among suddenly ancient ruins
that join the Temple of Jupiter
at Baalbek
to the gutted apartments
of Beirut
its buildings glutted
with collapsing life
with bodies
like fragments of statues
newly classical

Boy in a hospital
your olive skin has the pallor of smoke
you have had your moment's attention
there is no sanctuary here
there is panic here
the wounded are wounded again

How black your eyes stare into the world
that tore from you
mother father sister brother
tore off your legs

There was no food or water
the walls kept going down
the burning sky kept falling

Boy in a hospital
you are the way to Beirut
the road of pain
the road of shouting corpses
of amputated legs thrown into the street
with newspapers and expectations

to dance the *dabke*
to share your sister's and brother's laughter
rushing up the stairs
to your apartment
to taste your mother's stuffed grape leaves
from the enamel pot
to run along the beach
your hand safely in your father's

🐚 IMAN MERSAL 🐚

Solitude Exercises

He sleeps in the room next to mine, a wall between us.
I don't mean any symbols by this,
only that there is a wall between us
that I can fill with pictures of my lover
smoking, or thinking.
But I must find a neutral place for them
and be mindful of the distance between us.

It seems God does not love me.
I am old enough to believe:
God has not loved me for a long time, not since
He loved the math teacher,
and gave him sharp vision
and colored chalks
and many opportunities to punish a girl like me

who cannot figure the relation
between two unattached numbers.

But it's not important that God loves me.
No one in this world—even those who do righteous deeds—
can provide a single proof that God loves him.

I can open the door, and shut it behind me
quietly, so my beloved will not wake.
A girl goes out to the street
with nowhere to go.
This is not a dramatic situation at all.

When Dostoevsky said:
"One must have a home to go to,"
he was talking about quaint people
who wore long sideburns
and overcoats resembling loneliness.

I don't like "drama"
and find no reason to pluck a flower from its joy
to match it to the death of someone dear.

If I leave now
I will seize the hand of the first person I meet.
I will force him to accompany me to a side-street café.
I will tell him that a man sleeps in the room next to mine
without nightmares,
his mind no match for my body; he failed to be
a garbage pail for me, not even once; he left everything
to flow into the main streets.
And that I am an orphan
and I used to think that that was enough
to write good poems,
which did not prove to be true.
And that I didn't look after myself,
to the point that a small inflammation in my sinuses
now threatens to become malignant,

yet I continue to lie.
One ought to become angelic a while before death,
long enough that friends will not
become weary in searching
for one's noble qualities.
And that my death
will be easier than moving my right foot
if he were to leave me alone.

At a side-street café
I will tell a man I do not know many things at once,
and I will press my vocal cords
on his old wish to be helpful.
Maybe he will take me to his house and wake his wife.
I will watch her walking toward me
as she tramples on a filthy rug
like a village countess, and I will fabricate
a shyness to comfort her, and make her satisfied
with her husband as he advises me to start again, and as
I promise him that I will learn to play a musical instrument
that matches my small frame,
and that we may meet again during the holidays.

I threatened all who loved me
with my death
if I were to lose them.
I don't think I will die for anyone's sake.
Suicides—no doubt—
trusted life more than they should have,
and thought it was waiting for them elsewhere.
I will not leave here before he dies in front of me.
I will place my ear on his chest where silence is clearer
than any attempt to make me doubt it, not even
the cat that has the claws of a disappointed woman,
and that tries to topple the dustbin filled with the remains
of our day together,
the bin I place outside my door
to show the neighbors I have a peaceful family.

I will hold your fingers,
contemplate a precision befitting a surgeon
who needs no scalpel
to remove pustules from a body devouring itself.
I will place your hand in an ice bowl where there are no shivers
And I will leave here
clad in loss, and light.

You must die in front of me.
The death of loved ones is a great opportunity
to consider substitutes.
On the East Delta train I always select a suitable lady
who opens the coffers of her sympathy to me when I tell her that
my mother died when I was six.

The truth is
it happened when I was seven
but for me "six" seems to have a greater effect.
Middle aged mothers are addicted to sadness,
maybe to get accustomed to mourning before its time.
These touch-ups in the telling
have a magic
that can't be understood by those
who never had to steal sympathy from others.

Translated by Khaled Mattawa, with the author

❧ DUNYA MIKHAIL ❧

Rain

THE FIRST DROP

When the rain of God falls down
                    please, my friend,
keep silent for a while
so that speech does not get wet!

SECOND DROP

Close to the Dead Sea
the grieving flute yawns
and the dead rise up from the sea.
I was dallying...
                But behold!
Here are my good old dead,
          rising!

THIRD DROP

—What is it?
        My heart?
              Take it away
nothing throbs within it.
Yet, where shall the birds spend the night?

FOURTH DROP

A seagull gazes around
seeing millions of mirrors
millions of torn wings in the mirrors.

FIFTH DROP

Passages have my heart
passages that lead to doors
doors that lead to hallways
hallways that lead to windows
windows that lead to your heart.

SIXTH DROP

Within me is a heart
in the heart—walls
in the walls—cracks
in the cracks—dead wind.

SEVENTH DROP

The coffee is cold!
Friend, what shall I do?
There remains no space for me to jump in
no bird for me to drop down like a tear
no green except my heart.
The sunflower is not turning around this day
and language recognizes no pronoun but *I*.
My friend, what shall I do
now that the coffee is cold?

EIGHTH DROP

I have returned to you
but I have not brought with me
        the blueness of my soul
        nor the greenness of reproach
        nor the blackness of dawn
        nor the whiteness of drowsiness
therefore,
        have I not returned to you?

NINTH DROP

By day
I visited your tomb, where the birds lay their eggs of memory.
By night
    I had a dream
in which I was the witness.

TENTH DROP

The evening is white
and the heart is an icy carnation.
The evening is white
    history is snow
        the eyes
            Baghdad Observer
            your hands
                the appointments'
                    snow.
The waiter came over
dropped two ice cubes in my glass
and I dropped my heart in the glass.
Is it why the heart clamors for icy friends?

Translated by Samira Kawar, with Nathalie Handal

The Dawn Fairy

You are changing...
        You have changed greatly
I dare not look at you...
for fear that I will not see you.
                —Barbossa, *The Inferno*

That is the dawn fairy
                she comes to me every evening
building for her dreams

a homeland of air
and then goes towards the river
        scattering her sorrows into the stream

  that they may be eaten by the fish.

Kings sprout up in her wounds
    but without a kingdom she remains.

Upon life's wall she used to draw
    a dawn of myrtle
and embroider out of the night of gloom
           a moon
upon which the birds of drowsiness fed...
    Life opens a window
that overlooks your first tear,
    a tear shared out by the poor.
She promised herself to an illusion
    to a moment that swings
between the promise and the sky
      and for the sake of the promise
      and for the sake of the sky
          ... she prays...
—Our Father who art within hearts
    Give us this day our daily love
    And forgive us our trespasses
    And out of our longing make
        a home for all the birds.

Translated by Samira Kawar

The Chaldean Ruins

Then they sat on the ground with him for seven days and seven nights.
No one said a word to him, because they saw how great his suffering was.
                —From the *Book of Job*

Ascetic
    he emerges from its belly into the grave.
    His days enter no calendar
    and he picks up none of what is scattered:
    earthquakes do not shake him nor refer to death without him,
    was he born before the earth, or after it had wailed?
A wind passed
    and the tree did not shake.
They said: It was no wind
           but his sighs.
               He is the disturbed Chaldean
and it was no tree
           but the elongated roots of his village
stiffened.
    He sends water into the fields
    then upon the hill he brays
    and during the day with the darkness he is content.

Homeless
exile squeezes him
and throws his peels
        to the skyscrapers.

Waiting
    he lights a candle before the Virgin
    hoping she will move the borders to him
    Hallelujah... Hallelujah
    He celebrates the coming of his sheep
    and holds a vigil at their graves
            until the morning.

Confused
    he moves the mountains from hand to hand
    in search of a fragment of homeland.

Away from his tent
    he pulls the ropes
        and piles up as sand
           in faraway countries.

Preserved in a can
        he writes on his forehead:
                "Made in Ruins"
and feels that the word "ruins" is enough to refer to
what happened, or what is left.

Translated by Samira Kawar

⚜ HALA MOHAMMAD ⚜

4
What am I chasing!
From afar I beheld him
like a magic carriage
trailing lights
bells
and stories.

Every time
I stepped towards him
a fleeting moment
replaced my footsteps...

No trace of him
no trace.

24
At the door of anticipation
I sat
weaving seconds
on a tiny straw chair;
under the hearth of time
I rekindled the ashes of memories.

I invite no one to come
even if, on these ashes,
I have chairs lined up…

The straw chair
is for lingering on
and I am waiting,
at the door of anticipation,
for nothing but time.

43
The man who offers me his chest
To whose chest I give my five senses
has long been placing
just a cage under my head,
not knowing that I have long
been giving his chest
just a head.

58
Love burned out the light
With all my possessions
I listened to it
with my clothes
my closet
my window
my walls
until the darkness was burned.

Translated by Cornelia al-Khaled

❧ Brenda J. Moossy ❧

A Notion of Grace

A sudden blow: a great bird lifts us
at the nape and holds fast. There is so much
to regret. We are all willing victims swept
up in the great wide wings of want, no vague
fingers or tightening thighs. We open our mouths
and legs, ignore the sweep of taloned feet.
This is our nature, to deny the moon—
worship the sun. We forget they are bound,
one string tied to the other.
So, we endure the pang for the comfort
of warm skin pressed against our own, knowing
a cold bed awaits us.
                              In vain, we want.
Finally, and from birth, we are bound up
in our own skins, plead for revolution
or love, sudden cracks of deliverance.
Swift as thunder, a bolt to slay the bird's
fierce heart, we want redemption from this flight
we beckon from first breath. We fail to see
light prism off the shirred and feathered tip,
hear the song of Heaven's aching silence,
feel the embrace of air in our descent.

I Can No Longer Care for the Dying

I

My muse was imprisoned once
six months encased in stone
outside of Hebron.
She learned to sleep through torture,
to smile as they split her tongue.

She no longer throws stones
or hoists unfurled flags
She was shipped by night,
North across the Dog River.
North over the Chouf Mountains
to Byblos by the sea.

She is mute by day
she picks almonds and olives
for the greengrocer's cart.
Feeling the heft
judging by weight
estimating the knot
for Goliath's head.
She follows simple orders now,
incapable of schemes.

By night, she crouches
on jutting parapets
older than her name.
Her split tongue ululates
a spiral song to the moon
pulled from her throat like string,
the waves carry it to sea.

I can no longer care for the dying
can no longer grasp the hand
awash and drowning
"Throw out the Lifeline
Someone is slipping away"
Can no longer lose contact,
Feel nails rip into the meat of the palm

II

My muse sits in her garden
a pillow to her back
a baby to her breast

under the grape arbor, dappling
green shadows from a coastal sky.

She sits in the garden
a stain from her unused breast
spreading like the map of Israel.
Baby pulling
almost hurting,
the brown areola weeps milky tears.

She sits in the garden
White porcelain bowl
nestles to her hip, nearly tipping from fruit.
She cradles a fig in her outstretched palm:
Brown leather, ripe and pendulent.
She bites into crimson sweetness,
honeyed fruit flows down
the back of her throat.
She crunches
the seeds between her teeth.

I can no longer care for the dying
Can no longer bear to mirror their eyes
When I find them,
face pressed to the floor,
Buggered and bloody,
When they know,
finally and for certain,
they are mortal, after all.

When Fat Women Fear Famine

When fat women fear famine,
they arrange their canned goods
alphabetically
Stacking soups after sauerkraut
Butter beans before beets.

When fat women fear famine,
they stock their freezers
with sides of beef and butchered lamb.
Packages gleam white as snowbanks.
The red ink states:
stew bones
lamb chops
knuckle roast.
It splatters across each pristine surface.

When fat women fear famine,
their kitchens spew forth
stewpot after frying pan after casserole
of long-remembered recipes for
eggplant
parsnips
and 101 ways to prepare ground beef.
Their families flee from the flood of foodstuffs.

When fat women fear famine,
not even children are safe.
Their babies are coddled like three-minute eggs.
Their toddlers are wrapped like the breading
on fat, juicy sausages to protect against
the first cold winds of October.
As they grow, they are fussed over
like the Holiday turkey.
They are watched like the pot
that never boils.

These women are vigilant
against the threat of wanting.
They are full-fleshed warriors
waging war against an enemy
they cannot see
they cannot hear
They bear the battle-scars.
They know the pain of the gnawing heart,
the ache of the hollow bone.

❧ RAWIA MORRA ❧

From Ghurba

Powerless

what we are guarding
has been violated
again and again
in front of our eyes.

The spiders
are weaving their web
behind our ribs.

Death
rocks the child of our thoughts to sleep
while we crawl
like resurrected corpses
from one huge grave
to another.

We think we
are on the way
to what was once called
the greatest love.

Inside here
are those
who were born too late.

Out there lie
those who died prematurely.

Poetry survives
obstinately
amid the burned branches
in the churchyards
on those thirsty
lips
that have forgotten
long ago
what it means to forget.

Neighing at night
is a poem.

The pile of rubbish at the crossroads
is a poem
and the poet
cannot but
die.

My grandfather has an ashtray
a cup of coffee
tens of grandchildren
and his turban.

He reads from the Koran
the words are stuck in
his throat
when he looks up.

The leaves have no tree
to hang on to.

~

We must not fall asleep now

Not before we have crawled out
out of this quagmire
which God has drenched with his tears

we must not fall asleep now

Not before we have flown
high above this rubbish heap
of paper
years
visions
words
and truths

We must not fall asleep now

On this heap of rubbish we have
our own paper
our own years
visions
words
and truths

In the small hours
every word
is a rope
which once was
our own place in time.

Can we learn
to be quiet
during the chase?

Are we allowed to groan
while we suffocate?

~

Nothing smells worse
than dead love

There are no corpses here
no spirits
stammering out
a promise
for today
or eternity

~

I rinse you with my
exhaustion
and make your body
a cliff
that faces an ocean in the color of apricots.

You may rise tomorrow
dance
for the whiteness
of white light
for the magic circle
which underlines the dark
of darkness.

You may howl tomorrow
for the falling arrow
which is shaped like an arch
of diamonds
and you may hate me
if it fades away.

Today we are the cave people
and we shall sleep
for a hundred years.

~

The broken window
was once your mirror
the dusty trees
were your neighbors

The distance between your navel
and the word frightens you…
someone prolongs the trip
between the window and the bed sheet.

~

Your open wounds
gave me a room

Your sorrowful
screams
gave me a ceiling

I touch the knife
without raising any questions
and without mentioning
the kisses which
poets speak of

I give you a name
a face
and you disappear
in a stream of names
faces

~

I am as crazy
as ever

but I have learned
to love
pine cones
the gray clouds
and a cat
and when I feel cold
I dream
of a wine-red
velvet shawl.

I have learned
to wander
on the border between
me and myself
without being a stranger
or tired.

I have not found my home
but I have learned
to live
in my voice.

Translated from the Swedish by Magdi Abdelhadi

❧ AMAL MOUSSA ❧

Love Me

I carry me on my fingertips.
I carry me on the galloping of my vision.
I wrap myself with a swaddling of my skin.
I embrace me longing for myself.
I bless my flowing, my gushing.
I cradle me in my chest.
I glove these budding hands with poetry.

I claim revelation,
my engravings are on stone.
My image carries water to thirst,
and bait to fishermen's nets.
I spend the time of the tolling
of evening bells
sculpting.
I sleep in my own shade.
I wear my Bedouin nature
to spite cities.

I stroll within me
when I weary myself.
I enter a garden
that does not entice myself against me.
I love my impossible self,
the one whose feet
the earth does not know.

Translated by Khaled Mattawa

Autumn Rose

In crystal
I slept for three seasons,
then the drunkenness of sleep awoke me
to drink
the remains of springs.

I strike through the earth,
a female
pregnant with a damned river.
Grass bursts forth,
and in autumn
my rose blooms.

Translated by Khaled Mattawa

A Formal Poem

In the old house
where my grandfather composed his formal poems
I live as a concubine in my kingdom,
my dress wet,
and on my head I place a crown.

In the old house
where the jug is titled
water seeps out
mixed with prayers.

In the old house
where my first cry echoed,
I spread the soil of lineage
for us to sleep on,
one soul stacked next to another.
In the old house
where my grandmother was throned a bride
I search for her shawl
and place it for my shoulders to kiss.

In the old house
I cross ancient nights
and carry food to dervishes.

In the old house
I hand away my embers as a dowry
to lovers bathing in rain.

In the old house
love wears us like a cape
and the courtyard becomes
twice its size.

Translated by Khaled Mattawa

❧ SA'ADYYA MUFFAREH ❧

The Spell of Blazing Trees

When I'm smiling
It's only to stop crying
　　　—From an African-American song

His laugh:
silver
a horse neighing
a fragrance
of warm regret

the calm, noble joy
of horses
scattered in distant
plains

an ecstatic warmth
shattered
by a flock of doves
taking refuge
in shady
rest.

～

His laugh:
endearing like the trinkets of young girls
the lisping of a shy child

sharp like a sword
hung on his brow
by tribal elders

straight
like a well-lit street
fenced in
by infinite
details

beautiful women
water
palm trees and pebbles

proud silver droplets
a sudden summer rain
on the wide ocean
of my gloom

I shake myself
like a wet bird
dispelling sorrow
driving away
sleep

and paint a face
splendid and proud
to rival yours
which finds its way into
the features of my heart
like a mount
with a rider
who knows this territory

~

His laugh:
commanding love,
war
words
governing
melodies

a laugh
trickling out in
all directions

like the spell of the blazing tree
flowing
ebbing

transforming into a sun
but not intending
to set
for very long

Translated by Mona Fayad

❧ HABIBA MUHAMMADI ❧

In the forests of sleep
The lion of waking roars
And takes revenge
On a part of my dreams

The ink in the bowels of the pen
Is some
Of that oozing from the wounds
Of the ones we indite

I admire this earth
And its tireless turning.
Which one of you then
Has need of straightness?

This paper is our friend
It holds ever steadfast
Against the repeated stabbings
Of our pens

No one can stand
In the face of the sun
It alone knows
The way to the sunset

⁓

I write
To shout
To live
You write
To shout
To live
But who will silence
The shouting between us?

⁓

Whiter
The secret of your heart
The rock of manhood in you
Whiter than this paper
Tempting me with embraces
Whiter than the spirit
Than fresh milk
The milkman pours into cups
From Mecca Street to Abu Bakr Siddiq
Are not these snapshots of whiteness enough
For the picture of love to be complete?

⁓

A nap my heart takes under
Your trees
Hoping love will not bear fruit
In betrayal

~

I lay my head on the pillow every night
To sleep
But you haunt me in my dream
And reach for the seasons of the woman
In me
I then wake to find
The nectar of childhood
Sucked dry

~

The hearts raided by loneliness
Lead the conquests of the word

The lamps that some leave lit
When sleeping
Are naked blades against
Dreams that betray

~

In my room far away
I write the memory of dead paper.
In a barren space
Loneliness speaks words of love
To me
And light travels far
On a sail made of paper

~

Every day I try to wake up
Early
So that the dream
May not become
Taller than me

~

I love only you
And names only
Fill my cupboard

Men smell
The only fragrance
All women exude

Your heart is a mine open to the sky
And words are clouds
That bring no rain

~

All writings are ancient
But contemplation glows
Like sunrise every morning

I search for a day
In which I will rise
Without a memory
That my pillow may have room
For dreams without heads

On my bed sleeps
The bliss of thought
But when I reach out for it
With tenderness
I am ravished by words

Translated by Ibrahim Muhawi

❧ MAY MUZAFFAR ❧

Spinning

When from remote lands the wind rose,
all the city's trees prepared to crumble,
flower clusters dangled like bats,
the rotation started, and left no trace...
The world returned to its beginning...
The stars became orbits thrusting into the night...
                 and night fissioned.

Translated by Tahia Abdel Nasser

A Flash

Your face is the unexplored earth...
a night's sea and parades.
Your visible veiled face moves in the clouds,
so that whenever I try to open my eye...
               and stare
into the chests of darkness,
the wind takes over, hides it and laughs...
amid the pigeons' wings.

Translated by Tahia Abdel Nasser

Friends

A.
Like the water's outflow, the dream continues to bleed
and the men
go past seats that remain empty.
They were here...
      No they were not...

But their footsteps in the shadows were
grievous voices the night brings.

B.
Slowly the moon will burn...
It will continue to bleed its fire
and night will tyrannize, the images will be wiped out
slowly... throats will tremble with words
and no message but pigeons' moans will come.

Translated by Tahia Abdel Nasser

The Voice

Nothing but a resonance
of your distant voice remains for me...
Coming from the rain's rhythm
night heaps up a yearning silence...
All the doors of the stories
                              close up,
and the walls double up on their people—
the streets empty...
So no susurration rises to the people's ears
but a sandpiper's song emanating from a place...
to cross the space in the twinkling of an eye.

Translated by Tahia Abdel Nasser

Reticence

Yesterday
when I found
the curtains of the neighbor's floor
hold their silence over their windows,
and saw the bars' iron
intersecting in their windows—

I opened all the doors
and let the night overtake me.
There was nothing close to me but a utensil
a water jar
and the remnants of a derelict cage
which belonged to a bird—
pellets which dried and melted.

Translated by Tahia Abdel Nasser

The Absent

When pigeons returned
to the roof of the house, we said,
maybe the absent one has returned.
After the torrents of fire were removed
               and emptiness spread
outstretched arms around the city…
Sorrow was buried in the earth.
               The waters concealed him.
On the roof of the house the pigeons gather news…
it comes from the unknown or the unknown comes to us.
            We said,
during the day
draughts come through the door's openings…
Then they say:
Pass by me from amid the valleys of the night.
On the roof of the house we fed the pigeons,
wrote upon the clouds' palm a symbol
and hid within the folds of words.

Translated by Tahia Abdel Nasser

❧ HOUDA AL-NA'MANI ❧

The Stone Will Talk

Even in bronze curtains, I pierce the white ceiling,
my hands rocking like a returning ship,
my hands mocking the night,
painful like wounded limbs,
like a desert.

The batter stretches his arms
close by the net.
The others turn their backs
callow, having no ears.
Light stutters as it descends.

With a dagger-colored voice,
white-winged eyes,
breast like a wall,
one shadow sleeps,
a taste of grassy steps.

No spring inhabits the glass
no birds, no sky, no warmth.
In the glass purple genies dance.

Mother, calls the little fish, mother.
She hears but silence.
Lips of agony pierce—
winter could be tears,
could be happiness,
cascades of light...

But like Athena's dawning
the stone will talk
and the moans of the dead
     will be heard.

Translated by Houda Na'mani

The Purple Thought

It is ghosts that kill you without a drop of blood,
live within you never satisfied
with a tamed heart that tells you,
        "you are of that tree."
Then silence
a thousand fingers tenderly
carry fear into your face.

It is the blue that imprisons you between a wave and a wave.
A gift of a lifetime—you think—that lasts a day or more at most.
The valley hugs you to its rocks
then on your teeth patches of coal appear.

It is memories that hide you in a small bottle
until thirst fills your being
and you fall in pain drop after drop.

It is children who laugh and step on you.
You smile at them instead of weeping
among their toys, your nights your tomorrows
a well of your past.

It is things that slap you in your face
carrying under their nails your purple tears
and wounds.

Oh, Fear, drunken and tipsy as a mystical tree
your hands reel...
By yourself, paralyzed, you stay by the window
watching the tempest pass,
the lightning didn't even surprise you—
the winter curved in your eyes...
What might perhaps impress you—
a walking mountain?

Translated by Huda Na'mani, with Richard McKane

✠ SALWA AL-NEIMI ✠

Temptation

Marital quarrels are not poetic
nor are the cries of children,
the torture of public transport,
the reading of newspapers.
The poem falls from the faucet
like a fish, down onto my hands
while I wash the dinner dishes.

Translated by Subhi Hadidi and Nathalie Handal

Paranoia

I was a ripe fig
they almost squashed me
(I saw the horseshoes of their sandals)
I opened my palms
and there, they fell down from between my fingers:
one male after the other
one female after the other.
And now, putting my empty hands in my empty pockets,

I stride casually and whistle jovially:
      What's the name of this city?

Translated by Subhi Hadidi and Nathalie Handal

Dracula

Revolting against the lips
the long pointed fang was facing me
(despite all clumsy attempts to hide it).

I kept stealing glances at it,
dreamed of it pricked deep down my neck,
I bite my lower lip,
and blush beforehand.

Yesterday,
when he smiled, showing his aligned teeth
         (and dentistry can make miracles)
my face jolted,
myopic, I pretended to watch the passersby.

Translated by Subhi Hadidi

ADELE NE JAME

Song of a Thousand Empty Hands

I will build you a house of windows to let
the light in, to see the ocean, even the rain
each time you raise your eyes no matter where.
There will be no dry kiawe,
sun-bleached taro, no dark song. The west rooms
will show the Ko'olaus lush from rain,
the nightly rain, common as breathing
and cool verdant air to blanket you.
The wind from the sea on this cliff will take
the dryness from your bones, the dark song
from your heart. You will have only to lift
your eyes to see these succulents, the night-blooming cereus,
and jade, I've planted them all
for you, the deep cup-of-gold along the drive,
hundreds to gather the night rain, not human tears.
I will build you a house of windows to let
the cool light in, the golden morning mist,
the rolling light of verdant hills.

I have a thousand hands for the damp earth, for oleander
and along the ridge, a rush of yellow ginger,
a cathedral of light. You will see
stars, common as breathing, by daylight,
you have only to raise your eyes to see
my body, a tree growing skyward.

About the Men

The white moon, perfect
in the desert sky, in its precisely
dark and moving place.
Making a sound the heart knows:
the violence of beauty we want
to call tenderness, the exquisite moment
of entry, the pleasure of sudden stillness,
that fine body, his arms, thighs. The heat.
Then going past the long dreaming
strewn light,
to the distraction
of dogs barking in the distance
somewhere, the inaccuracy
beginning.

Somnambulist

In the pale light of the half moon, she sees him
opening the door, moving toward her
as if awake. He sits at the edge of the bed, tenderly stroking
her hair, inhaling deeply the heavy scent of
wet violets, the evening breeze along her arms.

She loosens her nightdress for him,
in the pale light of the half moon, she opens
her hand revealing desire of her heart.
His burning mouth against her palm,
even in sleep he groans as if defeated.

She has come to know his reluctant heart,
his body's struggle against itself,
to know even in this moment, he might turn away
suddenly, lift her from the bed,
carry her out into the night air
across the dampened field,
across the narrow foot-bridge, lay her down
there among the dark stones of the river bank.

Waking alone in their bed
how comforted he would be by her absence.
This night though, he does not walk out among
the trees, towards the flooded river.
He holds her close as if grieving.

His kisses are deep roses, the flutter of birds.
Their arms are so tightly clasped
together now, she longs for the river's swift current.
She fears the sound of the thrush. Even as they kiss,
she trembles, fearing the moment of his waking.

The World Is a Wedding

For my father

He might as well be dead if he does not know
the world is a wedding
            —Delmore Schwartz

After a supper of roasted lamb and eggplant,
fish baked with tahini and lemon,
Mother offers everyone demitasse.
She places the small gold cups
just so on the Quaker lace.
Her brothers and cousins crowded around
the table, one twirls his fedora, telling stories
of a summer spent at Sheep's Head Bay. The women.
Scolding him, and blessing herself in Arabic,

Mother pours more thick coffee; her hand glitters
with diamonds and platinum, gifts
my father insisted in the beginning she have,
offered to her like Van Gogh's profusion of stars.

After weeks of silence, worn out
from overtime, the daily commute into New York City,
Father sits drinking Four Roses as if his dream
might be constructed by the sheer recalling of it.
As if he were still mapping small countries
from the air, risking it all for the perfect shot.
Though he no longer tells the stories,
my uncles insist on the one of New Guinea,
of the dark woman in the photographs,
her heavy hair bound up in long cloth,
tattoos like lace on her shoulders,
strands of beads crossed over small breasts.
And her eyes darting into the camera like that.

He passes it off with a shrug, pours more drink,
defers to Mother. She quickly reminds everyone
that he carried *her* pictures
all over the world those years
before they married.
I was his girl even then, she says.

When the house is empty
Mother sits alone
in front of the TV watching
an old movie, the hero smoking a cigarette.
Father's already asleep in the small room
off the kitchen, having given himself up
to the next small loss, to King's Display
where, in a shabby darkroom
on West 45th Street he will turn out more prints,
10-foot blowups of movie stars,
heroes on the marquee, the crowd passing by.

❧ NAOMI SHIHAB NYE ❧

Arabic
(Jordan, 1992)

The man with laughing eyes stopped smiling
to say, "Until you speak Arabic—
—you will not understand pain."

Something to do with the back of the head,
an Arab carries sorrow in the back of the head
that only language cracks, the thrum of stones

weeping, grating hinge on an old metal gate.
"Once you know," he whispered, "you can enter the room
whenever you need to. Music you heard from a distance,

the slapped drum of a stranger's wedding,
wells up inside your skin, inside rains, a thousand
pulsing tongues. You are changed."

Outside, the snow had finally stopped.
In a land where snow rarely falls,
we had felt our days grow white and still.

I thought pain had no tongue. Or every tongue
at once, supreme translator, sieve. I admit my
shame. To live on the brink of Arabic, tugging

its rich threads without understanding
how to weave the rug... I have no gift.
The sound, but not the sense.

I kept looking over his shoulder for someone else
to talk to, recalling my dying friend who only scrawled
I can't write. What good would any grammar have been

to her then? I touched his arm, held it hard,
which sometimes you don't do in the Middle East, and said,
I'll work on it, feeling sad

for his good strict heart, but later in the slick street
hailed a taxi by shouting *Pain!* And it stopped
in every language and opened its doors.

The Whole Self

You put your whole self in
You put your whole self out
Whole self in and you shake it all about
 —The Hokey Pokey

When I think of the long history of the self
on its journey to becoming the whole self, I get tired.
It was the kind of trip you keep making.

Over and over again, the bag you pack and repack so often
the shirts start folding themselves the minute
you take them off.

I kept detailed notes in a brown notebook. I could tell you
when the arm joined, when it fell off again,
when the heart found the intended socket and settled down to pumping.

I could make a map of lost organs, the scrambled liver,
the misplaced brain. Finally finally we met up with one another
on a street corner, in October, during the noon rush.

I could tell you what I was wearing. How suddenly
the face of the harried waitress *made sense*. I gave my order
in a new voice. Spoke the word *vegetables* like a precious code.

Had one relapse at a cowboy dance in Bandera, Texas,
under a sky so fat the full moon

was sitting right on top of us.

Give me back my villages, I moaned,
the ability to touch and remove the hand
without losing anything.

Take me off this mountain where six counties are visible at once.
I want to remember what it felt like, loving by inches.
You put in the whole self—I'll keep with the toe.

But no, it was like telling the eye not to blink.
The self held on to its perimeters, committed forever,
as if the reunion could not be reversed.

I jumped inside the ring, all of me. Dance, then, and I danced,
till the room blurred like water, like blood, *dance,*
and I was leaning headlong into the universe,

Dance! The whole self was a current, a fragile cargo,
a raft someone was paddling through the jungle,
and I was there, waving, and I would be there at the other end.

The Small Vases from Hebron

Tip their mouths open to the sky.
The turquoise, amber,
the deep green with fluted handle,
pitcher the size of two thumbs,
tiny lip and graceful waist.

Here we place the smallest flower
which could have lived invisibly
in loose soil beside the road,
sprig of succulent rosemary,
bowing mint.

They grow deeper in the center of the table.

Here we entrust the small life,
thread, fragment, breath.
And it bends. It waits all day.
As the bread cools and the children
open their gray copybooks
to shape the letter that looks like
a chimney rising out of a house.

And what do the headlines say?

Nothing of the smaller petal
perfectly arranged inside the larger petal
or the way tinted glass filters light.
Men and boys, praying when they died,
fall out of their skins.
The whole alphabet of living,
heads and tails of words,
sentences, the way they said,
"Ya' Allah!" when astonished,
or "ya'ani" for "I mean"—
a crushed glass under the feet
still shines.
But the child of Hebron sleeps
with the thud of her brothers falling
and the long sorrow of the color red.

Yellow Glove

What can a yellow glove mean in a world of motorcars and
governments?

I was small, like everyone. Life was a string of precautions: Don't
kiss the squirrel before you bury him, don't suck candy, pop balloons,
drop watermelons, watch TV. When the new gloves appeared one
Christmas, tucked in soft tissue, I heard it trailing me: Don't lose
the yellow gloves.

I was small, there was too much to remember. One day, waving at a stream—the ice had cracked, winter chipping down, soon we would sail boats and roll into ditches—I let a glove go. Into the stream, sucked under the street. Since when did streets have mouths? I walked home on a desperate road. Gloves cost money. We didn't have much. I would tell no one. I would wear the yellow glove that was left and keep the other hand in a pocket. I knew my mother's eyes had tears they had not cried yet, I didn't want to be the one to make them flow. It was the prayer I spoke secretly, folding socks, lining up donkeys on windowsills. *To be good,* a promise made to the roaches who scouted my closet at night. *If you don't get in my bed, I'll be good.* And they listened. I had a lot to fulfill.

The months rolled down like towels out of a machine. I sang and drew and fattened the cat. Don't scream, don't lie, don't cheat, don't fight—you could hear it anywhere. A pebble could show you how to be smooth, tell the truth. A field could show how to sleep without walls. A stream could remember how to drift and change—next June I was stirring the stream like a soup, telling my brother dinner would be ready if he'd only hurry up with the bread, when I saw it. The yellow glove draped on a twig. A muddy survivor. A quiet flag.

Where had it been in the three gone months? I could wash it, fold it in my winter drawer with its sister, no one in that world would ever know. There were miracles on Harvey Street. Children walked home in yellow light. Trees were reborn and gloves traveled far, but returned. A thousand miles later, what can a yellow glove mean in a world of bankbooks and stereos?

Part of the difference between floating and going down.

OnGoing

The shape of talk would sag
but the birds be brighter than ever

O I needed the birds worse & worse as I got older
as if some crack had opened in the human scheme of things
& only birds with their sharp morning notes
had the sense for any new day

The people went round & round
in the old arenas
dragging their sacks
of troubles & stones & jaggedy love
I could not help them
I was one of them
the people pitched advice
in its flat hat back & forth
across the table

But the birds so far above us
hardly complete sentences
just fragments & dashes
the birds who had seen the towns
grow up & topple
who caught the changing wind
before anyone on the ground did
who left for Mexico when we were not
paying attention
what could they tell us
about lives in heavy bodies

what could they tell us
about being
caught?

❧ Maysoun Saqr al-Qasimi ❧

The Morning of Every Sin

2

I'm not sleeping now
leave me like that
like a scandal dying down in the light
When water creeps down its charm shall be complete
Who will knock at my window?
The rain!
Who will rub its legs upon my threshold?
The dogs!

No shadow in the long hallucination
Oh, how much I deserved this body.

6

Salty like my seashores
and like your fierce whales
you eat my fingers with frightening lust
I shudder each time you pant closer to my ear
each time I sleep on your lips

Dense shadows fall over my bed.

7

The voice is never enough
like when, time and time again,
we are born of this sea
and useless
is the pus of death along the streets

It's fair, that we feel satisfied
by kisses.

Translated by Subhi Hadidi

The Cusp of Desire

He is the source of hot forests
the yearning of him rises
and he oozes sweat whenever a sorrow pours down.
He is the white one with a crown of hair
as gentle as always
smooth like the desert
coy in front of invaders
frightened and the soaked
bearer of identical values
guardian of the fleshy breast
oasis for birds nibbling him
cage of secrets
master of embraces
the cusp of desire
moon of the round body.
When his light fades out
when he clings to harm
and is frozen in his plate of secrets
it's then that he shrinks…

Translated by Subhi Hadidi and Nathalie Handal

A Dream Recalling a Temptation

… And when he was awakened by the cold, she was washing her hair,
with tenderness feeling her buttock. The fuller she is, the more
    charming.
A great sadness began to hang loosely from her right breast.
When she got used to his serenity, she grew closer to his moments of

grief,
distracted by the danger of bringing the body to the moment of
    resurrection.
She could not believe she was capable of slow suicide.
As for the buttock aroused by the touch of longing,
as for the sleeper on her belly,
that can no more condense the moments beside her...
All in all on the verge of transfiguration.

Translated by Subhi Hadidi and Nathalie Handal

◈ MICHAELA RAEN ◈

La Sombra *of Who I Am*

Who was my grandmother?
What died with her
and is buried in the
soil *antigua debajo*
the burning sun?
¿Quienes eran mis abuelas ancinas?
Una mujer de los espíritus,
a spirit woman
darker than my *jedu*
visits me.
I am compelled by her to places within myself
never thought to exist.
She knows that I have Lebanese and Jordanian blood;
that I can cook only in the language that is not mine;
that I have built my life rebelling against those uncles
who said I was too independent/outspoken
as I watched them send to
our homeland
for their next wife.
She would for them give freely of her fertile soil,

sow seeds and govern their growth,
be lost in an Anglo utopia
surrounded only by English words
and few others like her
brought/bought from
their homeland.

I,
white skinned opinionated queer girl,
am valueless to men.
I,
lesbian (of color if only deep inside),
am to them a freak.
I want to know
the women in my blood.
I need to know
the entirety of what it is I have chosen to rebel against.
Maybe, I tell myself,
it's not as bad as my childlike eyes have seen it to be.

I am unacquainted with the ways
of those who wear scarves to cover their hair
and a *thoob* to "defemminize,"
disempower,
create obedience towards men.
I have never shielded my hair from the sun
nor covered my entirety from the wind.
I have never cooked traditional bread in a *ta'boon*
only *warraq enab*
on a gas stove
with bottled grape leaves and lamb meat bought from the Arab butcher.
I have no ingrained tolerance for maleness to lift me to freedom
freedom from men
freedom to cushion my new realities.
I am unacquainted with tradition,
its severity of punishment for all that is considered *haram*,
and the censoring of their voices,
                    devaluing of their importance,
                         beating them into submission.

Can I,
young lesbian whiter looking than most Anglos,
silence my own voice,
succumb to male superiority,
so I can discover my *ahli,*
and my grandmothers?
If woman only has power through man,
can I hide my "lesbian-ness"
my love for *todas las mujeres,*
can I stop the burning desire for desert women?
For love between women is much more than *haram*
it is impossible,
here.

I am,
what for many women
they are not allowed to be,
a strong female warrior
collecting power from those whose wings
conquered the great wind.
Who is this visionary woman
who is pushing me closer
to those whispering in my blood?
How much of myself
must I sacrifice to satisfy this hunger
to collect and to know
the feathers of these women
inside of my soul?

I am *bint.*
Soy una niñita del sol
an outsider looking inward to search for the visionary
Palestinian woman
who is calling to me
with her curly hair flying in the wind
dancing on the sandy soil of my past.

¿Es ella la Diosa,
    the earth mother,
    sappho's messenger,
    my grandmother
    or
    a culmination de *todas mis abuelas?*

I miss my grandmother's hands
watching them
as she washed the grape leaves
mixed the lamb with lemon juice
kneading with both hands in a large bowl.
Watching her hands
turn the pages of my herstory
to her nightlight as we slept,
I,
in the bed of my dead grandfather.
Watching *sus manos*
work endless cross word puzzles
not knowing how to love me
or even if she should
things she loved had a tendency to die.

Our Arabic language
lost in one generation
as she watched her daughters grow
and marry white men.
In the closest of cousins, at least,
she had the reflection of herself,
her son did not marry white.
She was my only *taitah,*
my *jeda,*
Umm Richard,
and I looked nothing like her daughter.

Todavía la mujer comes to me
dancing *con la música en mi alma.*
I must
to complete the circles of my life

follow the visionary *mujer*
wandering backward not forward to find myself.
Mientras la sombra
of who I am is widening
and soon will be overtaken by the darkness,
se desaparece,
se obscurece,
in the night sky;
as the same wind
that once caressed her face,
now ancient,
holds mine to the stars.

Notes: *ahli*–family; *bint*–daughter/little girl; *haram*–absolutely forbidden behavior; *jeda*–grandmother; *jedu*–grandfather; *thoob*–long black dresses for women with black stripes of embroidery; *taitah*–grandmother; *ta'boon*–traditional outdoor oven for baking bread; *Umm...*–mother of (add the name of the first born *male* offspring); *warraq enab*–a dish using grape leaves stuffed with lamb and rice; *sombra*–shadow; *antigua debajo*–ancient underneath; *¿Quienes eran mis abuelas ancinas?*–Who were my ancient grandmothers?; *Una mujer de los espíritus*–A spirit woman/A woman of spirit; *todas las mujeres*–all women; *Soy una niñita del sol*–I am a child of the sun; *¿Es ella la Diosa?*–Is she the Goddess?; *todos mis abuelas*–all of my grandmothers; *sus manos*–her hands; *Todavía la mujer*–Still the woman; *con la música en mi alma*–with the music in my soul; *Mientras la sombra*–While the shadow; *se desaparece, se obscurece*–disappears as it becomes darker.

⚛ NADIA HAZBOUN REIMER ⚛

To an Old Friend

I saw you smoldering,
sipping black coffee with
wheezy breath; wrinkles meandered
on a face fogged in behind the smoke
of a cigarette—butts everywhere.

What happened to the dream,
the holy spirit within you,
the plans designed in vers-libre:

graduation, a goddess wife and two
children, just like you—both boys.

Fifteen years went by
and dropped you off at the same café,
where we used to study Andromache
and sing a home-made song.

Now you sit there, dreamless,
a betrayed mortal. I walk by,
say hello. You gaze at the wall,
where we once scribbled names
and sipped rich coffee with cream—
with cubes of sugar.

The Middle East

no, it is not only the date clusters
in the palm trees
but also the oil, the phosphate,
the potassium, the olives, the citrus,
the salt,
the milk and honey,
and the manna that falls from heaven.

People kill to share this land,
while the verse on their holiday letter
reads:
"Peace on Earth!"

Workaholic

My hands are smooth, the grooves—
just wrinkles from age, thin skin veils
wild branches of green and blue veins,

displays sunspots, repeated burns
from sputtering cooking grease.

Seconds drag when I wait for another day
to collect laundry, wash pots and pans
that don't fit in the dishwasher,
straighten up my words, turn them over
and over on the screen like chickens
in an Mid-Eastern rotisserie—part dark,
part just right, the rest still raw—too raw.

Who forgot to make his bed today?

There's birds shit all over the car,
and the neighbor's cat
left muddy paw tracks on the hood.

Outside of me, the world spins,
whispers behind my back,
goes round and round,
marking off birthdays, anniversaries—
leaving me behind, a caveman
to sleep the centuries, to be discovered
some day by victims of haste,
just like I once used to be.

❧ Su'ad al-Mubarak al-Sabah ❧

Mad Woman

I am quite mad and you are wholly sane
From the mind's paradise I've sought to flee
You are all wise, yours are the summer months
So leave the winter's changing face for me.

I'm sick with love and I'm past any cure
Oppressed in body, that is woman's plight
My nerves are taut and should you only whisper
Into the empty air I would take flight.

I'm like a small fish lost in the great ocean
When will you lift the siege? You've hidden away
The key to unlock my house in your own pocket
And enter my life's details day by day.

O love, my passion whirls me dizzily
Gather my scattered soul whose fragments fly
For you are standing at the frozen pole
And I beneath an equatorial sky.

O love, I stand against the ten commandments
History behind is only blood and sand
To love I owe allegiance. Lemon trees
Within your breast my only native land.

Translated by May Jayyusi and John Heath-Stubbs

⚜ DORIS SAFIE ⚜

Danger, Men in Trees

Quietly, they take on the color and shape
of their surroundings. The danger lies
in the knowing. He said he had to find
the animal in himself. I said I already knew
where it was. But he went anyway,

when the branches were bare and full
of regret, as if time had a shape
that hangs from a straw. By the time
the leaves came, as they must
when rain and sun collude in spring,
I couldn't even see him. I looked

for the other women, and we talked,
over tea. We talked and talked until

the children came running in and shouted,
We can see them through the fox rain!
Sure enough, we could make out their limbs—
poised on the edge of raindrops
slanting gently down the sun's beams—
on the verge of gliding past the horizon.

That night, the wolf moon's yellow grin
slid past my window, daring me spy
into its clouded face. And I remembered
the first time I saw him, across the street,
holding an open umbrella, when it seemed his lips
were as close to mine as mine were to my mouth.

What excited me was their unknown quantity,
the feeling that makes you cling to straws.

I grew bored looking through windows, went out
to the indelible night, urged by the memory
of the thud inside me when he'd casually toss
a newspaper on the sofa. Or the rattle
cups made in their saucers, each time his arm
brushed the air in reaching for salt.

I looked back at the house, and the lights
grew dim, but I knew the power company
would have no record of it. I looked back
at the sky, and knew if I watched him
I'd change his course forever.

Meditation by the Xerox Machine
For Ethel Weinberger

Such a gloomy day
rain rain rain
sound of soldiers
in rain this gray
because of the rain
to believe something
in this small town trapped
by rain, mountains frame
the window, my hand
on the glass, coming out gray
on gray two three four
promising black and white
two three such ennui

in terms of global warfare is
vicious, has an edge, a child
of cities paved with children whose
bones echo, empty
drums. I copy and copy
and copy, dead paper
flies out like dry tongues, craving

the art of a poem you want
about peace. And I'd give you
the sun and its light dreaming
of seeds that burst
so flowers might bloom, a leak
of imagination and love to break
dams, melt ice, soften this earth too
subtle with hope, but this rain
these dead children gnaw at me gray
with numbness. I watch
two drops merge, like your dream
of a horse with wings connecting
continents at war. It's a choice
of no choice, this art in me
that wails, claws at the soul
like rain scratching
the window. The man in me
envies conviction, the woman
fears it, the child waits, the child
who says it likes rats
and moles, especially dead
ones. I know it's just a phase but
these crucifixions cling
like burrs. I keep trying
and trying and trying to find
the jewel in the machine in this room

that tolls the music of dead
masters, lost in the whirr of the machine
that blurs the tender craft of those
who see, as I copy and copy and copy...

❧ Amina Said ❧

one day I know the page
will cease to translate silence
into human speech

the words themselves
will stop knocking at my door

time will watch me die
perhaps far from the sea
embraced by the horizon

the star which shines for me
will softly fade out

and night will fold me peacefully
into death's dark egg

then the dawn of my first childhood
will remember me

the ancient tree who saw me leaving
and all the birds
who crossed my sky

when my shadow
shall be touched by light

I will know she was myself
exactly doubled

only a shadow of flesh
can walk this earth.

Translated from the French by Lucy McNair

L'écho de ce pays est sur
       —René Char

I present myself to the world
to my jumbled shadows
a cry alone can greet this earth
this sky and this face I will become

here the sun is a scorching fire
I present myself to the world
which has rocked forever
to the rhythm of days and nights

here the pines plant their needles
into reddish clay
water remains scarce
I still ignore what the wind carries

I present myself to the world
to the sea offer my first glance
a fish an open hand
to protect the houses' inhabitants

here waves are messengers
of the horizon's red ring
they dance on the fringed shore

calligraphies of seaweed and mist
but the women of the coast
walk the path of the earth
no one has ever sought
to deny the horizon of its freedom

I present myself to the world
the new star the crescent
shines over my shoulder
tomorrow again the sirocco

to my forehead sticks a black lash
I have my family's sight
grandmother noticed it
at the bottom of the big mirrors

seated by the fires of their reflections
draped in shimmering clothes
she would invoke her dead
her tomb has since been lost

here the dowsers of oblivion
cannot find wells anymore
whole gardens disappear
beneath the sand-choked tongues of birds

the earth is heavy with humanity
beings and things which adorn it
are works of here and of that elsewhere
the dead fix their eyes on

here earth and rock are memory
the saints lie in obscure repose
promising enchantment
here even miracles are discreet

in this primary place
bodies outstrip their shadows
toward which mysterious continent
does the dream of closed eyes point

I present myself to the world
here what lives liberates itself
by discovering the thread
in the labyrinth's hollow

here all ages reign
faces adjust to faces
and distance ends
by confounding us with ourselves

time is a lagoon sated to the brim
a tongue of earth rising from the waters
a mythic mountain eternal and blue
a column raised upon the bay

here the death and rebirth of centuries
nourishes men's desires
they leave to better return
here the absent are never wrong

for departure is never voluntary
beyond is that mirror
where the quest is for another image
a path leading us to our own story

here the light strips you naked
it is time to rediscover its source
it is time to decipher the day
encrusted with salt and fire

here the light is a living pillar
between the sky and the blind peak of the stones
it supports the slow
unfolding of night

and as everyone worries
about darkness's return
chants burst with ardor
to be pacified by joy

here the desert also sculpts
a song to its own measure
that men go to gather
from dune to dune

here other laws hold
in the aviary of words
each chooses with care
the one which will amaze her

here each day born
reminds the sky of its promises
here the earth is thirsty
for a rain of stars

here reality is visible
only to the heart's eye
the unseen haunts us
with conflicting images

here the moon-bathed night
is tuned to the living
I reach out to grasp the full circle
slips away its hammered face

falling into the belly of the cistern
it trembles on the black surface
then dissolves
I cannot drink this water

a cock crows at high midnight
in the morning that knows nothing of good-byes
these indolent lands wake
from the secret of a long siesta

cistern or whirlwind of spirits
on the terrace of legends
two turtledoves of sand
suddenly take flight

Translated from the French by Lucy McNair

❧ LAILA AL-SA'IH ❧

Intimations of Anxiety

You do not know how hard it is,
transfiguring blood into ink—
emerging from one's secret dream
to voicing the dream.
Perhaps I need years to understand
what swirls within me when we meet.
Do you know that constellations of cities and paths tangle
restlessly in the sand?
I do not know the name
for such sweet incandescence.
Even now I have not discovered all the stars
fanning out in the soul and body
like eloquent shining symbols.

Under a mass of snow
a violet is patiently waiting.
Each opening rose partakes of
the patience of ages.
These are the things we must share,
and how the word takes shape within me.
Pulled between a world that created me
and a vaporous world I wish to create,
I begin again.
Each time you transform me
into a haze,
Wait for my anxiety
for this nameless creature thumping
in my breast.
I begin again
with your book,
from your book,
reading the first pages
over and over, dazzled, amazed,

enveloped by vast days and puzzling depths,
saying: The moment will come
in which I discover language,
voice of the sun's fruits,
dialect of waves engulfing my heart.
Maybe then I will be able to add
a single syllable to this existence—
this arduous impossible task.

Translated by May Jayyusi and Naomi Shihab Nye

❧ SANIYYA SALEH ❧

Exile

For grief
he wore those colorful bells,
a mask of joy.
He bound his stories
        to his tongue's tip
so they would not betray him
        at the crucial moment.
And he walked
        lightly
                in jewel-studded shoes—
alone as the night
with no stars waiting
buy my eyes.

Bird, hovering over the horizon
remember
bullets are everywhere—
Remember
me
        the perpetual traveler—

All my life
I have willed to go forward and have not
advanced beyond
the borders of my grave.

Translated by Kamal Boullata

Choking

Every time I am bound towards you
my roads turn into dust
one step
and they vanish.
Mother
Cry out!
There is no sky
but
our throats.

Come back to me:
Bitter wilderness of childhood
           more vast than a child's fantasy
           where terror
           was concealed.

As you search for their graves
declare to the world:
           only the winds blowing without mercy
           could silence them for the night
           caution sealing their lips
           —guards before barred cells.

Do you remember who went out at night
           to meet the winds?
Only we children
only we
restless ashes.

Go back to your death
mythic woman.

Translated by Kamal Boullata

⚜ MUNIA SAMARA ⚜

Door of Roses

MINT

doomsday of wind
talk of the garden
ambush of rubies
hiding in its sleeves
the leaf of the scene
and painting
the tea of the poor.

MYRTLE

bolder than mint
for every morning
it rocks the peasant's beds
and prepares the jugs of ablution
and when it is caught
it falls bleeding
under the martyr's feet.

RED ANEMONE

bolder than myrtle
and more fragile too.

NARCISSUS

if it possessed the boldness of myrtle
and had shut its eyes a little
while looking into the book of red anemone
it would have retired, away
from the front of the scene

JASMINE

embellishments on the shirts of houses
and a perfume for the hands of the passersby
it amuses the picture of time
and when wind shakes it
it releases its seagulls
toward the villages.

THE DAMASK ROSE

age
spreading the perfume of youth
on the lines of its face
it flirts with
bygone days
from behind the gardenís fence
it has never sat
on the thresholds of geography
and never found its way
to the history book
everything in it
reveals hateful desire.

Translated by Amal Amireh

Door of the Cities

JERICHO

the scandal of this universe
and its joke
awakens the chaos inside the gods
and tests death.
One day
before the adulteress finishes her last dance
and the exiles spill their last glass
on the bed
it will tear off the shirts of the earth
and release the scream no one awaits,
except me.

JERUSALEM

All that the great gods
and fairies of the epochs have left,
from the drizzle of bright lightning
to the clouds which graze near the springs,
all quivers there,
under the closed arches.

It has not surrendered her keys to one prophet
and it has not run to the harbors of the invaders.

So it remained in its place
wrapped in its volcanic cloak
practicing magic on this world.

BETHLEHEM

the door of the earth
and the side of the cross,
it fills the empty bottle
with drops of lime
and drives away the donkey of the venerable sheikh

who wrote the lines of the old miracle
and cuts the roots of the oak trees
so that the virgin completes
what is left of the heads of saints.

NAZARETH

when the Nazarene returns to it
surrounded with murderers
in order to throw his miracle in the faces,
some faces darken others whiten
and the patriot lifting his pantaloons
runs
and a marginal youth
who no one ever heard of
smiles
then extends his hand to the ancient boards
and writes
at the beginning was
the word
and erases from its walls thousands of slogans.

ACRE

Sliding towards the mirrors of water
it opens its windows
and throws a bone
to the barking Napoleon around her walls.

Coming out of the mirrors of water
in all its adornments
it spreads its carpet for the Bedouins,
eats breakfast with them
and gives them its blue scythes.

Before it returns to the sea
it gives her desire
to a small child who has not yet reached the dream,
His name is Canaan.

a burning wound in the side of the earth
the burns of poverty play in it
and on its borders bark
the enemies' rifles.

Translated by Amal Amireh

✵ GHADA AL-SAMMAN ✵

The Lover of Blue Writing above the Sea!

It is not true that the shortest path between two points is the
    straight line!
That is what I learned when I was with you!
Dialogue? It is the longest path between the heart and the lips,
between my voiced waves and your silent waves.
Intuition alone led me to you...
It screamed one night without sound
that candles had gone out, that we were finished.
Parting poured poison in our coffee...
Once, I gave you my heart, naked like a white sheet of paper.
I wrote on it the plot for my murder... and my death certificate!
You did not forgive me, for leaving my death with you
and going with the gulls to the sea...

Who will lead me to a city that is a stranger to bombs,
that I might live there?
Who will lead me to fields, stranger to furtive burials
of a murdered man tortured to death?
Who will lead me to trees
that have never heard a woman moaning for her hijacked lover?
Who will lead me to a sky

whose blue is a stranger to injustice or harshness
or a thought that has been raped?
I am tired of your love, your time,
of men like you who compete in violence...
Their love is blue writing above the sea...
Who said: the love of men is not like water through a sieve?

~

We parted, and here is the last whiteness... becoming soiled
like snow in stations when trains fill them with soot...
Once, my hand was a bird trembling in your hand
begging you not to release it...
But your hand was releasing bullets and weaving slogans...
I am filled at once with the nation, with death...
The echo runs in my caves like lost souls...
I dedicate myself to our parting...
I guard the spider that is calmly spinning
its threads over your image in my eye...
The dust piles up on your lips,
the bat hangs from the black of your eyes,
and inside your clothes, snow pours down into your depths...
Plants, witness our time together
speed away to the street,
and climb up into neighboring balconies...

~

How did we let parting breed for years...
In the desolation of electrified violence,
let hypocrisy wear us for parties?
How did we commit the treachery of the rain,
renounce purity in the bars of voluptuousness,
betray the winds, side with the veils,
and claim that they had given birth to the storm?
Here the traces of the camp stop at our present, laugh mockingly
not finding us worthy of tears!—they flow like rain,
like a mother washing her two children spattered with mud...

~

Here is the city falling in on the sky,
fat women feeding their children
crying in the kitchen's dark corners
because of the betrayals of men
gambling both love and the nation...
Women weave threads of grayness with white bitterness...
... Here I am, running alone in the rain, without a man or a nation—
thousands of windows gaze at me with aggressive, burning eyes...
Like any rebellious black ewe
I weave the threads of my freedom far from the paths of the flock...
I try in vain to create a third fate
for a woman coming from the third world.
"Do you want to know the secret of my power?
No one has ever really loved me..."
Here I am, falling
but I insist on leaving traces of my steps, traces of my pens
on the darkness of the abyss... and the whiteness of the page!

Translated by Saad Ahmed and Miriam Cooke

The Lover of Rain in an Inkwell

When I die
these letters will still carry me to you,
my great love, without anything really changing...
When I die, search well inside this paper.
Go to the depths of my words and you will see me on the lines—
I fly silently like the owl of amazement.
If you are sad and burn the edge of my book
I shall come to you
like the genie in my grandmother's Damascene stories...
If a lover burns a strand of her hair, she will give it to him.
When I die,
if you tear this page in anger
you will hear me suffer...
If you lavish the love of your eyes on it, wherever you are
the sun will rise above my tomb in Beirut!

Translated by Miriam Cooke, with Richard McKane

⚛ MONA SAUDI ⚛

Blind city,

in its streets my visions multiply
in the chaos of objects
in the labyrinths of insomnia
I hear voices of silence
the stillness of time and sea
the death of night.
I warm myself with weeping pavements
there, life glows in an instant
born in a puddle of light.

Translated by Kamal Boullata

So drunk am I with the night, the air, and the trees

so drunk, I enfold the seas of forgetfulness.
When the shore appears, I bend away with my mast
         towards the endlessness of the waters
counting the waves: wave by wave
I yell at the sea:
         more of your remoteness.

Fortitude is futile, frustration and conversations
go on and on around the fireplace.
The days have numbers, the faces have names.
And the masks mime according to the time
         recorded on the clock in the
         piazza of the city.
Selling is a god. Buying is a god. And you,
         they have abandoned you. They let you fall
         into oblivion, yes, you:
         the distant traveling of the unknown in the
darkness: the drunkenness of the night and the air.

So drunk am I with the night, the air, and the trees

I have carried you, Sea, upon my forehead
you that carry no name, the journey to the unseen
through you and in you, the whole
     universe is reduced to the circles of the water:
     the tides of death and birth
and the silence of the migrating birds
between the poles.

You, migrating birds:
go tell the shores you are reaching
the sea is coming to wash the cities
to sweep the masks that are numbered
according to the rites of the marketplace
(the bowing, the creeping, and the fear.)

The sea is coming with the verses of the
     pregnant stones:
Action is the word and Refusal of the old.

The sea is coming. Open up the way
     for the procession of The Sea.
May glory be to the god of The Sea.
There is no god but
     that which is coming.
Coming with changes: illuminations
New crystallizations procreations through death
     and birth.
Coming in the absent present
     in the present absence
in a sweeping sea of circles.

Translated by Kamal Boullata

Saudi's poems reprinted from *Women of the Fertile Crescent: Modern Poetry by Arab Women,*
edited by Kamal Boullata. Copyright © 1981 by Kamal Boullata. Reprinted with permission
of Lynne Rienner Publishers, Inc.

ৰ MAI SAYIGH ৱ

Departure

In this the moment of departure,
point your red arrows,
disarm the lightening, and open wide
the gate to my exile.
Close the sky's open face, and ride away.
I long so deeply that the shores unfold their seas
and horses bolt!
Hooves have trampled my heart a thousand times,
a thousand waves have broken over it!
Now I'll carry the roads and palm trees in my suitcase,
I'll lock my tears in the evening's copybooks
And seal the seasons.

Let's begin our song: here is Beirut *wearing* you
        like her own clothes.
You must sit well on the surface of her glory
abandoning tears
In her blue froth
she contains you like eternity
like the sense of beginning that comes with certainty

—How can you be dead, yet so absolutely present?

Let the rivers abandon their sources,
the winds abandon their skies,
and the seas dry out!
Everything in the universe has an end
except my spilled blood...
Each time I think of it
you remain as large as your death.
The war planes choose you, discover you, plant
their blackness in you.
From all those clouded last visions,
how will you begin the story of harvest?

War planes select you,
at the start of your sleep,
at the end of your sleep.
How often did the sky explode over you
    with hatred?
How often were you taken aside?
How many massacres did you survive?
Now you collect all the wounds, taking refuge with
    death,
wearing dreams as wings.

Translated by Lena Jayyusi and Naomi Shihab Nye

❧ SEKEENA SHABEN ❧

tempest

there is little inspiration
tonight; air cool and wet
my heart a little dry and flat
white fabric pins open my midnight window

a slice of light
moon driven i hope
slides into my room

rain sings on
the tin window sill
slow hum of the fan
the winds now passed
like good-bye kisses
straight down from the sky

all night the creaking
of a loose window pane

and now this
unbearable stillness

thirteenth ode

with the window sliced open
in a circle
on the brightest part of your length
was a definition of explicitness
of your hands lit up in acute darkness
your youth diminished
loves composed on your forehead
reminded me of beautiful things
things we crave
things that leave us in shadows
the inward way
you learned to sustain yourself
through a crack in the sky
light filtered in and severed you half-naked
the gap between nothingness opened
the division of your limbs
emptied a place for me

fourteenth ode

i'm not sure of my age; descending pale
robes distant fluttering
all that is certain is time spirals
so elusive it winds me down stairs
the sirens beat my center
wash my aching swollen need for comfort
love here is occasional
dependent on the arms of an unwound clock
its face downcast; smitten with tricks
it can play

i reach out and grab my reflection
to shake it present
but cadence looms; skin fades and lines deepen
strange to be so far away from sequence
as it presses down my spine
garbage trucks roll outside my open window
it must be 4 am.

❧ GHADA EL-SHAFA'I ❧

A Scene for the Mornings Preceding the Fire

A beam of light in the mouth of azure
sucks the blood of darkness.
The night sneaks from the door,
wrapped up
with a garment of sleeping dust
on the fingers of asphalt.

Like a woollen cat,
you gaze
on feet made of the fluff of tropical shadows—
a cat comes to a balcony of time, seized by birds—
birds arriving very early with straws of long tales in their beaks.

A dream-painted sun
licks the waist of the cypress tree.
On the breasts of the grain field
pours once, a sip of morning,
escaping the windows of childhood days.
Here you are
throwing away a blackboard from the sky,
spotted with a handful of the old chalk's blood,
taking off the mineral-rich water from the planets' skin.

You go in the dancing crowd
to the last room in the forests' net,
drawing a scene for childhood's cypress tree,
an angle to follow the river in the midst of an enemy,
—maybe—a mirror of God's details...

How many times was your skin rubbed
by the grass,
raising its head from the heaped wood...
How many times was your mouth
reached by the echo of seagulls,
passing spaces in which eyelashes touch a glass
filled with the juice of your soul,
throwing you wings, flying in a thorny emptiness.

Here you are
pouring a drop of the oil of your remains
into the jar of time.

There is a forest with scattered trees
in the time of awakening...
a forest raises a foot filled with thorns and matches,
awaiting fires to stretch
to the shoulder of the plain—
a shawl the fields wear...

Translated by Atef Abu-Seif, with Nathalie Handal

Interlaced Lines for the Same Moment

Has it ever happened—
you forgetting: your hands hung on smoky trees,
your steps dwelling in the winds of yesterday...
You shelter in the shadow of the walls' cement shoulder,
searching the wardrobe of time for a shirt that might fit,
for lost hours of
happiness

Has it ever happened—
from the forests of the sun
you picked up thorny grass
placing it on graves the gods jostle
smashing their own reflection
in the mirror

Has it ever happened—
you carry a sea in your pocket
then pour it on sidewalks
cleaved by the daily grind,
circling like a horse
which half runs after the second half of the square

Has it ever happened—
you carry your head between your cut fingers,
rolling it like a ball in the bottomless pit
of oblivion?

Translated by Atef Abu-Seif, with Nathalie Handal

❧ DEEMA K. SHEHABI ❧

The Glistening

There are mountains on this earth
that savor the sun at the end of the day,
a sun drawn from the blurred bludgeoned
belly of the East,
spilling bleeding streaks of exile
across the rocks.

There are mountains on this earth
that breathe the white light of autumn
into hospitals
where the comfort of swollen strangers
is a reunion with love.

In the dark, worn-out night,
mountains drip secret layers of perfumed mist
into the cheeks of young girls
and the moon is a solitary man
who waits in anguish
for the unveiling of luminous violent courtyards hidden
just beneath the mountain tops.

Restless breathing mountains of the East
enclosed in swells of desert light
tumble down, like moving hymns
into the waiting lips of prayer-filled people
creating the giant hush
of an eternal resistance.

Bountiful mountains of the West
hum softly into blue slumber
and rise past the valleys strewn
with the roots of wide-eyed children
creating the deep gnawing of love,
a love which makes you want to leave your skin behind.

And where is that mountain of fire
the prophet prayed for
to separate Mecca from its enemies,
that yellow mountain, face of black,
meteor of heaven?
And where is that mountain
that will fold us inward slowly, that infinitely laboring
bald beautiful mountain,
enemy of melancholy, ally of life,
glistening darkly
in silence.

The Cemetery at Petit Saconnex

For my father

No earthbound morning is this
when we walk together
past the huge exalted folds of ancient tombstones
through an open wild mist that severs our throat
and a deep green so warm like love
past the Christian and Jewish quarters
to a piece of earth
where we bury our dead.

We talk of tombstone colors
in hushed intimate tones
you do not like gray
it does not breathe.

I wonder if you think of exile,
and how this land now fills our blood
with roots of belonging.
Later I wonder how green tombstones
and red flowers flow out of the fragrant depths of your mind.

We climb a little and approach the spot
where the soil spreads like water
over her body.
We lift our palms to pray,
but all I can think of is you in 1962
a proud man with a wound of some sort
bending to a moon layered with migrant hymns on the Potomac
dreaming of the claylike swell of the Nile
stripped by the warmth in the play of her eyes.

I see you resting beneath
eucalyptus trees
your head on her lap
your sleep filled with breezy afternoon dreams.

And through this trembling
I swear I see beautiful floods
just beneath the crescent of my brother's eyes
waiting, unnamed,
the translucent love bond between mother and son.

My mother's voice rises above the sound of waterfalls,
past a thousand orchards
of love,
she sheds the tread of pain imprisoned in her body
and drops beside you
depositing petals that glow melancholy in your ear.
And we return
to the parched blossom of time,
wrinkled with longing.

Breath

You come to me from the oldest wound of wind
traveling like a long breath across the globe
through the full July moon of a hundred sleepless nights
and centuries of dew.

You come to me from mountains
bathed by powerful, musky angels,
through the scarred throat of fog
and archways drizzled with twilight.

You come to me from minarets
rising smoothly from sky to sky
through voices of muezzins
and parched pilgrims.

You come to me from rows and rows of orange trees
rows and rows of lemon trees
rows and rows of olive trees

from the smell of sleepy earth in my love's hair
from the call to prayer at 5 a.m.
from spreading my fingers over the scars of apple trees
from hummingbirds that race into the buds of fuchsia.

Not so long ago,
you showed me how the air grows soft
when the sun crawls from rock to cloud.
Not so long ago,
you showed me the stillness of death.

And I would pray to everything sacred
and I would bow and stare deeply at the earth
and walk through old cemeteries to find the dead
softly gazing.

Sometimes, I see the beautiful broken fighter
and his lonely mother
and I see you breathe red poppies over the hills in Palestine
and I see girls with orchards of almond trees in their eyes
and old men strolling silently
among fallen villages.

And I can't say how I love my people

and I can't tell my love how to leave our land without weeping
and I can't always love this land.

People who sit by the sea
find you there through the rough water.
Others see you in the faraway crescent moon,
only to find you breakfasting at their table.
Some yearn for years
and suddenly catch you in the deepest edges of their children's eyes.

◈ Fawziyya al-Sindi ◈

Banners of the Heart

I confess
  I disperse,
        like blood shed from the soil's raindrops,
        the adapted capitals transformed in secrecy,
        between the palms of my hand,
        into platforms for collective laughter.
I wander
        my journey's provision: thirst of the deprived
        my biography: alienation to the bone
I play
        with the cold letter, the verge of possibility,
        I sing my hymns to a drop of the morning mist
        emerging from the back of a letter
                that will not kneel
        no comfort for me,
                I go forward.

2. My love
        blossomed like a forbidden love
        my arms collapsed throughout secret moments

of love,
of grief and yearning,
I burned
for the rose of your passion.

3. Ardor

wear out,
Oh! Banners of coffins spun in the heart,
this step hurts
the retreat is a nightmare looking for a foot
my feet like my heart
are masked with white hatred,
a veil dripping through heartless times.
Blood inflamed for awakening,
so, wear out
reread my heart
banners for exiled birds,
so that I can follow in my steps
wear out... wear out
the banners collide in my heart.

4. The secret

somehow, we met. Two lonely people on the
sidewalk of despair and the pricking of writing.
Rain stumbled on the echo of our steps.

Still, we

the chill of distance and virginity of water; we
shared
strangeness.

You said: The city is fear,
and daggers like birds migrate,
so seek only my shade.
My heart expanded and poured out.
Rain came, collected the evening and the
            tale's secret,
and it wasted the city.

Dialogue:
Trade me your joy
    Oh, crane to whom in meditation,
    I give the wings of blood... its remainder
    Of suitcases made of love and ceramic,
    shoes to await happiness.
Fires of my passion
    of songs glittering in the silence of poverty.
Trade me your sadness
If you wish, we would bring back the miserable sea with us.

6. Apology
    Oh, cloud dweller!
    Oh, farer in the melody of words.
    Light is not sufficient
    to kindle the secret lurking in this vein
    and the agony of metaphor,
    the hall is too narrow,
    for me to read to you
    the announcement of public death.
    So, the unveiled moment—
    the homeland that ascends in my head like a
        gallows.

    I glimpse the treading of suspicious steps at
        the end
    of the line,
    the roaring of exhausted years
    beseeches me
    I read
    Oh! courage no longer fascinates me
    chains notch my letters
    shear away my heartbeat.
    Letters stand erect in my heart
    flow as an indeclinable river,
    I collect the aroma of paths,
    to give my voice the perfume of the earth.
    I glimpse every extended hand,
    I retreat, a few steps for the creation,

the platform approaches me.
My words wave their fist and besiege me
cells of desire explode upon my lips
Recite:

"... in the name of agony that cultivates
in the hearts of people fields of wrath,
in the name of green grass emerging from
   rocks..."
               I calm down
               I resume my panic
Accept my apology,
               Oh, dweller of the mythical sea whose name is
               Word.
               My joy is wrapped around the world,
               my voice besieged as a river as it reads.

Translated by Joseph T. Zeidan

Awakening

Awaken,
               Oh, boughs of passion
               saddle the wind with your exhausted words,
Awaken,
               like roots craving the taste of salt
               like melancholic eyes, like an echo wandering in a
                  rainy night
Read
               who is there, awaiting the bitter drug in those streets?
               the dangerous ambers of life...

Stare
               you will find in me a mirage that awakens, and sleeps
               with the desert's sun.
               For my limbs are exhausted from the cold
               and the chill sun
               panting after the dead stone

Oh, chill stone,
my limbs pierce me,
they are kindled by the banners' bewildering chill,
the strong arms of a future nation.
My limbs are publicly plowed by death,
they resist,
like the panting of palm trees in this land,
this saline land,
they resist
I beseech this panic
                    to leave...
(The roads are a lighthouse,
the climate of alleys in bygone cities,
mazes
to those who cannot see the dreams of the poor
on these walls.)

Awaken

for the sweet numbness gathers my limbs
sharpens me as a spear
roaming among the heart's folds, exploding
the arteries of words.

Awaken

my voice is incapable of whispering,
it exudes blood,
perfume of the seventies,
comrades haunted by these prickings,
in doubt, I read only the soil of the past,
my blood is exuded from me.
It awakens prior to the birth... abandons me,
I search in a sinful time for a blood drop haunting me
for a diaspora that knows the taste of estrangement,
my homeland flees from me.
Who, among you, has not read the aches of his blood,
has not questioned all his cells
about the secret of its flowing which kindles this heart
secure on its throne.

I ask you,
I awoke to ask you
who among you?

(3)

Converse with me, smug time!
Shackles have baptized my limbs with murderous rust,
my boughs with doubt
        and have alienated me in my homeland
Awaken,
        Oh, handful of wind known as my homeland
        bind up your grief
        the bullet is a killer
        if I do not vomit your thirst
        ... the bullet is a killer.
        If I do not retain your blood within me,
        ... the bullet is coming
        if not...
Like the sea,   awaken
        in waves or a woman
        in my voice, the path of your wounds now burns
        my eyes are kneaded with fear,
        in them, your passion will grow
        so, awaken.

(4)

Muhammad wandered
these roads begging for a cry
pregnant with insanity—death.
You were
a child, a rose...
A book holding the sea between its palms
was reading whiteness, delirious with one flood,
a dream exposing the confession of gulls,
steps gathering rocks in a hectic time,

a homeland, upon its edges the heart leaps with pride,
and he ended up at the guillotine.

(5)

In my voice cells, you sprung up like water
you were the beginning:
a night, and you are my lighthouse
rain or shine.
I passed through childhood,
this is my youth wrapped in timidity,
how can I begin
                    when panic questions?

(6)

Oh, boughs of lust panting in my palm
awaken
on a homeland or a horizon...
You will find my eyes enchanted,
shaking the boughs of fear and love...
awaken.

Translated by Joseph T. Zeidan

❧ SUMAIYA EL-SOUSY ❧

Voices

One day, I decided to postpone believing the tale until the school bell rings.

The courtyard completely empty,
the lads' bodies filling the street with the oil of speech,
the cinchona tree stripping
a few old leaves,
postponing drowning, the colour is different—
—this departure futile—
no room for you in the lifebelt.

Her hands like the depth of Moroccan superstitions
carry the smells of the incense-spiced body
with burned *zaatar* loaves,
from a place drawing its lust with a secretive accent.
The other swells the language.
Her silence
is like the click of a chess piece being moved.
She has not decided on the next move,
to be honest the king did not fall.
A prince from a story book,
who has a grandmother's plait
dug into the evening,
the voices becoming crazy,
the prince having no way back into the story.
A primitive dance,
the clothes not included in the text nor in the letters...
I know very well what I say,
the token is confused with *Eid*'s fresh sweetness,
the little girl preparing what remains in her pocket
puts her hand
in a hole bigger than her little finger...
We celebrate:
Eid is not yours alone,

you have never been mine,
you always could have power over me—
holding my umbrella.

You, the other with no stories—
can we escape?

Translated by Atef Abu-Seif, with Nathalie Handal

Notes: *Zaatar* is a mixture of the powdered leaves of thyme, which grows on the mountain
slopes of the Levant, and other ingredients such as *summaq* and roasted sesame seeds.
Eid is Islam's New Year. Islam's most important celebration, which comes after the fasting in
Ramadan and the pilgrimage to Mecca.

﷽ LINA TIBI ﷽

A Voice

Leave me to the night
to the darkness drifting out of the sun's window,
to the dry leaves
sadly rustling,
playing airs on the bamboo flute,
sobbing in its own way...

Leave me to the absence,
letting it
open my heart
sweeping away the dust—
gently, bringing me closer to itself.

Translated by Subhi Hadidi and Nathalie Handal

If only...

If only God were a violet
opening wide in a glass of water near the bed.

If only God were the evening prayer
wiping the day off our foreheads.

If only He were a tear
that we can repent by.

If only He were a sin
that we adore.

If only God were a rose that withers every evening
so that we change it.

Translated by Subhi Hadidi and Nathalie Handal

Failure

I

I can't talk to you now.
Water and water
in the hallway of my darkness,
I saw what kindled my awakening...
I can sleep no more...
I drown, deep there, where the daylight shines.
I have water
a boat
and a lot of keys
to lose.

II

Long-necked horses chase me,

and make their way across my path.
All that I see is over-stretching, overflowing,
slipping away and expanding.
All that I see is lost in the vision.

Water.
Water streaming in the midst of my ablution,
sweeping me away from my prayers.
I pray for the morrow,
and each day for which I pray shall be dead,
born, then dead.

(...)

Light me a lantern,
let me see my hand.
Light up this darkness, let it die out.
You shall have my hand saved for you:
let it rise to reach you.

Each time
I am unable, I fall silent.
I scatter speech,
with my lips recollect it, cry over it.
Water rose high over the sand,
and I rose too, for thus I sleep.

III

Because I cannot disclose everything
I watch them slip away.
Because I left them untended
they blossomed in the wilderness
and withered in my flowerpot.

Sleep in resurrection:
and now,
only now,
I see the resurrection.

Across merciful soil I run,
splitting apart its dust.
I can do nothing.
These waves that rise up
drown me.

Soaked. Salty.
I left my boat behind—
all that remains is no more mine,
all that I have is what I lost in the flood.

Whenever your name is far away
I will stretch my loneliness
a bed,
for you to sleep.

Translated by Subhi Hadidi and Nathalie Handal

Suicide

The mouth that gave me your voice,
was nothing but a shadow on the water—
the morning—a witness,
I—water.

Have you seen
your voice, your voice given to me,
abandoning the shadow?
Have you seen me becoming its water?

The farther away you get,
the more your shadow
becomes your cup of coffee,
the more the cup becomes a shadow
shivering under the sun.

Have you seen the morning arrive
and steal me off to your shadow?
I tremble,
become the terror lurking in the garden,
a fish fleeing the night.

Did you see?
The farther your shadow goes,
the closer I approach.
I take refuge in the last cup of coffee,
where I hide my weakness.

The night saber breaks down its shadows,
takes me out toward shadeless mornings
where I come closer...
Did you see me,
no longer touching your shadow?
I became the bier reluctant to leave you,
the bier killing itself willingly
hungry for the sand of God.

Translated by Subhi Hadidi and Nathalie Handal

XXVII

Striding, shuddering
I leave behind a summer, a winter.
The inner mind I shut down,
my call loud,
yet silence quenches my thirst, and that's my voice,
that's my cruelty having me adopted in time.
I walk and shatter into pieces,
the air swiftly passes by
and snatches the fluff of childhood.
The gleam shrieks, smashes the window.
The fist of time—passing.
The tremor of water.

I hunt for news, all alone in the abyss.
Let me have your hand...
The air penetrates deeply into sleep,
opens my window up to the splitting night.
Let not my soul cross, let it not be measured by fever.
It is just an idea,
that one might have another hand while dying.

It is only when listening to you
that I love my life.

Translated by Subhi Hadidi and Nathalie Handal

❧ NADIA TUÉNI ❧

Beirut

Let her be courtesan, scholar or saint,
a peninsula of din, of color and of gold,
a hub of rose sailing like a fleet
which scans the horizon for a harbor's tenderness.
Beirut has died a thousand times and been reborn a thousand times.
Beirut of a hundred palaces, Beryte of the stones
where pilgrims from everywhere have raised statues
that make men pray and wars begin.

Her women have eyes like beaches where lights shine by night,
and her beggars are ancient as Pythonesses.
In Beirut each thought inhabits a mansion.
In Beirut each word is a drama.
In Beirut, thoughts deliver filibusters of the mind,
and caravans bear priestesses and sultans' wives.
Let her be nun or sorceress or both,
or let her be the hinge
of the sea's portal or the gateway to the East,

let her be adored or let her be cursed,
let her be thirsty for blood or holy water,
let her be innocent or let her be a murderess.
By being Phoenician, Arabic or of the people—
Levantine—or of such dizzying variety
as strange and fragile flowers atop stems,
Beirut is the last place in the Orient
where man can dress himself in light.

Cedars

I salute you,
you who draw life
from a single root
with the night as your watchdog.
Your rustlings have the splendor of words
and the supremacy of cataclysms.
I know you,
you who are
hospitable as memory;
you wear the grief of the living
because this side of time is time as well.
I spell your name,
you who are
unique as *The Song of Songs.*
A great cold enfolds you,
and heaven itself is in reach of your branches.
I defy you,
you who wail in our mountains
so that we hear the sound in our blood.
Today, which is yesterday's tomorrow,
crosses your forms like a setting star.
I love you,
you who depart with the wind as your banner.
I love you as man loves breath.
You are the first poem.

Baalbeck

When the sun strikes a tall dead tree
and when the moon blossoms,
the roads of Baalbeck know the blueness of dances;
things are coated with silence like oil.
Stones and the universe reveal secrets.
Memories ride on horseback like heavily armored knights,
pulling prayers and gods behind them down the roads.
Night comes out of its dark cell
like a vulture from a white repose—
Heliopolis under storm clouds.
Beneath each column a sleeping star
bursts into double novæ on the peak of noon.
Its language luminous, its gestures architectural,
Baalbeck is a gift from the world of measures.

Tripoli

This is the city of three leaves.
Wide as a smile,
it offers neither temples nor prayers to make the earth turn.
It is like a sea that reveals a ship
as plainly as the sky accepts a bird.
Ancient troubadours sang at its dawn.
It is where the orange tree inherits history.
Man and death live in an hourglass of love.
Tripoli is a fort outlined in pencil.
The narrow souks roll up like a headdress
secured with pins of spun sugar.
The alleyways dance with color.
Here the fishermen, sons of Paladins,
spread out their nets each morning like fine garments.
Here the minarets speak to us of voyages.
Here time at times takes the wrong road.

In the Lebanese Mountains

Remember—the noise of moonlight
when the summer night collides with a peak
and traps the wind
in the rocky caves of the mountains of Lebanon.

Remember—a town on a sheer cliff
set like a tear on the rim of an eyelid;
one discovers there a pomegranate tree
and rivers more sonorous
than a piano.

Remember—the grapevine under the fig tree,
the cracked oak that September waters,
fountains and muleteers,
the sun dissolving in river currents.

Remember—basil and apple tree,
mulberry syrup and almond groves.
Each girl was a swallow then
whose eyes moved like a gondola
swung from a hazel branch.

Remember—the hermit and goatherd,
paths that rise to the edge of a cloud,
the chant of Islam, crusaders' castles,
and wild bells ringing through July.

Remember—each one, everyone,
storyteller, prophet and baker,
the words of the feast and words of the storm,
the sea shining like a medal in the landscape.

Remember—the child's recollection
of a secret kingdom just our age.
We did not know how to read the omens
in those dead birds in the bottom of their cages,
in the mountains of Lebanon.

Tuéni's poems translated from the French by Samuel Hazo

❧ FADWA TUQAN ❧

A Prayer to the New Year

In our hands is a fresh yearning for you,
in our eyes songs of praise and unique melodies,
into your hand as choral offerings we will thrust them.
O you who emerge as a sweet fountain of hope,
O you who are rich with promise and desire.
What is in store for us that you hold?
What have you got?

⁓

Give us love, for with love the treasures of bounty within us
burst forth...
With love our songs will grow green and will flower
and will spring with gifts
riches
fertility.

⁓

Give us love, so we may build the collapsed universe within us
anew
and restore
the joy of fertility to our barren world.

⁓

Give us wings to open the horizons of ascent,
to break free from our confined cavern, the solitude
                                        of iron walls.
Give us light, to pierce the deepest darkness
and with the strength of its brilliant flow
we will push our steps to a precipice
from which to reap life's victories.

Translated by Samira Kawar

Elegy of a Knight
To Gamal Abdul Nasser

-1-

SEPTEMBER

Death's carnival was at its height, Amman
transformed into a coffin and a grave.
The tyrants drunken and enraptured
by what the sea of insanity washed up.
The fishing nets were full
one thousand slaughtered, two thousand, thousands.
Any more to come?
Give us more, O insane sea.
Death's desire burns brightly,
give us more, for the table
has been laid, blood's wine enlivens them, and this day
is a feast.
Give us your catch, O sea, for this day is a feast,
Oh what a feast!

-2-

THE REDEEMER

In the paroxysm of blood and fire, and the flood of insanity,
the redeemer, love's prophet, spread his hands over us
and redeemed us.
Oh, how costly the redemption
he brought us!
Oh, how high the price!
Beset by the pricking nails of pain
and by fatigue's cutting knives
he laid down his head and lowered
his eyelashes and fell asleep...
His eyes filled with visions of love and dreams of peace.

~

Oh, it was not time for him to dismount.
The bereaved mare twisted beyond grief.
Her eyes roamed across
the roaring ocean of crushed humanity.
Who would redeem her hero?
Who would release the dear manacled knight
from the fetters of death? Who would restore him,
the haggard lover, to the saddle, the arena?
Who would restore him?
The bereaved mare twisted beyond grief
and exposed her sorrow with sigh upon sigh.
Who would release the dear manacled knight?
Oh, it was not time for him to dismount.

~

Said the wind: He shall come,
his death is birth, he shall surely come
with the sun in his hands, the very same sun,
and in his eyes a yearning, the same yearning and passion
of devotion.
From the wounds of the earth he shall come,
from the years of famine he shall come,
from the ashes of death he shall come,
his death is birth, he shall surely come.

Translated by Samira Kawar

◈ NAJAAT AL-UDWANY ◈

A Boat on the Pacific

Age is wheat chaff
that shudders
in the palms of the tempest.
Hence, I ride the poems,
I follow the winds...

The fish toil with a moon
that rolled off my two palms,
wearing the cape of night,
and wandering in the songs.

The rose of its mouth
on my body,
and around us the sea
on fire.

We merged—a male bird
with a female bird—
fleeing two jaws
crushing the jasmine
on a slave girl's bosom.

The waft of trees was
his path,
his hand reached for my dress
roses fell off,
and from his breath
I hurried
gathering the beads of my scattered necklace.

We were covered with water and roses,
we dozed off:
a woman's moan in smoke,
—extinguished lanterns

holding on to the arms of the street—
marching naked on the palm of the dollar.
She wrapped around her waist
Abi Jahl's headgear
and she danced
over a broken helmet.

In our wings
the fuzz fluttered,
the sea became
a boat.
We spread out our wings
over the sails,
her gloomy face disappeared
in the dyes.
Her wound kept following us,
her breasts fleeing the harbors of life.

She is calling upon us
to come to her bosom,
which is swollen with woes!

Translated by Moulouk Berry and Ali Farghaly

Butterflies of Anxiety

A vein under my skin
Sneaking.
Your blood,
which reminds me of the swords
of the Arabians' slaughtering.
The prophets
and their camels
pierce me.

I close my window
off a street

from which blows
the waft of slain tears,

and off a woman
whose communion with the beloved,
has stolen her blood.

How am I to meet you
while you are armed with
swords and armaments,

and how am I to embrace
a face turning to illusions
away from me,
showing me
—from heaven and hell—
paintings twisting around my neck,
uncovering the veils off my soul?

My body sways between
a smile,
and the tooth—
between the piece of *al-marqrud*
and the hammer of hate?

To whom should I raise my complaints about you?
And our prayers no longer belong to one Lord?

Should I split my blood
from a species to which you belong?

Extend to me
a song
by which I would comb the lashes of the night...

The butterflies of anxiety
overflow around me.

Should I doze off once
while your hand passes like a rose over my mouth?

O Mother!
extend to me your face
to swim in it
with two eyes in which sleeplessness
has nested.

I am
incapable of swimming.

I burned my boats
and I have not found behind me
a sea
nor found
before me someone to fight!

Translated by Moulouk Berry and Ali Farghaly

Note: *al-maqrud* is a Tunisian sweet.

Carthage

I am the desert
between my folds—
the memory laments.

The sea had risen
between us,

you have never left
the tongues of utterances.
Over a butterfly's wing
we used to meet.

And now,
no sea,
no whistles,
no wings...
—between us—
a castle
which buries my dreams
in the winds...

How could the wound heal
while my cottage cries:
cover me with your wings of roses?

You are there,
standing tall
in the face of those coming to you—
pilgrims and tourists.

They said:
you are the daughter of a woman,
ruined by her fidelity.

Here I am,
another woman,
burning inside a shell...
Would you accept
my suicide?

Translated by Moulouk Berry and Ali Farghaly

❧ THURAYYA AL–URAYYID ❧

Thirst

When your longing spans the earth
an ancient root
thirsty for a drop of water...
When faces are once again
reduced to shadows of silence and loneliness
do you ask about me
my blood pouring forth into the question?

Was Life ours one day?
Did we chase the coursing pulse of streams?
Did sparks of Light set our dreams ablaze?

Here we are
today, at the crossroads of separateness...
Thirsting, body and shadow.
Apart as earth and sky.
United by separation.
Forever moored on the margins of knowledge.
Deep in the cloud of illusion.
Together tending an impossible dream.

When I glimpse the prancing of a doe in the grass,
innocent as my dreams
my heart skips.

My heart leaps wildly
when in the dusty expanse of sky
the sun reflects a glimmering seagull
a flash of wings
then she is gone.

Here, I stay behind in the pale shadows.
A seagull with wings bound,

a soul yearning for far horizons,
in the grip of shackles
transfixed.

Translated by Farouk Mustafa, with the author

In the Stealth of Stillness

Do we see in what we see
anything but what we wish to be?
Maybe...

When my soul is overrun
by the yearnings for my self,
do I find it reflected in others' eyes?
Maybe...

Did I ever see it
as flashes trailing raining clouds?
Shattered mirrors
flying splinters
the stillness crashing?
Maybe....

My body standing between me and myself,
how can I transcend it?

When the fog of silence fills my eyes,
how can I still see?

When I listen to my echoes, my silence,
the fear of death gripping me—
is my soul killing me with my own voice
or centuries of forced silence choking my voice?

Will the mystery remain hostage to my intuition—
deluded in the myth of my past and fables of the future?

Is my birth and my death
an abridgement of my life?

When I look for my self
and see you boasting about it
do I lose it since you have it?
Should I make light of it?
Or is it that, when you sing its praise—
we become?

Wherever the distances keep calling us,
is the secret of the walk in the distance?
Are the echoes of the secret within us?
When we draw near, run away
or when the distances collapse within us?

When we deny it
when I erase you from my being
and when you erase me.
Does myself still remain myself?

I defy it—it doesn't mind my being buried alive in it,
it defies me.
I cancel it.
Sometimes I ransom it
whenever I can't kill it within me
and I see her in my blood,
a little girl, victorious.

Perhaps that which is left of it...
Ecstasy of the heart
was no sin
as they told us one day
when it came pouring out of the eyes.
Perhaps you were no illusion
as I had thought.
Perhaps I was no figment of a wild imagination,
rather we were together, without a doubt,

victims,
my soul whispers
in the stealth of stillness.

Translated by Farouk Mustafa, with the author

❧ LORENE ZAROU–ZOUZOUNIS ❧

Embroidered Memory

Arabic tapestry embroidered
into my soul
      is my memory
        of home

Red on black pyramids
octagons, lines and vines
each village distinct
bedouin purple and fuchsia
red poppies and tulips
my mother, sixteen—creating
vibrant peacocks on linen
circle around
down, up
up, down
A fine needle in and out
An artist's tool piercing
fabric, weaving culture

Women of this art
fill my heart with hues of
red and orange fruit orchards
filling the air with aroma
of a culture of olive,
almond and fig groves

kept safe and warm
in the many suns
and many moons
        of a chosen land

Sacred grounds belonging
to holy men and women
of ancient days, of new days
bathing in the heat of their
        many suns
fantasizing in the light of their
        many moons

Oasis in the center of the world
Timeless paradise, center of my heart
Hermitage beneath the sky's palms
and mountain's waterfalls
implanting fresh thoughts
forming a cool memory
so vivid amidst
wind and splash

Wandering child in a land
        of stars and sand
of milk and honey
embroidering my memory
intricate arrays of vibrant
magentas and blues in valleys
Scents of wild anise, jasmine
Visions of prophets
Gibran and his cedar trees
on mighty mountains
        finding a childhood
among the poplars, oaks
finding past lives

A common thread
of memory beyond eyes

Stories of truth and myth
taken aback, my time
in lost and kept time
Memory fine as a needle
growing with design
            to touch, wear, display
                a memory
                of home

Her Heart is a Rose Petal and her Skin is Granite

A woman refugee arms herself with pride and faith
generation after generation
occupation after occupation
still thriving, giving birth and love
fights for her right
with all her might

A Palestinian woman
made of stone, water and light
sustains like the earth's oceans and trees
withstanding abuse and being taken for granted

She exhibits what a true female of God
a goddess
can really do, say and stand for
while an ever-present force so powerful
as to change a culture and a nation
breathes through her very soul

She heals the wounds of a broken family
after an adolescent, regretful Israeli soldier
loses his humanness
but only temporarily
while his innocent child victim
loses humanness permanently

She journeys through a lonely desert
no longer hers
to imagine kissing her husband's tortured body
after not knowing his whereabouts
only to return home to a one-room tent,
five hungry children,
and greeted by enemy handcuffs

She endures torture while pregnant in prison
for carrying on where her incarcerated
freedom-fighter husband left off
giving birth to a child that survives this hell
because inside this woman, all along, is a white light
and an eternal flame that exists in the child
who carries on where mother left off

She stands up against steel bullets coated in rubber
faces her occupier head on to defend herself,
her family, her people and homeland
then turns her back to resume
a daily life in the fields,
fetch water from a well that has run dry
tend to children sickened by open contaminated sewers
running along their front door or curtain

A Palestinian woman has her heart that bleeds rose petals
in a bloodstream of tainted water
and sweats the colors black, green, white and red
through a granite skin that stretches
but never breaks

❧ AMIRA EL-ZEIN ❧

The Land of Mirrors

When your water reaches me,
the cup trembles
and throngs of people vanish from my sight.
When I drink the water
the snow melts.
Longing for the water
rings of gold unfasten.

I enter the cup
and join the rings and return to you,
O land of mirrors,
led to you by women
whose coughing blows the air
and covers me with dust.
When I reach you, I hear
the rain fall from my being
and I see the streams of my valleys
swell and flow toward your mouth
and see your houses
hanging in the mirror,
glowing between two suns,
their curtains neither open nor shut,
between a question of darkness
and a reply of light.
I enter, I enter a boat of gold
and return to you,
O land of mirrors.
The strands of my pain sprout.
I see in the mirror a skein of gold.
I hug it and untie it
and hold the thread.
It writhes with pain with the needle.
As I darn my dress in the land of mirrors,

the river flows from my dress.
As the thread rises and falls with my breath,
the cloth becomes tight
and my feet wither
while the streams of my valleys swell
and flow toward your mouth,
O land of mirrors.

I return to you without memory
to see you as dough in the hands of women
and see you flee toward the fire
and burn without memory.
Shall I gaze into the mirror,
to drink my coffee and invent
a memory for you?
Shall I gaze, to find
the horizon in smoke,
to find myself clothed
with the feathers of a black raven
and the sky drinking coffee with me?
I weep to see you burning
with my memory.

I have forgotten that I was
a river in your earth.

Is this the reason why I rage and cry
from head to toe?
Is this the reason why all the colors
of my forests turn dark
longing to your suns?
Is this the reason why I see you
without my memory
as rings of gold open one by one
and are thrown into the water?

Yesterday, I lifted the veil of fate
and gazed into its depths

and saw obscurities teaming
with creatures of the dark,
using their claws for mirrors,
leaving your hills an eaten cluster of grapes.
Do your moons hide from me to test themselves?

O land of mirrors,
I hid my garden in my pocket
and said, "Tomorrow I will write you a poem."
When I awoke, I found the old chief of my memory
shaking hands with the sacred tree
and conversing with it.
O chief, how did you fill my poem
with the leaves of the tree?
How did you dig up the past
like a piece of cloth you folded
and threw under my window—
bits of my memory:
squares, triangles, pyramids, a pinch of salt—
while I wept and wrote my poem for you?

I open the rings of gold
and throw them in the water,
saying, "I will find you."

O land of mirrors,
the howling of the wolf
reaches me from your valleys,
bringing me news of tall giants
who carry your body to the horizon's pit.
The singing of sparrows
reaches me from your mountains.
Water rises in my mouth
like bare trees.
Ah! I choke, I bend, I double up with pain.
The pain comes to me
and when it goes away,
the water flows.

Your breezes come to me and touch me
while a headache rolls over me
like stones from your mountain peaks.

How can I return to you,
now that you are without memory?
A liquid voice comes to me, asking,
"How did you write your poem?
And why do people whisper around me
and wild flowers shake their heads?"
I shiver with cold and dig up
the floor of my room
to see you lying
in the grave of my memory,
O land of mirrors!

Translated by Husain Haddawy

⚜ SABAH AL-KHARRAT ZWEIN ⚜

Tableau 66
From The Inclined House

I have already lost the style and maze of language. I have already fallen in the death of speech, in speech I was unable to say, and even had I been able to say, I would have died, my voice remained in my heart, and my sonority remained within, I remember the window that was always closed, the same window that saw me dying within, the glass, the glass that reflected my faded shadow and my sunken face, the window that saw me twist and embrace my pain, I was in the setting of language, only a few features on the walls, only markings of madness in the corners of the hall, the deadly silence, and the tyrannical time which has not passed was stacking up on the inner and outer glass, time stacked up in the labyrinth of my place, time was tyrannical, and we were in the haziness of the place, on the edge of that window, we were shackled by the reduction of the text, we said nothing, we only looked at the remnants of the outside when the night became wet, and inside we gazed at our silence, and the place inside was inclined, I could see but remnants of us, our pale shadows on the yellowish walls, the shadows of memories, the hall sank in the memories of pictures, the body remained in its laceration, looming between one gesture and another. Those gestures reduced speech, and the text was being completed in silence, and became secluded in the wounds of speech, language was unable to express itself, it was in the incapacity of our time and space, we were looking around beyond the window from time to time, we were seeing remnants of houses, gazing at our incomplete faces, we were embracing the falsehood of space and the fragility of our hours.

Translated by Kaissar Afif

From As if in Flaw, or in the Flaw of Space

An abysmal circle is in the sky. At the moment we are an infinite line
    headed towards it.

~

Your few moments uplift me to a whiteness that we know. This is our
    whiteness.

~

One diminished form is headed toward the abyss.
But the line is spreading toward it.

~

That is how I see you in my center whenever I want to approach. But
    whenever
I want to approach, we vanish.

~

I see you throwing yourself in the hollow circle; time has stopped in
    your space.

~

In my disappointments, I rise daily to the crest of your solitude.

~

You glimpse at me as if we have become one open line headed towards the bottom.
I glimpse at you as if the purity of our encounter accumulates within me.

~

As if it was one more time and always.

~

The form was dwindling.

~

Emptiness is in the center.
There is an anguish in the expansion of the particles.

~

The decline is linked to the lower movement.
We only have to add the doors to the inner motion.

~

I have started to lose the form of the lines.
I was not able to lean.

~

Every particle separates daily.
Nothing enters eternity.

~

She was holding a bouquet of light in her hand.

~

So that I finish, the day was about to finish.
I put my upright body facing the white wall.

~

I was always seen from behind.
The white body against the brightness was light and elevated.
Darkness was sneaking.

~

I am aslant, I always bend in that direction.
Then, I turn into the dwindling light.

~

Now I stand below the arch of the old window, the opposite window.
Today, the face is in the sky.

Translated by Kaissar Afif

ABOUT THE POETS

Elmaz Abi-Nader is a poet and writer of Lebanese origin. She got her Ph.D. at the University of Nebraska in fiction and non-fiction writing, and an M.F.A. in poetry at Columbia University. Abi-Nader has taught at the University of Nebraska, State University of New York at Albany, John Jay College–CUNY, San Jose State University; she is currently associate professor in the English department at Mills College, California. She has won many awards and honors, including a faculty development grant, the Quigley Summer fellowship at Mills College, and the *Best All-Around Award*—Writers' Harvest, Share Our Strength, Annapolis. Her work has been published in numerous magazines and anthologies, and she is the author of *The Children of the Roojme, A Family's Journey* (W.W. Norton, 1991), and a poetry book, *In the Country of My Dreams* (Sufi Warrior Publishing,1999). Abi-Nader has also written a storytelling performance, *Country of Origin.*

Huda Ablan was born in 1971 in Yemen. She obtained a B.A. in political science and economics from Sana'a University in 1993. Her work has appeared in numerous newspapers and literary journals all over the Arab world. She has been invited to numerous literary festivals, and is a member of many writers' organizations including the Yemen Writers' Association. She is the author of three books of poetry.

Fawziyya Abu-Khalid was born on August 17, 1955 to a traditional Bedouin family in Riyadh, Saudi Arabia. She obtained a degree in sociology at the American University of Beirut, then went to Lewis and Clark College in Portland, Oregon (1985), and is currently a second year Ph.D. student in the sociology department of the University of Manchester. She was a lecturer at King Saudi University in Riyadh from 1985–1996. Abu-Khalid teaches interdisciplinary courses in sociology and literature. In the past seventeen years, she has published over 200 articles on social, political, and literary issues, in numerous daily newspapers, weekly, monthly and periodical magazines in Saudi Arabia and the Arab world. Abu-Khalid has published three poetry books, including: *Ila Mata Yakhtatifunaki Lailat al-Urs?* (Until when will they abduct you on your wedding night?; Beirut, 1973), which was attacked by critics in Lebanon and banned entry into Saudi Arabia, and *Secret Reading in the History of Arab Silence.*

Zulaykha Abu-Risha is Jordanian, born in Palestine, and raised in Syria and Jordan. She is a poet, researcher, journalist, and activist. She obtained a B.A. in Arabic language and literature and an M.A. in Arabic literature from the University of Jordan, and received a diploma in education and a diploma in Islamic studies from the Islamic Studies Institute in Cairo. Abu-Risha has done extensive research on Arab women's issues, and is recognized at an international and national level by the UNIFEM (United Nations Development Fund For Women) as an expert in gender and the status of Arab women. She has published numerous poetry books, namely: *Water Gypsies, Shelling of Disguise, Mud Text, Memory, He Who Landed On Earth, His Holy Names, The Afflicted Anger, No Body But the Crazy Says*. She has published a book of short stories entitled *In the Cell,* and she has also published more than twelve books of and on children's literature; and also numerous essays and books of literary criticism and feminist thought, namely, *The Absent Language: Non-Sexist Language*. She is currently living in England, where she is finishing her Ph.D. at the University of Exeter, on the image of women in novels by Arab women in the twentieth century.

Etel Adnan was born in 1925 in Beirut, of a Syrian Muslim father and Greek mother. She studied philosophy at the University of Paris, at U.C. Berkeley, and at Harvard. Adnan taught the philosophy of art and humanities at Dominican College in San Rafael, California from 1958 to 1972. She is a bilingual poet and writer (French and English) and a painter and tapestry designer with an international reputation. In 1984 she was commissioned to write the French part of the multi-language opera *Civil Wars* by the American stage creator Robert Wilson, which was performed at the Lyon Opera House and in Paris. She has also written the texts for two documentaries on the war in Lebanon that were shown on French television as well as in Europe and Japan. Her work has been published worldwide, and she is the author of more than twelve books, most of which have been published by the Post-Apollo Press in California: *The Arab Apocalypse* (poetry), *Sitt Marie-Rose* (novel; winner of the France Pays-Arabes Award in Paris; translated into six languages), *Of Cities and Women* (Letters to Fawwaz), *Paris, When It's Naked* (fiction), *The Indian Never Had a Horse & Other Poems, The Spring Flowers Own & The Manifestations of the Voyage* (poetry), *Journey to Mount Tamalpais* (essay), *From A to Z* (poetry), *Moonshots* (poetry), *Five Senses for One Death* (poetry), *"Jebu" Suivi de "L'Express Beyrouth—Enfer"* (poetry), *Pablo Neruda is a Banana Tree* (poetry) and most recently, *There: In the Light and the Darkness of the Self and of the Other*. Adnan lives in Paris, Lebanon, and California.

Laila 'Allush is an Arab-Israeli. Her work has appeared in many magazines and journals in the Arab world. She is the author of two books of poetry: *Spices on the Open Wound* and *Years of Drought, My Heart*.

Lamia Abbas Amara was born on December 5, 1927 in Baghdad, Iraq. In 1950, she received a B.A. in Arabic literature from the Higher Teachers' Training College, Baghdad, Iraq. She later became the vice-representative in the Iraqi Delegation to UNESCO in Paris, from 1974 to 1976. Then Amara returned to Iraq and was appointed Director of Arts and Literature at Technology University, Baghdad. Her work has appeared in numerous magazines sand newspapers since 1944, and she has received a number of prizes including the Lebanese Cedar Medal. She has published more than seven books of poetry, and currently resides in San Diego, California.

'Aisha Arnaout was born in Damascus, Syria on October 13, 1946. A poet and short story writer, Arnaout studied French literature at the University of Damascus, and worked in children's programming at the Syrian National Television. She has continuously been involved in national projects fostering creative talents among children, including collective poetry writing and painting. Her work has appeared in many literary magazines in the Middle East, and she has published three collections of poetry.

S.V. Atalla is a poet and translator. Her work has appeared in *Prairie Schooner, Mediterraneans, Passport, Two Lines*, and others. She currently lives in California.

Thérèse 'Awwad was born in Beirut in 1933. She studied in the French Lycée for Young Girls in Beirut and then went to Paris to finish her higher education. Her work has appeared in numerous magazines and journals in Beirut and throughout the Arab world. She has published several books, namely, *Cobwebs* (poetry) and *The Pulley* (a play). 'Awwad lives in Rashana, a Lebanese mountain village.

Fadhila Chabbi was born on January 24, 1946 in a town in southwestern Tunisia bordering the Sahara. Her work has been published in newspapers and literary journals throughout the Arab world. She has been invited to read her poetry at literary conferences and festivals all over the Arab world, and in Paris, Spain, and Italy. Her work has also been translated into many languages, namely, French and Italian. She is the author of numerous books of poetry.

Andrée Chedid was born in 1921 in Cairo, of Syrian-Lebanese parents. Chedid was educated in French schools and then studied at the American University in Cairo. She moved to Paris in 1946, where she still lives. Chedid has published nineteen collections of poetry, nine novels, five plays, three collections of short stories, and other writings. She has been awarded numerous important prizes in literature: The Louis Lapier Award for Poetry (1976), the Aigle d'Or for Poetry (1972), The Royal Belgian Academy Grand Prize for French Literature (1975), the Mallarmé Award for Poetry (1976), and the Goncourt Prize for her collection, *Les Corps et le Temps* (Bodies and Time, 1978). Chedid was awarded an honorary doctorate by the American University in Cairo in 1988. Her work has been translated into many languages.

Siham Da'oud is an Arab-Israeli writer. She grew up in the sixties, in the only Palestinian family in the Jewish neighborhood of Ramla (a very prosperous Palestinian metropolis before 1948). Da'oud started publishing at sixteen in the literary supplement of the daily newspaper of the Israeli Community Party, *al-Ittihad*. She moved to Tel Aviv after finishing her high school, and then to Haifa, where she has been living for almost 25 years now. Her work has appeared in numerous journals and magazines, as well as her collection of poetry, *I Love in White Ink*. Da'oud currently works for Arabesque Publishing House.

Safaa Fathy was born on July 17, 1958 in Minia, Egypt. She received a degree in theater studies from the Paris VIII, St Denis in 1985, and then a Ph.D. on Brecht and Britain's epic theater (John Arden and Edward Bond) from the Sorbonne in 1993. Fathy's poems are published in numerous Arabic journals and magazines, and her articles on theater and poetry have appeared in many French and other European literary and cultural magazines. She has directed eight plays, most recently, her play, *Terror* in 1995, and *New Voices in Arabic Poetry* in Paris in 1996 (stage production in French and Arabic). She has also worked on numerous documentaries; *Hidden Faces* (made for British television in 1991) won many prizes at different festivals, including the festival in Créteil and in Chicago. Her two poetry books are *Little Wooden Dolls...* and *...and One Night.* She has also published plays and edited anthologies, and is co-author with Jacques Derrida of a book that is forthcoming in 2000. Fathy resides in Paris.

Mona Fayad graduated from the University of Illinois with a Ph.D. in comparative literature. She has taught graduate and undergraduate classes in women's studies, post-colonial studies, and Arabic and English literature at a number of universities in the United States, including UCLA, Colorado College, and Oregon State University. Recently, Fayad completed a novel, *Chameleon Tracks,* set partly in the Middle East and partly in the United States, and dealing with the experience of an immigrant family. She is a regular contributor to the Arab-American arts and culture journal, *Al Jadid.* Fayad currently teaches in the English department at Salem State College, Massachussetts.

Claire Gebeyli is originally Greek, born in 1930 in Alexandria, Egypt. She married a Lebanese and has lived most of her life in Lebanon. She writes fiction, billets, and poetry, and has won numerous awards. Gebeyli is presently an associate editor of the Lebanese French daily *L'Orient-le Jour.* She also lectures in francophone literature at St. Joseph University in Beirut.

Noujoum al-Ghanim is the author of two books of poetry: *The Evening of Paradise* and *Transgressions.* She lives in Abu-Dhabi.

Nada el-Hage was born in Beirut on May 9, 1958. She graduated from the Sorbonne with a degree in philosophy. She then returned to Lebanon where she started her artistic career with a role in *Jesus' Judgment,* a play directed by Raymond Gebara. Her first poems were published in the late seventies in *Annahar Al A'rabi Wal Dawli.* From 1981 until 1995, al-Haj was editor of the cultural column in the monthly magazine *Fairuz,* published by Dar Al Sayyad. She translated from French into Lebanese dialect important plays such as: *The Tot Family* by Stephen Orkini (1982), *Life Is a Dream* by Calderon (1984), *The Border House* and *The Patients* by Marojik and Odeberti (1985). Many of the plays were later directed by Joseph Bou Nasser for the Professional Local Theater, established in 1981. She also translated with May Menassa, Nada Tuéni's collection of poems,

Sentimental Archives of a War in Lebanon. She has published three books of poetry: *Prayer in the Wind* (1988), *Touches of the Soul* (1994), and *Journey of the Shadow* (1998). She lives in Lebanon.

Laila Halaby is the daughter of a Jordanian father and American mother. She was born in Lebanon, grew up mainly in Arizona, and lived for brief periods in Jordan and Italy. Halaby received a B.A. in Arabic and Italian, and a minor in French from Washington University. She then graduated with an M.A. in Arabic literature from UCLA, and an M.A. in school counseling from Loyola Marymount University. She is fluent in all of the above languages and also in Spanish. Her work has appeared in numerous anthologies and literary journals, including *Food for Our Grandmothers, Emergences, Rattlesnake Review, Mr. Cognito, Tucson Weekly,* and *The Space Between Our Footsteps.* She has finished a novel, *Flowers from My Roza,* narrated by three adolescent girls, all first cousins, who are separated from one another by distance and culture (Hala is in the United States and Jordan; Mawal is in the West Bank; Soraya is in the U.S.); and *Tracks in the Sand,* a collection of Arab folktales gathered on tape and in writing from Palestinian and Jordanian children whom she met in private, government, and UNRWA (United Nations Relief and Works Agency) schools. Halaby currently resides in Los Angeles with her husband, Raik, and their son, Raad.

Suheir Hammad was born in Jordan to Palestinian refugee parents in October 1973. She lived in Beirut for a brief period during the civil war and then moved with her family to Brooklyn. In 1995, she was co-recipient of the Audre Lorde Poetry Award at Hunter College in New York City. She also received an honorary mention in the Morris Center Poetry Award for her poem "nothin to waste," included in this anthology. Her work has appeared in many anthologies and magazines, and she has given numerous readings. Hammad is the author of *Drops of this Story* (essays, 1996) and *born Palestinian, born Black* (poetry, 1996). She is currently working on a new collection of poetry, *zaatar diva,* on a novel, and editing *Butter Phoenix,* a literary magazine.

Nathalie Handal was born on July 29, 1969. She has lived in the United States, Europe, the Caribbean, and has traveled extensively in the Middle East and Eastern Europe. Poet, writer, and literary researcher, she is presently living between Boston and London, where she a researcher in the English and drama department at the University of London, and a chair of the Pushkin Club (Russian Literary Center). She has an M.A. in literature and a B.A in international relations and communications from Simmons College in Boston, Massachusetts. Her work has appeared in numerous magazines, literary journals, and anthologies in the United States, Europe, and the Arab world. She has also interviewed many American writers including Allen Ginsberg and Charles Simic. Handal has read/performed poetry widely, and has given lectures on Ethnic-American literature at the Sorbonne, Yarmouk University, University of Jordan, University of London, and numerous other universities and conferences worldwide. Her book of poetry, *The Never Field*, is published by The Post-Apollo Press, California; and *Traveling Rooms*, a CD of her poetry and music by Russian musicians, Vladimir Miller and Alexandr Alexandrov, was produced in the United Kingdom, and released in 1999. She is currently finishing an *Anthology of Arab-American Literature*, and a second book of poetry.

Dima Hilal was born in Beirut, Lebanon, and has lived most of her life in California. Halal obtained a B.A. in English with a focus on writing and poetry at the University of California, Berkeley. Her work has appeared in various journals and anthologies, and she has given a number of readings, including an appearance on NPR's radio program, *Flashpoints,* with host June Jordan.

Hoda Hussein is a poet, novelist, and translator, who was born in Cairo in 1972. She received a degree in literature and French from Cairo University in 1993. Her work has appeared in many journals in Egypt, the Arab world, Switzerland, and France. She is the author of two books of poetry: *Let it Be* (1996) and *Once Upon a Time* (1998). Hussein has also published a novel, *Amiba's Lesson* (1998), and translated the short stories of Marguerite Duras (1996) and two novels by Annie Ernauld.

Donia el-Amal Ismail was born in 1971 in Egypt of Palestinian parents. Since 1994, she has lived in Gaza, where she works as a journalist. She has written many book reviews for Palestinian and Arab newspapers and magazines. Ismail published two books of poetry: *Everything is Separate* (Cairo, 1996) and *The Resonance of Solitude* (Gaza, 1999). She has also published an autobiographical account, *I Have Seen Gaza*, which describes her return to Palestine after 23 years in exile. She is a member of the Palestinian Writers' Union, and founding member of the Group for Creativity in Gaza.

'**Enayat Jaber** is a Lebanese poet, critic, and journalist, born in 1958. She currently works at *al-Safir* newspaper in Beirut, and is also a film critic. Her work has appeared in many literary journals in the Arab world, and she has read her poetry worldwide. Jaber has published four books of poetry, including *The Ritual of Darkness, Losing Mood,* and *Simply Things.* She is married and has three sons.

Annemarie Jacir is an activist, writer, poet, and filmmaker of Palestinian origin. She grew up in the Arab world and moved to Texas when she was sixteen years old. Jacir got her undergraduate degree in California, and then moved to New York, where she is currently finishing her M.F.A. in film at Columbia University. She is a winner of the Kathyrn Parlan Hearst Award in screenwriting at Columbia University. She has written, directed, and produced a number of short films and is currently working on her latest film project. She also writes creative non-fiction, and has published work in various literary journals and columns. Jacir has taught at Bethlehem University and Birzeit University in the West Bank.

Salma Khadra Jayyusi is a poet, critic, and anthologist. She was born in 1926 in Salt, in East Jordan, of a Palestinian father and Lebanese mother. She went to the American University in Beirut where she got a degree in Arabic and English literature, and later obtained a Ph.D. at the University of London. Her first collection of poetry, *Return from the Dreamy Fountain,* appeared in 1960. She taught at the universities of Khartoum, Algiers, and Constantine, then at the universities of Utah, Washington, and Texas. Her poetry and critical writings have appeared in many journals in the Middle East and abroad. In 1980, she founded PROTA (Project of Translation from Arabic), in order to spread Arabic literature in the West. Under PROTA, she has edited about thirty volumes, from single author works to large anthologies, such as: *Trends and Movements in Modern Arabic Poetry, Modern Arabic Poetry, The Literature of Modern Arabia, Modern Arabic Fiction, Contemporary Arabic Drama,* and *Modern Palestinian Literature.* Her most recent book is *The Legacy of Muslim Spain* (Brill).

Amal al-Juburi is an Iraqi poet born in 1967. She is also a journalist and translator currently living in Germany. She got her B.A. in English in 1987 from the University of Baghdad. Al-Juburi has been published in many newspapers in Europe and the Arab world, and she has translated Herbert Mason's *The Death of al-Hallaj, A Dramatic Narrative* (1979). She has published two collections of poems, and her second book, *Release Me O Words* was recognized as an important contribution to contemporary Arabic poetry because of the themes she used and her evocative language. Her forthcoming collection is *Enheduanna Prietesse of Dispersion.*

Joanna Kadi is a writer, editor, and grassroots community organizer of Lebanese descent. Her essays and short fiction have appeared in *Colors, Working Class Women in the Academy: Laborers in the Knowledge Factory, Sojourner: The Women's Forum, Sinister Wisdom,* and *Hurricane Alice.* She teaches classes in critical thinking for the Center for Arts Criticism and the GLBT Programs Office of the University of Minnesota. Kadi also studies Afro-Cuban, West African, and Arabic drumming, and performs throughout the Twin Cities, where she currently resides. She is the editor of *Food for Our Grandmothers: Writings by Arab-American & Arab-Canadian Feminists,* and author of *Thinking Class: Sketches from a Cultural Worker* (both published by South End Press, Boston, MA). She is working on her first novel.

Mohja Kahf was born in Syria, and came to the United States when she was young. She obtained a Ph.D. in comparative literature at Rutgers University in New Brunswick, New Jersey, and is presently assistant professor in the English department and Middle East Studies program at the University of Arkansas. Her articles, translations, book reviews, essays, and poetry have been published in different anthologies and literary journals, namely, *Exquisite Corpse, Jusoor, Banipal, Visions International,* and *Islamic Horizons.* She has given numerous lectures and readings, and is the author of *Western Representations of the Muslim Woman: From Termagant to Odalisque* (University of Texas Press).

Pauline Kaldas was born in Egypt, and immigrated to the United States in 1969 when she was eight years old. She returned to Egypt in 1990 for three years to teach at the American University in Cairo, and then moved to New York. She received her Ph.D. from SUNY-Binghamton. Kaldas's poetry has appeared in various magazines and anthologies, namely: *Lift*, *Michigan Quarterly Review*, *International Quarterly*, *Food for Our Grandmothers*, and *The Space Between Our Footsteps*. Her essays have been published in *Nurture, Teach, Serve*, and *The Family Track: Keeping Your Faculties While You Mentor*. She currently resides in Roanoke, Virginia with her husband and two daughters.

Fatma Kandil was born in 1958 in Cairo. Poet and short story writer, she is an important contemporary voice in the literary scene in Cairo. Kandil received an M.A. in literature, focusing on the textualization and the poetry of Egyptian poets in the 1970s. Her work has been translated and published in the Arab world and abroad, and she has attended countless literary conferences. She has published one play, *The Second Night After the One Thousand and One Nights* (1991); and three books of poetry, including *To Be Able to Live* (1983) and *Curfew* (1987). She is the Editor of *Fosoul* (Seasons), a literary journal devoted to literary criticism.

Dhabya Khamees was born in 1958 in Abu-Dhabi. She obtained her B.A. in political science and philosophy from the University of Indiana, and an M.A. in modern Arabic literature from the American University in Cairo, and then went to the University of London to do her Ph.D. In 1987, she was kidnapped and imprisoned in Abu-Dhabi for five months without trial as a punishment for her writings and her booked were banned. Khamees worked at the Ministry of Planning in the United Arab Emirates, and helped form the Writers' Union in the Emirates. She also worked in television, co-edited *Awraq*, a literary review that was published for a few years in London. Since 1992, she has been working for the Arab League. She has translated two books, written three books of literary criticism, published three short story collections and numerous books of poetry, among them, *A Step Over the Earth* (1981), and *I am the Woman, the Earth, All the Ribs* (1983), *Scarlet* (Cairo, 1994), *Walking in Romantic Dreams* (Cairo, 1995), and *The Sea, the Stars, the Grass, all in one Palm* (Cairo, 1999). Her work has been translated into English, Russian, German, Dutch, Urdu, and Spanish. She has read her poetry worldwide, and participated in several literary events, including Kavita Asia in India (1988), and the Amnesty International Poetry Tour in Holland (1988).

Hamda Khamees was born in 1946 in Bahrain. She studied political science at the University of Baghdad, graduating in 1968. After her studies, she started working as a journalist at *Al-Azmina Al-Arabiyya* in the United Arab Emirates, and then at *Al-Faqir*, also in the Emirates. Her work has appeared in numerous journals in the Gulf, and in a variety of Arab periodicals. Khamees has published five volumes of poetry, including *An Apology for Childhood* (1978). She has been living in Cairo since 1989.

Nidaa Khoury is born in 1959 in the village of Fassouta in Upper Galilee. She received a B.A. in philosophy and comparative literature and is currently finishing a second degree in philosophy. She also has a certificate in administration, education, and arts and a certificate in communication and public relations. Khoury has published numerous books: *I Announce My Silence To You* (1987), *The Braid of Lightning* (1989), *The Barefoot River* (1990), *The Belt of Wind* (1990), *The Culture of Wine* (1993). She has attended many conferences in Europe and the Arab world, and she is a member of the General Union of Arab Authors in Israel and the General Union of Authors in Israel. She is currently the administrative manager at the Association of Forty, an NGO for human rights and for the recognition of the unrecognized villages in Israel. Khoury is the mother of four children.

Vénus Khoury-Ghata was born on December 23, 1937 in Baabda, Lebanon. She is a poet and writer, and has been living in France for more than twenty years. She was educated in Arab schools and then went to the Université Saint Joseph in Beirut. Khoury-Ghata has published nine books of poetry, and more than seven novels. She has won many distinguished prizes, namely, the Grand Prix de Poésie de la Ville de Paris, the Prix Max Jacob, the Prix France Quebec, the Apollinaire prize for her collection of poems *Les Ombres et leurs Cris* (*The Shadows and their Cries*, Belfond, 1980), the Mallarmé prize for another poetry collection, *Monologue du Mort* (*Monologue of a Death,* Belfond 1987), and the Grand Prix de la Poésie de la Société des gens de lettres de France (1993) for her entire body of work, and in 1995, she was awarded the Frankfurt Prize for *La Maitresse du Notable.* She sits on a number of literary juries, notably the Prix France-Liban and the Prix Mallarmé, and is a member of the Committee of the Literary Review, Europe. She currently works at France-Culture. Khoury-Ghata is the author of the following poetry books: *Terres stagnantes* (Stagnant Lands, Seghers, 1969), *Au Sud du Silence* (South of Silence, Editions Saint-Germain, 1975), *Qui parle au nom du jasmin?* (E.F.R., 1980), *Un Faux-pas du soleil* (Belfond, 1982), *Leçon d'arithmétique pour le grillon* (Milan, 1987), *Fables pour un peuple d'argile* (Belfond, 1992), *Iles* (eleven poems illustrated by the famous painter Matta, éd. des Amis du Musée d'art Moderne de Paris; 1993). Her novels include: *Les Inadaptés* (éd. du Rocher, 1971), *Dialogue a propos d'un Christ d'un acrobate* (E.F.R., 1973), *Le Fils empaillé* (Belfond, 1980), *Alma cousue main* (éd. Régine Desforges, 1981). She has been translated into Arabic by renowned Arabic poets such as Adonis and Unsi El-Haj, and into numerous other languages as well.

Wafaa' Lamrani was born on April 15, 1960 in El Ksar El Kébir, a small city north of Morocco. She started writing poetry at a very young age, and has been publishing in Arabic literary journals and magazines since 1980. She currently teaches literature and humanities in Mohammedia, and directs the poetry workshop, Clairière Poétique. She is a member of the Maison de la Poésie (House of Poetry) in Morocco, and became its secretary general in February 1999.

Lamrani has taken part in numerous cultural events and festivals in Morocco, the Arab world, and Europe. She had published four collections of poetry: *Toasts, The Wail of Heights, The Magic of Extremes,* and *For you I have Prepared Myself.*

Fatima Mahmoud is a Libyan poet. She worked as a journalist in Libya from 1976–1987, and then moved to Cyprus and started a magazine focusing on Arab women's issues, *Shahrazad Al-Jadeeda* or *Modern Sharazade.* Mahmoud later returned to her homeland but had a confrontation with, she says, the "dictatorial political regime" concerning the absence of freedom of speech. Therefore, she was forced to leave her homeland in 1995, and sought political asylum in Germany, where she currently resides. Mahmoud is the author of *Ma Lam Yatayasar* or *If It's Not?* (1984), and a new collection of her poems is forthcoming.

Lisa Suhair Majaj was born in Hawarden, Iowa, to a Palestinian father and American mother. She was raised in Jordan, educated in Beirut, and currently resides in Cambridge, Massachusetts. Her father was born in Birzeit and grew up in Jerusalem. Majaj received her B.A. from the American University of Beirut, evacuating out of Lebanon in the summer of 1982 during the Israeli invasion. She subsequently moved to the United States to continue her education. She is currently finishing a doctoral dissertation on Arab-American literature at the University of Michigan, and is co-editing three collections of essays on contemporary Arab and third world women writers: *The Politics of Reception: Globalizing Third World Women's Texts* (with Amal Amireh; forthcoming from Garland Publishing); *Intersections: Gender, Nation and Community in Arab Women's Novels* (with Paula Sunderman and Therese Saliba); and *Etel Adnan: Scribe of a Scattered Self* (with Amal Amireh; forthcoming from MacFarland and Company). Her poetry, personal essays, scholarly essays, and book reviews have been published in a variety of journals and anthologies, such as *International Quarterly, Forkroads: A Journal of Ethnic-American Literature, Visions International, Food for Our Grandmothers: Writings by Arab-American and Arab-Canadian Feminists,* edited by Joanna Kadi (South End Press, 1995), *An Ear to the Ground : Presenting Writers from 2 Coasts,* edited by Scott Davis (Cune Press, 1997), *The Space Between Our Footsteps,* edited by Naomi Shihab Nye (Simon & Schuster, 1998). Majaj has read her poetry and presented papers at conferences across the United States and the Middle East, including the First International Palestine Writer's Conference (Birzeit, 1997). In 1998–99 she was a visiting scholar in women's studies at Northeastern University.

Nazik al-Malaika, poet and critic, was born in 1923 in Baghdad, Iraq. She is a pioneer in Arab literature, because she broke away from the classical form of the Arabic *qasida* and helped lead the movement of modern Arabic verse. Al-Mala'ika was educated at the Higher Teachers' Training College in Baghdad and then at Princeton University, where she studied English literature. She has taught at the University of Mosul in Iraq, and at the University of Kuwait. By 1978, she was already the author of seven volumes of verse, including: *'Ashiqat al-Layl* (*The Woman Lover of the Night*, Baghdad, 1947), *Shazaya wa Ramad* (*Splinters and Ashes*, Baghdad, 1949), *Qararat al-Mawja* (*The Bottom of the Wave*, Beirut, 1957), *Shajarat al-Qamar* (*The Moon Tree*, Beirut, 1968), *Ma'sat al-Hayat wa Ughmyalil-Insan* (*The Tragedy of Being and a Song to Man*, Beirut, 1970), and three volumes of criticism of Arabic poetry. Her work has been translated and published all over the Arab world and abroad.

Zakiyya Malallah was born in 1959 in Doha, Qatar. She received a Ph.D. in pharmaceutics from the Collage of Pharmacy, Cairo University in 1990. She is currently the head of quality control in the laboratory/pharmacy department at the Ministry of Public Health in Qatar, and a writer in the cultural section of the journal *Al Watan*. Malallah is the author of nine books of poetry: *In the Shrine of Desires* (Cairo, 1985), *Love Variations* (Doha, 1987), *For You I Sing* (Cairo, 1989), *In Your Eyes the Violets Bloom* (Cairo, 1990), *Exodus Inside Ego* (Beirut, 1991), *Some Unspoken Words* (Beirut, 1993), *You are Pure Gold* (1993), *Stars in Remembrance* (Doha, 1993) and *Lights in the Morning Eyes*. She is also a member of the League of Modern Literature (Egypt), the Ahram Cultural Club, the World Academy of Art and Culture (USA), the World Poet Academy (India), and the Women's Union (Paris). She has won many poetry prizes, participated in numerous radio and television programs, given poetry readings worldwide, and her poetry has been translated into Spanish, Urdu, and Turkish.

Thurayya Malhas is one of the pioneering Arab women poets who have been writing since the early 1950s. She has published three volumes of poetry: *The Straying Hymn, Immolation,* and *Eye Sockets in the Caves*. Malhas lives in Amman.

al-Zahra al-Mansouri is a poet and journalist, currently living in Al-Mohammadia. Her work has appeared in numerous magazines and journals in Morocco and all over the Arab world. She is a member of the Moroccan Writers Union (L'Union des Ecrivains du Maroc), and a member of the House of Poetry, Morocco (Maison de la Poésie, Maroc). Her first book of poems, *Chants*, is forthcoming.

Maram Masri was born in Syria, and currently lives in France. Her work has been published in various journals in France and the Arab world. She is the author of two books of poetry: *A White Dove was my Warning to You* and *Red Cherry on a White Tile*.

D.H. Melhem is a poet, critic and novelist, and a former member of faculty at both Long Island University and the New School for Social Research. She was born in Brooklyn, the daughter of Lebanese immigrants (with some Greek ancestry). She earned a B.A. *cum laude* at New York University, an M.A. from City College, and a Ph.D. from the City University of New York. She conducts a workshop annually for the International Women's Writing Guild Conference at Skidmore College. Melhem has published four books of poetry, including *Notes on 94th Street, Rest in Love,* and most recently, *Country (An Organic Poem).* She has also published a novel, *Blight* (Riverrun Press, 1995). Her book *Gwendolyn Brooks: Poetry and the Heroic Voice* was nominated for a Woodrow Wilson Fellowship in women's studies and published by University Press of Kentucky (1987); her book *Heroism in the New Black Poetry* (also UPK, 1990) was undertaken by a National Endowment for the Humanities Fellowship, and won an American Book Award in 1991. Melhem has published over fifty essays in books, critical journals, and periodicals. Her *New York Times Magazine* article earned a New York Heart Association Media Award. She currently resides in New York.

Iman Mersal is an Egyptian poet and journalist. Her work has appeared in numerous magazines, journals, and anthologies in the Arab world. She got her Ph.D. at the American University in Cairo, and currently resides in Canada.

Dunya Mikhail was born in Baghdad, Iraq on March 19, 1965. She obtained her B.A. in English from the University of Baghdad in 1987. She has published the following books: *The Psalms of Absence* (Baghdad: Al-Adeeb Publisher, 1993), *Diary of a Wave Outside the Sea,* (first edition, Baghdad: Cultural Affairs Department, 1995, and the second edition, Cairo: Ishtar Press Books, 1999), *Almost Music* (Tunisia: Dar Niqoush Arabiyya, 1997), and *The War Works Diligently* is forthcoming. Mikhail was living in Amman before moving to Michigan in 1996.

Hala Mohammad was born in Syria in 1959, and currently lives in Damascus. She studied cinema at the University of Paris from 1983–1986. She worked as an assistant director and costume designer on four films, and has produced one short documentary film. She is also a journalist. Muhammad has published two volumes of poetry: *The Spirit Has No Memory* and *Upon this White Dimness.*

Brenda J. Moossy got an associate degree in nursing from the University of Arkansas, Fayetteville. She is founding member and co-chair of the Ozark Poets and Writers Collective and *Poets on Tour,* which is a roster for performance poetry and outreach. She has performed in countless venues, has won poetry prizes and her work has appeared in many magazines. Moossy has published a number of chapbooks, most recently, *Night Vision* (1995) and *Anaconda* (1997). She has also co-produced an audiotape, *Ozark Women Poets–Snake Dreams.* She is currently finishing her M.F.A. in Creative Writing at the University of Arkansas.

Rawia Morra was born in Beirut in 1966. In 1985, after spending the war in the refugee camps in Beirut and southern Lebanon, she went to Sweden. She has studied classical Arabic, Swedish, and Scandinavian literature. Morra has also worked as a translator and an Arabic language teacher. She writes for different newspapers and lectures on different topics, including the Palestinian question, and Islam and women. Her first collection of poetry was written in Swedish with an Arabic title, *Ghurba*. She is currently finishing a novel.

Amal Moussa was born in 1971. She received a degree in journalism, and currently works in the cultural section of the daily newspaper *al-Sabah*. Her work has appeared in different literary journals. *The Female Water* is her first book of poetry.

Sa'adyya Muffarreh is a poet, critic, and journalist from Kuwait. She studied Arabic language and education at Kuwait University. Her work has appeared in numerous Arabic newspapers and journals, and she has given many poetry readings. She has published four books of poetry: *He was the Last of Dreamers* (first edition, Kuwait, 1990 and second edition, Cairo, 1992), *When you are absent, I saddle the Horses of my Suspicions* (Beirut, 1994), *Book of Sins* (Cairo, 1997), and *Only A Mirror Lying Back* (Damascus, 1999). Muffarreh is currently the art editor of *al-Qabas* newspaper in Kuwait.

Habiba Muhammadi was born in Algeria. She received a degree in philosophy from the University of Algiers, and then went to Cairo to finish a degree in Arabic literature. Muhammadi works as a radio presenter and as a journalist, writing for the literary and cultural section of many Arab newspapers. She has participated in numerous conferences all over the Arab world and Europe. Muhammadi has published five books: three collections of poetry, a compilation of articles and essays she wrote on Algeria, previously published in various journals throughout the Arab world, and a critical study on the work of the Syrian poet Nizar Qabbani. She resides in Cairo.

May Muzaffar was born in Baghdad, and currently lives in Bahrain. She obtained a B.A. in English literature at Baghdad University. She is a poet, writer, and translator from Arabic into English. Her work has appeared in a variety of literary journals, and has been translated into different languages. She has published several collections of short stories, and three volumes of poetry, including *Fire Bird* and *Gazelle in the Wind*. She is currently a part time researcher at the Royal Academy for Islamic Civilization Research. Muzaffar is married to the painter and printmaker Rafa Nasiri.

Houda al-Na'mani is a poet and artist born in 1930 in Damascus. Al-Na'mani received her early education at the Lycée Français and the Franciscan's school. She later studied in the law school of the Syrian University, and then literature, Sufism, and Islamic Studies at the American University of Cairo. She has lived in London and Washington, DC, and currently resides in Lebanon. Her work has appeared in various journals internationally, and she has published seven books of poetry: *To You* (1970), *My Fingers...No!* (1971), *Love Poems* (1973), *I Remember I was a Dot, I was a Circle* (1978), *Haa, it is tumbling on the Snow* (1982), *Vision* *upon a Throne* (1989) and *Huda... I am the Truth* (1990). Al-Na'mani is currently preparing *Rim of a Lock*, a new collection of poems in English about the Lebanese war and diaspora, to be published by Syracuse University Press, with an introduction by Miriam Cooke.

Salwa al-Neimi is a Syrian poet and journalist, living in Paris since the mid-1970's. She got her degree in Arabic language and literature at the University of Damascus, and then obtained a degree in Islamic philosophy, theater, and cinema from the Sorbonne. Al-Neimi has worked as a journalist since the mid-1980s, and currently, she also works at the information section of l'Institut Du Monde Arabe in Paris. She is the author of a collection of short stories, *The Books of Secrets* (1994); and several books of poetry, including, *Parallel Things* (1980), *The Temptation of Death* (Cairo, 1996), and *All those whom I love have gone...*(Cairo, 1999).

Adele Ne Jame was born and raised in New Jersey, and is of Lebanese origin. She moved to Hawaii in 1969, where she continues to reside with her daughter. Ne Jame got her M.A. in English literature and creative writing, and currently teaches creative writing in Honolulu, Hawaii. She spent one year (1989–90) as artist-in-residence at the University of Wisconsin-Madison, and received a National Endowment for the Arts award (1990). She has won many prizes, including the Pablo Neruda Prize for Poetry. Her work has appeared in numerous journals such as *Nimrod, Ploughshares,* the *Blue Mesa Review, Equinox, Denver Quarterly, American Nature Writing, The Paper, Hawai'i Review, Literary Arts Hawai'i, Hawai'i Pacific Review, Poet Lore,* and *Manoa.* She is the author of one book of poetry, *Fieldwork,* published by Petronium Press/An 'I'iwi Book, Honolulu.

Naomi Shihab Nye is probably the best known Arab-American poet. Born in 1952 in St. Louis, of a Palestinian father from Jerusalem and an American mother, she grew up in St. Louis, except between 1966–67, when she lived in Jerusalem and attended St. Tarkmanchatz Armenian School in the Old City. In 1980, Nye's first book of poetry, *Different Ways to Pray,* won the Texas Institute of Letters prize and her second collection, *Hugging the Jukebox,* was one of the National Poetry Series books selected by Josephine Miles and one of the American Library Association's Notable Books for 1982. She published *Yellow Glove* in 1986, which was selected by W.S. Merwin to receive the Lavan Award from the Academy of American Poets in 1988. The same year she was the co-winner of the Charity Randall Prize for Spoken Poetry, given through the International Poetry Forum, Pittsburgh. Her fourth collection of poetry, *Red Suitcase,* appeared in 1994, and her most recent collection is *Words Under the Words: Selected Poems.* She has also published *Mint* (a chapbook of paragraphs), two picture books for children, *Sitti's Secrets* and *Benito's Dream Bottle,* and she is the editor of *This Same Sky,* a collection of poems from around the world. Most recently, Nye has published a novel for young adults, *Habibi,* and edited an anthology of poems and paintings from the Middle East, *The Space Between Our Footsteps* (Simon & Schuster).

Nye has participated in the translation of poetry from Arabic into English for four of PROTA's (Project of Translation from Arabic) anthologies. She has worked as a writer-in-residence and traveled abroad on three United States Information Agency sponsored Arts America grants—speaking tours throughout the Middle East and Asia. Nye is also a songwriter and singer. She currently resides in San Antonio, Texas with her husband and son.

Maysoun Saqr al-Qasimi was born in 1958 in the United Arab Emirates. She got a degree in political science from Cairo University in 1982. A poet and painter, she currently works as the director of the cultural department of the Ministry of Information & Culture in the United Arab Emirates. Her poetry has been published in numerous journals and anthologies in the Arab world and abroad. She is the author of nine books of poetry, most recently, *Home* (1992), *Another Place* (1994), *The Other in His Darkness* (1995), and *Harm Formation* (1997). Al-Qasimi has participated in many literary festivals, has exhibited her paintings internationally, and has designed many book covers.

Michaela Raen is currently a graduate student at Chapman University where she is earning an M.A. in creative writing. She also studied in Mexico, and spent a semester in Palestine. While in Palestine, she had the opportunity to visit her grandfather's birthplace, Ramallah, and locate his family. She has dedicated her life to supporting and advocating positive social change within her various socio-political communities and beyond. Her work has been published in various magazines, and she is the author of *The Part of Me That is You is Simply Love*. Raen in currently working on a collection of short stories centering on Palestinian-American themes entitled, *Woman of the White Sand*.

Nadia Hazboun Reimer was born and raised in Amman, Jordan. She obtained her B.A. and then became a translator for USAID projects. In 1978, she was married and moved to the United States. After seeing her children to school, she attended Eastern Washington University and earned a second bachelor degree with a teaching certificate and an M.A. in creative writing. She is currently a high school teacher of English and French. Reimer has given readings in Europe, the Middle East, and North and South America. Her work appeared in several literary journals in the United States, Jordan, and Ireland.

Su'ad al-Mubarak al-Sabah is an activist, economist, and a poet from Kuwait. She obtained a Ph.D. in planning and development from the University of Surrey. Al-Sabah has been an active participant in the fight for freedom and human rights. She has published numerous books, including *Kuwait: Anatomy of a Crisis Economy* and three volumes of poetry, including *A Wish* and *To You, My Son*.

Doris Safie's family emigrated from Palestine to El Salvador. When she was six months old they moved to Brooklyn and then Rye, New York. In 1969 she obtained a B.A. in Oriental studies and linguistics from Columbia University, and then an M.F.A. in creative writing from Vermont College. Her work has appeared in various journals. She has also written plays, and worked with the Vermont Repertory Theater of Burlington. She currently lives in Charlottesville, VA.

Amina Said was born in Tunis in 1953, of a Tunisian father and French mother. She spent her childhood in Tunis. Although exposed to both Arabic and French, she considers the latter to be her first language. At the age of sixteen she moved with her parents to Paris, where she studied languages and English literature. She went back to Tunis and taught at the Faculté des Lettres until 1979, and then decided to return to live permanently in Paris. Said has published eight volumes of poetry and two of them received prizes. Her first book, *Feu d'oiseaux* (Birds' Fire), was awarded the Jean-Malrieu prize by the journal *Sud*, Marseille, 1989, and the second book, *L'une et l'autre nuit* (One and the other night), received the Charles-Vildrac prize, given by the Société des gens de lettres, Paris, 1994. Her poems have been translated into Arabic, German, Spanish, Portuguese, Italian, Turkish, Dutch, and English, and have been included in numerous anthologies and journals all over the world. Said has also published two volumes of reinvented Tunisian folktales; and in 1996, started translating from English into French the work of the major Filipino writer Francisco Sionil José, who has been translated into 24 other languages and is the founding president of the Philippines PEN Center. She has given and/or participated in many workshops, poetry readings, interviews, debates, and lectures on poetry. *Québec français*, in 1989, referred to her as "a new force of Francophone poetry;" and in 1993, the Parisian review *Hommes et Migrations* wrote that she was "the best French-language Tunisian poet of our time." She continues to reside in Paris, where she works as a journalist.

Laila al-Sa'ih received a degree in psychology and philosophy from the Arab University in Beirut. She has worked as a literary journalist in Kuwait and other Arab countries. Al-Sa'ih has published a book of poetry, *Copybooks of the Rain*, and a diary on the 1982 Israeli invasion of Beirut, *Roots That Do Not Depart*.

Saniyyah Saleh was born in Misyaf in northern Syria in 1935 and died in 1985. Saleh lost her mother when she was very young, and that event had an important impact on her life and work. Her work was published in many magazines and journals in Lebanon and Syria such as *Shi'r*, *al-Adaab*, and *Mawaqef*. She is the author of two books of poetry: *al-Zaman al-Dayyeq* (*Straightened Times*, Beirut, 1964) and *Hibr al-I'dam* (*The Ink of Execution*, Damascus, 1970), which received the first prize for women's poetry from *al-Hasna'*, a woman's magazine. She was married to the poet and playwright Muhammad al-Maghut and was the mother of two daughters, Sham and Sulafa.

Munia Samara is a poet and translator. She was born in 1955 in Kuwait, of Palestinian origin. Her work has been published in many journals, and her collection of poetry is *The Book of the River, the Sea, and In Between*. Samara lives in Jordan.

Ghada al-Samman is a short story writer, novelist, essayist, and poet, born in Damascus. She received a degree in science and a degree in English from the University of Damascus. She then went to Lebanon and got her M.A. in English from the American University in Beirut. Al-Samman taught and then became a journalist. She is the author of many books. She divides her time between Beirut and Paris.

Mona Saudi was born in Amman, Jordan on October 1, 1945. She studied sculpture in Paris and has exhibited her work worldwide. Her poetry has been published in numerous journals in the Arab world. She has published a collection of drawings by and conversations with Palestinian children from the Baqa'a Refugee Camp, *In Times of War Children Testify/Shihadat al-Atfal fi Zaman al-Harb* (bilingual, Beirut, 1970), and a book of her poetry and drawings, *First Visions,* (Beirut, 1972). She resides in Amman.

Mai Sayigh was born in 1940 in Gaza, Palestine. She graduated in 1960 from the University of Cairo with a B.A. in sociology, and has been the president of the Union of Palestinian Women since 1971. Sayigh has published three collections of poetry: *Garland of Thorns* (1968), *Love Poems for a Hunted Name* (1974), and *Of Tears and the Coming Joy* (1975). In 1988, she published a prose account, *The Seige*, on the 1982 Israeli invasion of Beirut.

Sekeena Shaben is a poet and fiction writer born in Canada. She studied writing at the Jack Kerouac School of Disembodied Poetics in Boulder. Her work has been published in numerous literary journals in the United States and Canada. She is the author of a book of poetry, *Regular Joe*, and is finishing a novel. Shaben currently resides in New York.

Ghada el-Shafa'i is originally from Acre. She currently lives in Jerusalem and attends Hebrew University. Her work has been published in numerous literary journals in the Arab world, and she is the author of one book of poetry.

Deema K. Shehabi is a Palestinian poet. Her poetry has appeared in anthologies and literary journals, including the *Atlanta Review.* She works as a managing editor for a quarterly magazine in Northern California, where she currently resides with her husband, Omar.

Fawziyya al-Sindi is a Bahraini poet. She has been working for the Women's Association in Bahrain for fifteen years, and is a member of the Bahraini Writers Association. Al-Sindi has published five books of poetry, including *Awakenings* (1982), *Do I see what is around me, Shall I describe what happened* (1986), *Throat of the Absentee*, and *The Shelter of the Soul* (1999). She currently lives in Al-Manama.

Sumaiya el-Sousy was born on December 11, 1974 in Gaza City. She has a B.A. in English. In 1998, she published her first book of poetry, *The First Sip of the Sea's Bosom*, and her second collection, *Doors*, is forthcoming She is member of the Palestinian Writers' Union. She lives in Gaza, where she works for a research center.

Lina Tini was born on February 12, 1963 in Damascus, Syria. She has lived in Kuwait, United Arab Emirates, Lebanon, and Cyrus, and presently resides in London. Her first collection of poetry came out in 1989, *A Sun in the Closet*. Then she published *Self-Portrait* in 1994, and *Here She Lives* in 1996. Tibi's work has appeared in numerous magazines, she has read her poetry worldwide, and was the co-editor of *Al-Katiba*, an important literary journal of Arabic women's literature. She currently works at *Azzaman* in London.

Nadia Tuéni was born on July 8, 1935 in Beirut, Lebanon, and died in 1983. She was educated in the Lycée Français for Young Girls, the French Academy in Athens, and Université Saint Joseph in Beirut, where she graduated with a law degree. She was married to Ghassan Tuéni, the director of *An-Nahar* and former Lebanese Ambassador to the United Nations. Tuéni was one of the most prolific woman poets, with nine collections of verse in French: *Textes Blonds* (Blond Texts, Seghers, Paris, 1966), which received the Sa'id Aql Prize; *Juin et les Mécréantes* (June and the Unbelievers, Seghers, Paris, 1968), a poetic statement on the June War of 1967; *Poèmes pour une histoire* (Poems for a Chronicle, Seghers, Paris, 1972); *L'âge d'Ecume* (The Age of Foam, Seghers, Paris, 1974); *Le Rêveur de Terre* (The Dreamer of the Earth, Seghers, Paris, 1977) and *Liban: Vingt poèmes pour un Amour* (Lebanon: Twenty Poems for One Love). She has been awarded seven prizes in France and Lebanon, including the Prix de l'Académie Française in 1973, the order of La Pleiade, and the Gold Medal of Honor for Public Instruction. Tuéni's final books were known for their concern with the tragedy of Lebanon.

Fadwa Tuqan is considered to be one of the best avant-garde poets in the Arab world. She was born in 1917 in Nablus, where she continues to reside. She comes from a family of poets and intellectuals. Her brother, Ibrahim Tuqan, was one of Palestine's major poets. She was among the first to explore women's inner turmoil and protest, their reality in love and society. Tuqan has written many personal and political volumes, especially since the start of the June 1967 war. She is the author of nine books: *Alone with the Days, I Found It, Give Us Love, In Front of the Closed Door* (1967), *The Freedom Fighter and the Land* (1968), *Horsemen and the Night* (1969), *Alone on the Summit of the World* (1973), *Nightmare in Daylight* (1974), and her latest autobiography, *A Mountainous Journey* (1985). In 1990, Tuqan was awarded the Sultan Uweis Prize for Poetry and the Jerusalem Medal for Literary Achievement. Her poetry appeared in various literary journals all over the Arab world and has been translated into different languages. In 1997, her distinguished presence was requested in Paris for Les Belles Etrangères-Palestine, which was organized by the French Ministry of Culture.

Najaat al-Udwany was born May 4, 1956 in Tunisia. She is a poet, critic, and writer whose articles and poetry have appeared in numerous Arabic newspapers. She has attended many literary conferences in Europe and the Arab world. Al-Udwany has published three books of poetry, *In Each Wound a Lily* (Tunisia, 1982), *Roots to my Sky* (Beirut, 1986), and *The Going of a Steel Soul* (Tunisia, 1994); and one novel, *Mirror for one Cadaver* (Tunisia, 1997).

Thurayya al-Urayyid was born in Bahrain, the seventh child and sixth daughter of the well-known poet and critic, Ibrahim al-Urrayid. A poet in her own right, she started writing in the fifth grade and received many awards during her student years. She left Bahrain at the age of sixteen on a government scholarship to study at the Beirut College for Women in Lebanon, where she obtained a B.A. in education/teaching English, and then, an M.A. in educational administration from the American University of Beirut. After her marriage, she continued her graduate studies and received a Ph.D. in educational administration and planning from the University of North Carolina, Chapel Hill. She then returned to Dhahran, Saudi Arabia and started working for Aramco, as well as being active in literary, educational, and national development activities. Al-Urrayid is a known columnist, having published in many newspapers and journals, such as: *Beynana Kalimah, Mada, Al-Hayat, Shawarid, al-Wasat, and Madar.* She has written about politics, controversial socio-economic events, and the ongoing debates in the literary and social scene. Over the years she has spoken on issues of education, social development, and the welfare of women and children at many conferences regionally and internationally; she has also presented papers on women writing in Oman, United Arab Emirates, and Saudi Arabia. Her poems have been published in numerous Arabic literary journals, and in bilingual anthologies of poetry (Arabic and English). Al-Urayyid has published three volumes of poetry: *Crossing the Empty Lands Alone* (1994), *Where is the Direction of the Trees?* (1995), and *Woman... without a Name* (1998). Her poetry has been translated into English and French.

Lorene Zarou-Zouzounis was born in Ramallah in 1958. She came to the United States in 1964 with her parents and four brothers. She lived in Michigan until 1971, and then moved to California where she found herself as a poet, writer, environmentalist, and human rights activist. She has been published in more than five anthologies and numerous magazines, and has given over fifty readings. Zarou-Zouzounis is currently finishing a collection of poems. She continues to reside in California with her husband and two children.

Amira el-Zein was born in Lebanon, lived in Europe (Paris and London) for more than fifteen years, and currently resides in Maryland. She has lectured widely on Sufism, folk literature, comparative literature, and published many articles in Arabic, French, and English. In addition, she has translated numerous books from French into Arabic including Malraux, Genet, and Artaud. Her book, *The Seen and the Unseen: Jinn among Mankind*, if forthcoming from Fons Vitae USA

Publishers; and she is working on a book on Sufism with Seyyed Hussein Nasr. She is a professor of Arabic literature at Georgetown University.

Sabah al-Kharrat Zwein is a poet and critic, born in 1954 in Lebanon. She works for *An-Nahar*, a Lebanese daily newspaper, and is a regular contributor to other newspapers and literary reviews. Zwein translated *The Real and the Theatrical* by the Canadian writer Naim Katan, and a study on contemporary women's poetry in Lebanon. She is the author of numerous collections of poetry, namely, *On a naked sidewalk* (1983), *Passion or idolatry* (1985), *BUT* (1986), *Starting from, or maybe* (1987), *As if in fault, or in the imperfection of the place* (1988), *Time is still lost* (1992), and *The inclined house, time and the walls* (1995).

ABOUT THE TRANSLATORS AND READERS

Magdi Abelhadi is an Egyptian writer and journalist working for the BBC. He lives in London.

Atef Abu-Seif was born in Palestine on August 20, 1973. He is originally from Jaffa but was raised in Gaza. Abu-Seif obtained a B.A. in English literature, a diploma in translation from Birzeit University, and finished his M.A. in European studies at Bradford University in the United Kingdom. His critical essays and short stories have appeared in many Arab newspapers and literary journals in Palestine, Egypt, and London. Abu-Seif's poetry translations have been published in *Alayam* and *Shura's Literary Quarterly* in Palestine; and he was one of the translators for the book *Poetical Texts by Women Poets From Gaza*, published by the Palestinian Writers' Union in cooperation with the British Council in Gaza. He is the founder of the Group for Literary Creativity in Gaza, and a member of the Palestinian Writers' Union. He has published two novels: *Shadows in the Memory* (1997) and *The Tale of the Midsummer's Night* (1999). Abu-Seif has been working in the Palestinian Ministry of Planning and International Cooperation for the past three years.

Kaissar Afif was born in Saida, Lebanon. He obtained his B.A. and M.A. in philosophy from the American University of Beirut, and his Ph.D. in philosophy from Kensington University in California. Afif returned to Lebanon where he currently teaches philosophy and is the editor of the *Poetic Movement*, a review of modern poetry. He has translated many texts into Arabic, including the work of Octavio Paz, Elsa Cross, and Jaime Sabines. Afif has published three books of poetry: *Graffiti, The Word Became Poems*, and *The Trilogy of Exile*.

Saad Ahmed is presently finishing his degree at Duke University.

Salih J. Altoma is professor emeritus, Near Eastern languages and cultures, African studies, and comparative literature at Indiana University. He served as chairman of the department from 1985–1991, and as director of the Middle Eastern Studies Program from 1986–1991. Altoma has taught at many other universities in the Arab world and in the United States, including Harvard and Princeton. He has won many awards, fellowships and grants; and has published more than twenty books and over eighty essays, in both Arabic and English, which have appeared in books, encyclopedias, and periodicals.

Amal Amireh was born in Palestine, and obtained her higher education in the United States. She finished her Ph.D. in English (19th- and early 20th-century American fiction) at Boston University. Amireh has received many honors and awards, including a Fulbright Scholarship (1985–87). Her translations from Arabic into English, her essays, and papers have been published and presented in the United States and abroad. She is currently a professor in the West Bank.

Mona Takyeddine Amyuni is an assistant professor in the civilization sequence program at the American University of Beirut. She translates from Arabic and French into English. She has published on Lebanese women writers, war literature of Beirut, francophone literature, and Tayib Salih.

Moulouk Berry is a Ph.D. candidate in the department of Near Eastern studies at the University of Michigan. Her main areas of focus are Islam, Middle Eastern women, and modern Arabic poetry and fiction. She is also a fiction writer and a poet.

Kamal Boullata is a Palestinian artist and writer, born in Jerusalem on May 28, 1942. He graduated from the Academy of Rome, and has lived and exhibited his paintings in the Arab world, the United States, Canada, Asia, and Europe. His writings on art and poetry have been published in many literary journals. He has translated the work of numerous Arab poets, including the Palestinian poet Rashad Hussein, and has particularly translated many Arab women poets. Boullata now lives in the south of France.

Clarissa Burt received a Ph.D. from the University of Chicago in 1993. She has taught at different universities, including Ohio University. Burt has lived in and traveled all over Egypt, and is currently assistant professor of Arabic literature at the American University in Cairo. She teaches Arabic poetry of all periods, from pre-Islamic to the most contemporary; and more specifically, focuses on poetry by women. Among her current projects is a volume on the *Architecture of Tragedy in the Mythic Cycle of Harb al-Basus*, dealing with the diachronic social functions of retellings of the pre-Islamic tale of a blood feud war, intimately tied to poetry and cultural productions throughout the ages of Arabic literature. Her translations and critical essays have been published in numerous journals, and she has given many talks in the United States and the Arab world.

Julia Casterton is an English poet and teacher born in 1952. She is the author of *Creative Writing: A Practical Guide* (Macmillan), and three collections of poetry, the most recent being *Bottom's Dream* (Smith/Doorstop). She teaches writing courses at the City Literary Institute in London and a humanities course for the Open University. She has two daughters, and lives in London with her husband.

Suneet Chopra an Indian poet. He graduated from the School of Oriental and African Studies, University of London.

Miriam Cooke obtained a Ph.D. from Oxford, and currently teaches modern Arabic literature at Duke University. She has published many critical essays on Arabic literature, and translated numerous Arab women writers. Cooke has published numerous books, including, *War's Other Voices: Women Writers on the Lebanese Civil War* (1988) and *Opening the Gates: A Century of Arab Feminist Writing* (1992). In 1995, she went to Syria on a Fulbright scholarship.

Charles Doria is an American poet and translator. He studied classical and comparative literature at Harvard and SUNY, Buffalo. Doria has taught at numerous universities, including Rutgers University, and edited *Assembling Press* in New York in the 1980s. He has published many books of poetry, including *The Game of Europe* and *Short and Shorter.* His translations include: *Origins: Creation Texts from the Ancient Mediterranean*, *The Tenth Music: Classical Drama in Translation*, and Muhammad al-Mahdi al-Majdhoub's long poem, *Birth*, on the birth of the Prophet (1979). Doria has also published many articles on literature, particularly of the classical period.

Ali Farghaly is a lecturer in Arabic in the department of Near Eastern studies at the University of Michigan. He obtained his B.A. in English from the University of Alexandria in Egypt, his M.A. from the University of Leeds, and his Ph.D. in linguistics from the University of Texas, Austin. Farghaly has also taught in Egypt and Kuwait, and has conducted research on language, computers, and the human mind in the United States. He has given numerous lectures, written many articles, and translated two books into Arabic.

Nasser Ferghaly was born in Alexandria in 1964. He worked in Arabic television news in London from 1990–1998, and then moved to the United Arab Emirates. He founded the imprint *al-Arabaaiyun* in 1990, which produced four periodicals and six book-length publications. Ferghaly's work has appeared in major Egyptian and other Arabic journals and magazines, including *Al-Karmel, Mawaqif,* and *Ibdaa.*

Judy Gahagan is a psychologist, translator, poet, and short story writer. She is the author of numerous books of poetry: *Ghosting the Cities, When The Whole Mood Changed,* and *Crossing The No-man's Land.* Gahagan has also published *Did Gustav Mahler Ski?*, a work of fiction. She lives in London and Italy.

Husain Haddawy was born and raised in Baghdad. He taught at the University of Wisconsin, Wesleyan University, the University of Rochester, and is currently professor of English at the University of Nevada, Reno. He has translated numerous books from Arabic into English, including Mahmoud Darwish's *Psalms,* and most recently, *The Arabian Nights.* Haddawy has written on English literature, Arabic philosophy, and Islamic art.

Subhi Hadidi is a translator, critic, and scholar, born in Kamechly, Syria in 1951. His translations have appeared in numerous journals and magazines in the Arab world and abroad, and he has translated many books from English into Arabic, including Ken Kesey's *One Flew Over the Cuckoo's Nest,* Yasunari Kawabata's *The Sound of the Mountain,* and Edward Said's *Afterwards to Orientalism.* He writes extensively on Arab literature. Hadidi currently lives in Paris.

Nathalie Hallassou el-Hani was born in 1966. She received a B.A. in languages (Arabic, French, and English), and an M.A. in translation from the Université Saint Joseph in Beirut. In 1990 she attended the Sorbonne in Paris as a student of English literature. She then went back to Beirut and got a B.A. in geography. El-Hani is head of the English translation section in the School of Translators and Interpreters of Beirut, and in 1991 was appointed chair of the English department at the Université Saint Joseph. Then in 1996, she started teaching translation at Notre Dame University, and by 1997, was in charge of literary translation— Arabic and French into English—in the fourth-year translation school of USJ. El-Hani is currently working on her Ph.D. in translation at Heriot Watt University in Scotland.

Samuel Hazo is the president and director of the International Poetry Forum in Pittsburgh, Pennsylvania and is a professor of literature at Duquesne University. Hazo is the author of over fourteen volumes of poetry, numerous books of criticism, fiction, and translations of both French and Arabic into English. Among his most recent publications are *Silence Spoken Here* (poetry), *Still* (fiction), and *The Rest Is Prose* (essays). Hazo has received a Phi Beta Kappa honorary membership, the Forbes Medal, and the Hazlett Award for Excellence in Literature as presented by the governor of Pennsylvania.

John Heath-Stubbs is an English poet, critic, and translator. He was educated in Oxford, and has lectured at the universities of Alexandria, Michigan, Oxford, and the College of St. Mark and St. John in London. He is the author of many books of poetry, including *Artorius*, his long poem that won the Queen's Gold Medal for poetry in 1972. In 1978, he won the Oscar William-Gean Durwood Award. Heath-Stubbs has also published many plays, books of criticism, and has translated poetry and prose from Arabic, Persian, and Italian into English. He resides in Oxford.

Lena Jayyusi was born in Amman, Jordan to Palestinian parents. She was educated in England, obtaining an M.A. in economics and a Ph.D. in sociology from the University of Manchester. She later went to Boston University where she got an M.S. in film studies. Jayyusi was assistant to the producer on three documentary films about women in the Middle East. She has translated and written a number of books, including: *Categorization and the Moral Order, Sayf ibn Dhi Yazan* (part translation, part retelling). She also gives talks on different subjects pertaining to the Middle East, especially on Palestinian women.

May Jayyusi is a Palestinian scholar born in Amman, Jordan. She got a B.A. in philosophy from the University of London and then obtained a M.S. in film studies from Boston University. She has translated many novels and books of poetry from Arabic into English for PROTA. She has also worked as a production assistant on *Wedding in Galilee*, a film made by the Palestinian filmmaker Michel Kheifi. Jayyusi resides with her husband and two children in Jerusalem.

Samira Kawar currently lives in London where she is a translator and television journalist/producer for WTN. She has translated extensively from Arabic into English, including Liana Badr's novel *The Eye of the Mirror* (Garnet Press, United Kingdom), and the filmscript *Suspended Dreams,* directed by Jean Chamoun and aired by the BBC. Kawar has been involved in numerous assignments in several European and Arab countries, and recently translated the childhood autobiography of Abdul Rahman Munif, *Sirat Madina* (Quartet Books, United Kingdom).

Cornelia al-Khaled is part Syrian, part German. She got her Ph.D. in English, concentrating on nineteenth-century English women writers, from Leeds University in 1992. She then went to Syria, and became a lecturer of English from 1992 until 1996. In 1997, she spent a year at Harvard University as a Fulbright scholar, doing research on Arab and Arab-American literature. She has written numerous articles, and given many talks on Arab women's writings. Al-Khaled currently lives in London.

MiMi Khalvati was born in 1944 in Tehran, educated in Switzerland, and trained as an actor at the Drama Centre in London, where she currently resides. She has worked as an actress and a director of the Theater Workshop in Tehran and in the United Kingdom. She has also translated many plays from English into Farsi, and co-founded the Theater in Exile group. Khalvati is the Coordinator of The Poetry School, London. She has published three poetry collections, all from Carcanet: *In White Ink, Mirrorwork,* and *Entries of Light.* Her *Selected Poems* is forthcoming in spring 2000.

Smadar Lavie is the author of *The Poetics of Military Occupation: Mzeina Allegories under Israeli and Egyptian Rule,* and she is the co-editor of *Creativity/Anthropology* and of *Women Writing Culture.* Lavie was associate professor of anthropology and critical theory at the University of California, Davis until she moved to Israel.

Mike Maggio is an American poet and translator. He has traveled and lived all over the Arab world and continues to work in the region. His translations have appeared in many literary journals and anthologies.

Sarah Maguire was born in London in 1957. She was the first writer to visit Palestine and Yemen on behalf of the British Council. Maguire is the presenter of the series *Good Books* for the World Service, and frequently contributes to BBC Radio Arts. She has published two books of poetry, *Spilt Milk* (Secker, 1991) and *The Invisible Mender* (Jonathan Cape, 1997). She is presently editing a collection of poems about plants and gardens for Chatto & Windus, and continues to participate in the dissemination of Arabic literature.

Khaled Mattawa was born in Benghazi, Libya and moved to the United States in 1979. He obtained an M.F.A. in creative writing from Indiana University, where he taught creative writing and won an Academy of American Poets award.

He was a professor of English and creative writing at California State University, Northridge and was awarded the Alfred Hodder Fellowship at Princeton University (1995–96). His work has appeared in numerous prestigious magazines such as *Kenyon Review, Poetry, Poetry East, Iowa Review,* and *The Pushcart Prize Anthology.* Mattawa is the author of a book of poems, *Ismailia Eclipse,* and the translator of a book of Arabic poetry, Hatif Janabi's *Questions and Their Retinue,* which won the University of Arkansas Press Award for Arabic Literature in Translation. He is currently a Guggenheim scholar at Duke University.

Richard McKane was born in Melbourne, Australia in 1947. Throughout the 1960s and 70s, he traveled frequently, in particular to Turkey. He has translated over twenty books from both Turkish and Russian into English. His latest anthology of poems, new and selected translations is *Poet for Poet* (Hearing Eye, UK, 1998). McKane was the first non-US citizen to be awarded the Hodder Fellowship at Princeton University as a writer. His first collection of poetry, *Amphora for Metaphors,* was published in London in 1993, and his *Turkey Poems* was published bilingually in Istanbul. He is one of the chairs at the Pushkin Club (Russian Literary Centre), and is an interpreter at the Medical Foundation for the Care of Victims of Torture in London.

Lucy McNair was born in 1963 in Worcester, Massachusetts. She obtained a M.A. in Literature at the Université de Paris VIII, St Denis, a B.A. at the University of Massachusetts, and attended Universitat Freiburg in Germany for two years. She lived in Paris for many years, where she was a professional translator of German and French into English, and taught creative writing for non-native Anglophones at the American University of Paris. McNair has translated extensively, including the French poet, Bernard Noel. Her other translations have appeared in *Zoom-Zoom, Frank,* and *In Our Own Voice;* and her filmscript translations include, *La vie est immense est plein de dangers* (Life is huge and full of dangers) by Denis Gheerbrant, *Erfolg* (Success) by Lion Feuchtwanger and *Novembertagen* (November Days) by Marcel Ophuls. She was the co-organizer of the Paris bilingual poetry reading series, "Chaise pour 2 lan(ton)gues" ("Chair for 2 tongues"). She is a member of the association, L'image tend l'oreille (The Image Grabs the Ear), collaborations on diverse projects uniting a literary and an artistic approach. McNair currently lives in New York, where she is finishing her Ph.D.

Ibrahim Muhawi is a Palestinian scholar, writer, and translator born in Ramallah, Palestine. He studied engineering and then English and American literature. He is the co-author and translator of *Speak Bird, Speak Again: Palestinian Arab Folktales* (California, 1988), and the translator of Mahmoud Darwish's *Memory For Forgetfulness* (University of California Press, 1995). He has taught at many universities in the United States, Europe, and the Arab world. Muhawi was professor of folklore and rhetoric at the University of California, Berkeley before moving to Scotland and becoming professor in translation studies at the University of Edinburgh.

Farouk Mustafa was born in Egypt. He has translated widely from Arabic into English. He is currently a professor in the department of Middle Eastern studies at the University of Chicago.

Tahia Khaled Abdel Nasser was educated in Europe and Egypt. She is currently finishing her M.A. in English and comparative literature at the American University in Cairo. She writes short stories and poetry in English. Her work has been published in literary reviews in Egypt and in the United States.

Yaseen Noorani was born in London in 1966, and grew up in the United States. His family came from Kenya, of Indian origin. In 1988, he received his B.A. in history from the University of Virginia, and in 1997 got his Ph.D. in comparative literature from the University of Chicago. Noorani received two fellowships: Center for Arabic Studies Abroad Fellow, 1988–89 and American Research Center in Cairo Fellow, 1993–94. His languages of research are Arabic and Persian. He is currently a lecturer in Arabic literature at the University of Edinburgh.

Wen Chin Ouyang was born in Taiwan, raised in Libya, and educated in the United States. She got her Ph.D. in Arabic literature from Columbia University. Ouyang taught at Virginia University for six years, and is currently a lecturer of classical Arabic at the School of Oriental and African Studies, University of London. She has published numerous articles and given many talks on Arabic literature in the United States and Europe. Her book, *Literary Criticism in Medieval Islamic Culture: The Making of a Tradition*, was published in 1997. Ouyang is presently conducting research on Arab storytelling.

Carole Satyamurti as born in 1939 and grew up in Kent. She has lived in the United States, Singapore, and Uganda, and currently resides in London. Satyamurti has won numerous poetry prizes, including the first prize in the National Poetry Competition in 1986. Her work has appeared in numerous journals and anthologies, and she is the author of many books of poetry, namely, *Broken Moon* (OUP, 1987) and *Changing the Subject* (OUP, 1990). She teaches at the University of East London.

Joseph T. Zeidan is assistant professor of Arabic at Ohio State University. He has published two editions of the *Bibliography of Women's Literature in the Modern Arab World* and most recently, *Arab Women Novelists: The Formative Years and Beyond*. His translations have appeared in many magazines and journals in the Arab world and in the United States.

POETS BY COUNTRY